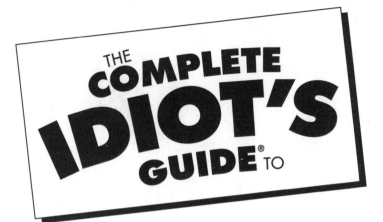

Visual Basic .NET

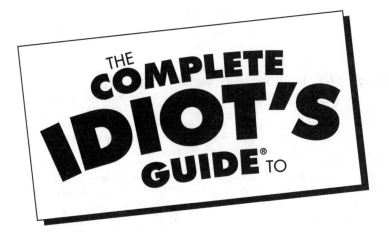

THE COMPLETE IDIOT'S GUIDE® TO

Visual Basic .NET

by Clayton Walnum

ALPHA

A Pearson Education Company

To Lynn

International Standard Book Number: 0-02-864231-7

Library of Congress Catalog Card Number: 2001098463

04   03   02   8   7   6   5   4   3   2   1

Interpretation of the printing code: The rightmost number of the first series of numbers is the year of the book's printing; the rightmost number of the second series of numbers is the number of the book's printing. For example, a printing code of 02-1 shows that the first printing occurred in 2002.

Printed in the United States of America

Note: This publication contains the opinions and ideas of its author. It is intended to provide helpful and informative material on the subject matter covered. It is sold with the understanding that the author and publisher are not engaged in rendering professional services in the book. If the reader requires personal assistance or advice, a competent professional should be consulted.

The author and publisher specifically disclaim any responsibility for any liability, loss, or risk, personal or otherwise, which is incurred as a consequence, directly or indirectly, of the use and application of any of the contents of this book.

Publisher: *Marie Butler-Knight*
Product Manager: *Phil Kitchel*
Managing Editor: *Jennifer Chisholm*
Acquisitions Editor: *Eric Heagy*
Development Editor: *Michael Koch*
Production Editor: *Katherin Bidwell*
Illustrator: *Chris Eliopolous*
Cover/Book Designer: *Trina Wurst*
Indexer: *Julie Bess*
Layout/Proofreading: *Steve Geiselman, Susan Geiselman, Rebecca Harmon, Michelle Mitchell*

Contents at a Glance

Contents

Appendixes

Introduction

If you're like a lot of people, when you sit down to work at your computer, you're probably curious about what makes your software tick. You might think that the answer to that mystery is a well-guarded secret that only a special few are privy to. But the fact is that computer programming is available to just about anyone. The only difference between you and the people who wrote that spreadsheet program you're using is that the latter folks have spent many years perfecting their craft.

Does that mean that you have to spend years learning about programming before you'll be able to do it? Not at all! You can start writing programs almost immediately after you learn a few simple commands. You won't be writing the next bestseller any time soon, of course, but that doesn't mean that you can't have fun as well as produce useful software. Just as with any craft, you have to take the first step. Luckily for you, you're holding that first step in your hands right now: a book that gets you started with the new computer language, Visual Basic .NET.

In this book, you'll discover most of the techniques used by any Visual Basic .NET programmer, whether a novice or an expert, to produce computer applications. And the best news is that learning these techniques isn't hard at all. It's actually pretty easy as long as you're willing to spend a few minutes understanding the concepts. By the time you complete this book, you'll have all the knowledge you need to not only write your own programs with Visual Basic .NET, but also to decide whether you'd like to be one of those computer "gurus" who goes on to become a programmer extraordinaire.

Whom This Book Is For

This book is for anyone who wants to get started with Visual Basic .NET programming. You don't need to know anything about programming to use this book. All the basic programming techniques are covered at the same time that you learn how Visual Basic .NET implements those techniques. All you need in order to understand this book is basic computer skills such as using a keyboard.

Note that there have been many versions of Visual Basic. The newest version, Visual Basic .NET, is the one this book is about. If you know how to program in earlier versions of Visual Basic, you'll still find a lot of good information here, because Visual Basic .NET is very different from any previous version of the language.

Software and Hardware Requirements

If you want to leverage the power of the Visual Basic .NET programming environment, you need a computer that meets the following minimum system requirements:

- Windows XP, Windows 2000, or Windows NT 4.03
- PC with a 450MHz Pentium II processor
- 64MB RAM
- Hard disk with at least 500MB free
- CD-ROM or DVD-ROM drive
- 800×600 screen resolution with 256 colors
- Mouse

Extras ...

This book also features extra tidbits called *sidebars*. These asides are designed to supply you with extra information, tips, and cautions. Here's what you'll find ...

Techno Talk

This is where you'll find definitions of the technical words you need to know as a programmer.

Check This Out

This is where you'll read about tricks and tips that can make programming more fun and convenient.

By the Way

This is where you'll read about interesting topics related to the discussion at hand.

Whoops!

This is where you'll find important information about problems you may run into as you write your programs.

Acknowledgments

I would like to thank the many people who had a hand in getting this book from my head to the bookshelf. Special thanks go to Eric Heagy for keeping me busy, Michael Koch for polishing things up, and Katherin Bidwell and the production staff at Alpha Books for a job well done. As always, thanks also go to my family: Lynn, Christopher, Justin, Stephen, and Caitlynn.

Special Thanks to the Technical Reviewer

The Complete Idiot's Guide to Visual Basic .NET was reviewed by an expert who double-checked the accuracy of what you'll learn here to help us ensure that this book gives you everything you need to know about programming basics. Special thanks are extended to Bonnie Biafore.

Trademarks

All terms mentioned in this book that are known to be or are suspected of being trademarks or service marks have been appropriately capitalized. Alpha Books and Pearson Education, Inc., cannot attest to the accuracy of this information. Use of a term in this book should not be regarded as affecting the validity of any trademark or service mark.

Part 1

First Steps

You can't build a house before you know how to use a hammer, and you can't program a computer until you know how a computer and its programming tools work. So, in this part of the book, you learn how computers take the program code you write and turn it into the words and numbers that appear on the screen. You also learn how to get started with the Visual Basic .NET programming environment.

A Basic Introduction to Programming

In This Chapter

◆ Discover reasons to program

◆ Find out what a program is

◆ Learn about different computer languages

◆ Explore how to write a computer program

Before you get started with computer programming, it might help to have a basic understanding of what it's all about. You undoubtedly have some ideas about what a program is and how it works, or you wouldn't have bought this book to begin with. Some of these ideas may be right on the money; others may be as crazy as a whale in a tutu.

Whatever your ideas about programming, this chapter gives you the skinny. After reading this chapter, you may find that your perceptions about programming are pretty solid; or you may find that you know as much about programming a computer as you do about building a submarine. In either case, you'll be a better person for having spent some time here.

The Surprising Secret

The computer-programming world has a well-kept secret. You won't hear programmers talking about it (which is, of course, why it's a secret). And if you've been using a computer for any time at all, you'll probably find this secret hard to believe. Nevertheless, it's as true as the sky is blue. So brace yourself. You're about to learn a shocking fact—computers are stupid.

A computer can do absolutely nothing on its own. Without programmers, computers are as useless as rubber razors. Computers can do only what they're told to do. And if you think for a minute, you'll realize this means that computers can only perform tasks that humans already know how to do. So why do we bother with computers? The great thing about computers is not that they're smart, but that they can perform endless calculations in the blink of an eye.

Programmers, of course, are the people who tell computers what to do. That's not to say that when you use your computer you're programming it. For example, when you plop yourself down in front of a word processor and hack out a letter to your congressperson, you're not giving commands to the computer. You're only using the commands contained in the program. It's the computer program—which was written by a programmer—that actually tells the computer what to do.

The bottom line is that if you want to give commands directly to your computer, you have to learn to write programs.

Why Learn to Program?

There are as many reasons for learning to program as there are raisins in California. Only you know what it is about computer programming that makes you want to learn it. For example, you may want to …

- Look for a fun and rewarding hobby.
- Be able to write the programs you really need—the ones you can't always find at the software store.
- Learn more about how computers work.
- Have to learn programming for school or work.
- Impress your friends.
- Please some misguided person, who gave you this book as a gift.

These all are legitimate reasons. You may have a better one, but whatever your reason, once you get started with programming, you'll find it can be both fascinating and addictive. Your significant other, however, may ban computers from your home and burn this book after he or she realizes just how addictive computer programming can be. Consider yourself warned.

What's a Computer Program?

A computer program is nothing more than a list of instructions that tells a computer what to do. The computer follows these instructions, one by one, until it reaches the end of the program.

Each line in a computer program is usually a single command that the computer must obey. Each command does only a very small task, such as printing a name on the screen or adding two numbers. When you put hundreds, thousands, or even hundreds of thousands of these commands together, your computer can do wonderful things: balance a checkbook, print a document, draw pictures, or blast invading aliens from the skies.

As you will see in the following section, computer programs can be written in one of many different languages.

Programming Languages

Computers don't understand English. They can't even understand BASIC, the computer language upon which Visual Basic .NET is based. Computers understand only one thing, machine language, which is entirely composed of numbers. Programming languages like BASIC enable people to write programs in an English-like language that a BASIC interpreter then changes into machine language so the computer can understand it.

Visual Basic .NET programs are a dialect of the BASIC computer language, which was developed not to help computers, but to help people make sense out of the numerical nonsense machines delight in. Visual Basic .NET replaces many of the numbers used by machine language with words and symbols we lowly humans can more easily understand and remember. Moreover, Visual Basic .NET enables a programmer to visually assemble a program's window from parts in a toolbox.

A BASIC program uses words and symbols (and a few numbers) that people can understand. How, then, can the computer understand and run BASIC? The truth is, when you load Visual Basic

By the Way
Often, you see the name of the BASIC language spelled with lowercase letters like this: Basic. Even Visual Basic .NET uses this spelling. However, BASIC actually started out as an acronym, which is why you also see the name spelled in all capital letters. The BASIC acronym stands for Beginner's All-purpose Symbolic Instruction Code.

.NET, you are also loading a compiler, which is a special program that takes the words and symbols from a Visual Basic .NET program and converts them into machine language that the computer can understand. Without the compiler's interpretation of your programs, your computer wouldn't have the slightest idea what to do with the program.

By the way, there are all kinds of computer languages, including Pascal, C++, FORTRAN, COBOL, Modula-2, and BASIC. Likewise, there are many versions of the BASIC language, of which Visual Basic .NET is only one. Older versions of DOS (pre-5.0) came with a version of BASIC called GW-BASIC. Newer versions of DOS came with QBasic. There was also a version called QuickBASIC. All these software packages enable you to create computer programs with BASIC, but they all implement the BASIC language slightly differently. However, of the versions of BASIC mentioned here, only Visual Basic .NET enables you to write Windows applications. The DOS versions of BASIC are now obsolete.

As a rule, all computer languages have one thing in common: They can be read by humans and, therefore, must be converted to machine language before the computer can understand them.

Techno Talk

Some computer languages, such as some types of BASIC, convert a program to machine language one line at a time as the program runs, using what's called an **interpreter.** Other languages, such as Pascal and Visual Basic, use a **compiler** to convert the entire program all at once before any of the program runs. In any case, all programming languages must be converted to machine language in order for the computer to understand the program.

A compiler changes your program into an executable file (for example, WORD.EXE or SIMCITY.EXE) that can be run directly, without a compiler or interpreter. An executable program is actually a machine language program that's ready for your computer to read and understand. With few exceptions, most computer programming languages come with a compiler.

The Programming Process

Now that you know something about computer programs, how do you go about creating one? Writing a computer program, though not particularly difficult, can be a long and tedious process. It's much like writing a term paper for school or a financial report for your boss. With these types of writing projects, you start out with a basic idea of what you want to do and write a first draft. After reading over the draft and resisting the urge to throw the pages into the fireplace, you go back to writing—polishing your prose until it glows like a gem in the sun. Over the course of the writing process, you may write many drafts before you're satisfied with the document you've produced.

Writing a Visual Basic .NET program requires development steps similar to those you use when writing a paper or report. The following list outlines these steps:

1. Come up with a program concept, document what you want the program to do, and sketch out on paper how it might look on the screen.
2. Create the program using the Visual Basic .NET toolbox and editor.
3. Save the program to disk.
4. Run the program and see how it works.
5. Fix programming errors.
6. Go back to Step 2.

As you can see, most of the steps in the programming process are repeated over and over again as errors are discovered and corrected. Even experienced programmers can't write error-free programs (unless the program is extremely short). Programmers spend more time fine-tuning their programs than they do writing them initially.

This fine-tuning is important because we humans are not as logical as we like to think. Moreover, our minds are incapable of remembering every detail required to make a program run perfectly. Most of us are lucky if we can remember our telephone numbers. Only when a program crashes or does something else unexpected can we hope to find those sneaky errors that hide in programs. Computer experts say that there's no such thing as a bug-free program. After you start writing full-length programs, you'll see how true this statement is.

> **CAUTION**
>
> **Whoops!**
> Bugs are programming errors that stop your program from running correctly. (Bugs are also nasty creatures with spindly legs and crunchy shells that make you scream when they leap out of shadows. But this book doesn't deal with that type of bug.) Before a programmer can release her program to the unwary public, she must be certain she has squashed as many bugs as possible.

Is Programming Easy?

After reading all that's involved in writing and running a computer program, you might be a little nervous. After all, you bought this book because it promised to teach you computer programming. No one warned you about such mysterious topics as machine language, interpreters, compilers, and program bugs. So, is programming easy or not?

Yes and no.

It's easy to learn to write simple programs with Visual Basic .NET. The Visual Basic .NET language is logical, English-like, and easy to understand. With only minimal practice, you can write many useful and fun programs. All you need is the time to read this book and the ambition to write a few programs of your own. In fact, what you'll learn in this book is enough programming for just about anyone who's not planning to be a professional programmer.

However, if you want to make programming a career, you have much to learn that's not covered in this introductory book. For example, consider a word-processing program like Microsoft Word, which took dozens of programmers many years to write. To write such complex software, you must have intimate knowledge of how your computer works. Additionally, you must have spent many years learning the intricacies of professional computer programming.

Still, there's a lot you can do with Visual Basic .NET, whether you're interested in writing utilities, simple applications, or even games. And, once you get the hang of it, you'll discover that programming in Visual Basic .NET is not as difficult as you may have thought. (If you're interested in programming Visual Basic games, check out my other book, *Teach Yourself Visual Basic Game Programming in 21 Days* [Sams, 2000]. But read this one first.)

The Least You Need to Know

- A computer can do only what a human instructs it to do.
- A computer program is a list of commands that the computer follows from beginning to end.
- There are many computer languages. The language you learn in this book is a form of BASIC.
- A BASIC program must be converted to machine language before the computer can understand it. The compiler in Visual Basic .NET does this conversion.
- Writing a program is a lot like writing a text document. You must write several "drafts" before the program is complete.
- Programming with Visual Basic .NET is as easy or as difficult as you want it to be.

Chapter 2

Cranking Up Visual Basic .NET

In This Chapter

◆ Get Visual Basic .NET up and running

◆ Tour the Visual Basic .NET main window

◆ Find the commands that control Visual Basic .NET

So, here you are. You're all excited and ready to get to work. Your brand-new copy of Visual Basic .NET is installed on your computer, and you swear you can actually hear it begging you to write a program. (Or is that your spouse nagging you to take out the trash?) There's only one problem—not only do you not know how to write a program, you don't even know how to get Visual Basic .NET started or what to do with it when you do. Look at it this way! In short, you've got a great excuse for not taking out the trash; you've got Visual Basic work to do!

Starting Visual Basic .NET

When you installed Visual Basic .NET (for installation details see Appendix A, "Installing Visual Studio .NET"), the Visual Basic .NET installer copied a heap of files to your hard disk and added Visual Basic .NET program icons to your Start menu. Starting Visual Basic .NET is as easy as opening your Start menu, finding the Microsoft Visual Studio .NET folder, and then clicking on the Microsoft Visual Studio .NET entry in that folder.

When you run Visual Studio, after a short wait, its main window pops up on your screen. That screen should look similar to the Figure 2.1.

Figure 2.1

Visual Studio's main window looks something like this.

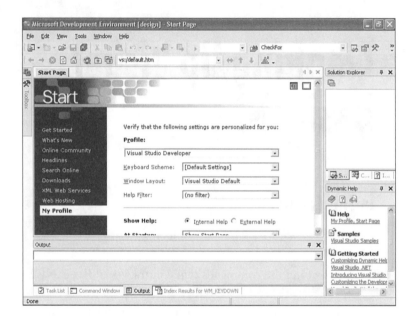

Starting and Loading Projects

That little window in the middle of the main screen is the Visual Studio Start Page, which is politely waiting for you to decide exactly what kind of Visual Basic .NET project you want to start. (Visual Studio is the name that Microsoft gives the software that enables you to create Visual Basic .NET programs.) If you're looking at the My Profile window, click the Get Started selection on the left to get to the page shown in Figure 2.2.

As you can see, the window displays three choices that enable you to access projects in different ways:

◆ You can load a recent project by clicking a project link on the list of recent projects.

◆ You can create a new project.

◆ You can load an existing project that doesn't appear in the recent project list.

The Visual Studio Start Page is extremely patient, so there's no point in sitting there and gazing at it any longer. I assure you, it will win any staring contest. So, to get things started, click the New Project button. This action informs Visual Basic .NET that you want to create a brand-new program. Don't worry; Visual Basic .NET doesn't know that you haven't learned to program yet, so it won't snicker at you.

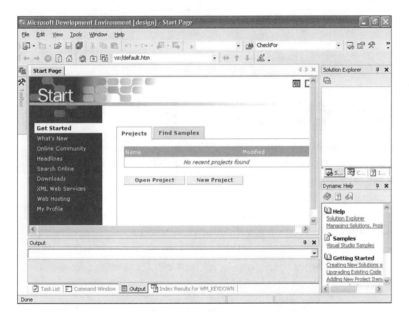

Figure 2.2

This is where you start creating Visual Basic .NET projects.

Now you should be looking at the New Project dialog box, which is shown in Figure 2.3. How this dialog box looks depends on what parts of Visual Studio you have installed on your system. In any case, select Visual Basic Projects in the Project Types pane. Then, double-click the Windows Application icon in the Templates pane.

Figure 2.3

The New Project dialog box enables you to choose the type of project you want to start.

Introducing the Parts of the Visual Basic .NET Window

When you start that new project, a lot of other exciting stuff happens. First, a set of controls appears on the left side of the window in the Visual Basic .NET toolbox. (If the toolbox doesn't appear automatically, press Ctrl+Alt+X to make it appear. You can make the toolbox stay in place by clicking the thumb tack image at the top of the toolbox.) Also, your new program's starting window—called a *form* in Visual Basic .NET—appears in the middle of the screen. And, as if that weren't enough, your new project's name and components appear in the Solution Explorer window, and the form's property settings appear in the Properties window. Figure 2.4 shows these wonderful new elements of the Visual Basic .NET main window.

Now that you can see these marvelous wonders on the screen, you probably want to know what they are. If you don't, you're probably reading the wrong book. Everyone who thinks he's reading *Misbehaving Misters and Misses from Missouri* should now quietly exit the room; you're in the wrong class. The rest of you take a look at the Visual Basic .NET toolbox.

See all those little icons in the Toolbox? (If the icons aren't visible, even though the Toolbar is, just click the Windows Forms tab on the Toolbox.) Those icons represent controls that you can use with your program. Controls are objects like buttons, text boxes, labels, images, and shapes that you can position on your form in order to build your program's *user interface*. If all this sounds strange, don't worry about it. You'll learn how to build a program in Chapter 3, "Creating Your First Project."

Toolbox   Form   Solution Explorer

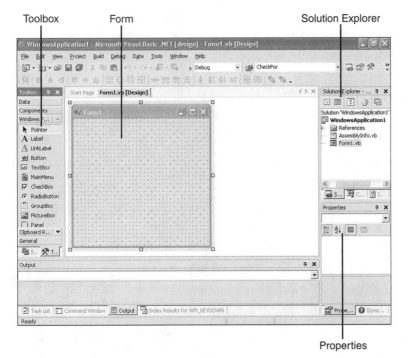

Figure 2.4

The Visual Basic .NET main window displays several different areas.

Properties

The window inside the Form1.vb [Design] window—the one with Form1 in its title bar—is your project's window. That is, when you run your program, this is the window that appears on the screen. Logically, then, this is also the window where you place the controls that make up your program's user interface.

The Solution Explorer window gives you an overview of the objects in the currently loaded project. Usually, a form is one of these objects. You may, in fact, have more than one form in some projects. By clicking the plus and minus signs next to folders in the Solution Explorer window, you can display more details about the project.

Finally, the Properties window displays the *properties* of the object that's currently selected in the form. (A thick, gray line and sizing handles surround the currently selected object.) Currently, the form itself is selected (if it isn't, click on it), so its properties appear in the Properties window. What are properties? You can think of properties as the attributes of an object. For example, your project's form has a

Techno Talk

A **user interface** is the part of the application that enables the user to interact with the program. A user interface usually includes various types of buttons, menus, dialog boxes, and other kinds of objects. By using the objects that make up the user interface, the user supplies commands and information to the program. Similarly, the program accesses the user interface in order to display information to the user.

property called Text, which is the text that appears in the form's title bar. If you change the text for the Text property, the text in the form's title bar changes, too, as shown in Figure 2.5.

Figure 2.5

A form's title bar holds the text from the Text *property.*

Changed Caption

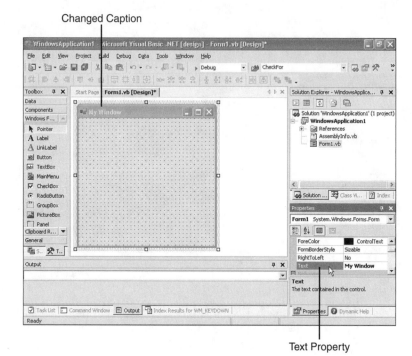

Text Property

Techno Talk

Properties determine how an object looks and acts. Many Visual Basic .NET objects, in fact, share similar properties. For example, all objects have a Name property, which enables a program to refer to that object. Most objects also have properties that determine the object's size, position, text, colors, borders, and much more. You'll learn more about properties as you work with Visual Basic .NET. You'll learn a lot about properties in Chapter 20, "The Inner Workings of Controls and Objects."

Revealing the Code Window

Although Visual Basic .NET enables you to build much of your project by placing controls from the toolbox onto the form, sooner or later, you have to settle down to writing some program source code. As you learned in Chapter 1, "A Basic Introduction to Programming," programs comprise many lines of commands that tell the program what to do. In Visual Basic .NET, you type these commands into the code window.

When you first start a new project, Visual Basic .NET doesn't display the code window. To bring up the code window, just double-click the form; your Visual Basic .NET window will look similar to Figure 2.6.

Code Window

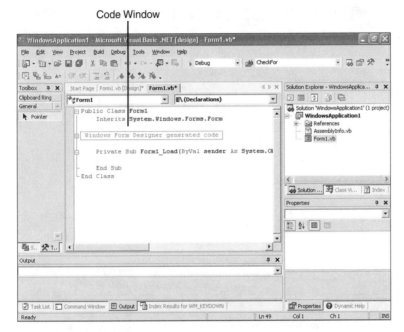

Figure 2.6

The code window is a text editor into which you type your program's lines.

The new window that appears is the code window. As you can see, Visual Basic .NET is pretty smart and often tries to guess what you want to do. In this case, Visual Basic .NET has started something called a procedure—a Form1_Load procedure to be precise. If you were actually writing a program, you'd probably finish the Form1_Load procedure by typing Visual Basic .NET commands between the two lines that Visual Basic .NET already provided for you. In fact, you'll see how to do this in Chapter 3.

Scoping Out the Menus and the Toolbar

Two important parts of the Visual Basic .NET main window are the menu bar and the toolbar. The menu bar holds a series of menus, each of which contains commands you need to make Visual Basic .NET do what you want. (To get Visual Basic .NET to listen to you, you could try glaring threateningly at the screen, but the menus tend to work so much better.) For example, if you want to add a new form to your project, you could select the Project menu's Add Windows Form command, as shown in Figure 2.7.

Many of the menu commands have so-called *hotkeys* that you can use to select the command directly from the keyboard. For example, in the previous figure, you can see the keystroke Ctrl+Shift+A listed after the Add New Item command. This means that you can send Visual Basic .NET the Add New Item command just by holding down your keyboard's Ctrl and Shift keys and pressing A at the same time. You don't need to open the menu at all.

Figure 2.7

The menu bar provides a home for many Visual Basic .NET commands.

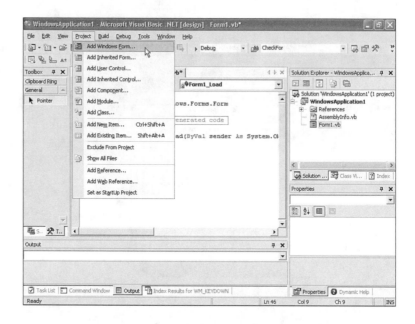

Check This Out

If you spend a little time now to learn the Visual Basic .NET shortcuts and hot keys, you'll be able to work much faster when you start programming.

The toolbar provides access to many of most commonly needed Visual Basic .NET commands. Most of the buttons on the toolbar are just quick ways to select a command from the menus. For example, see the button on the toolbar that looks like a stack of floppy disks? If you click this button, Visual Basic .NET saves all the files in the currently open project. Clicking this button is the same as selecting the File menu's Save All command, as shown in Figure 2.8.

If you're still paying attention, you may have noticed that the File menu's Save All command has the same icon next to it as the icon used on the toolbar button. When you see an icon like this next to a command, you know that the command is also available in a toolbar—if you happen to have that particular toolbar turned on. (Visual Basic .NET lets you turn different toolbars on and off.)

Now, wasn't that fun? Aren't you already starting to feel empowered? You should, because you've taken your first steps toward becoming a Visual Basic .NET programmer.

The Save All button

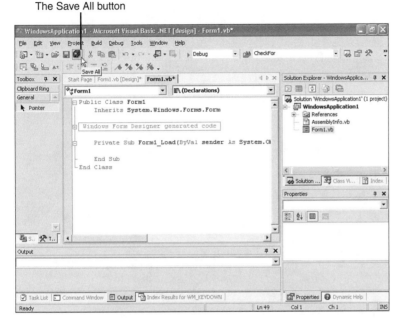

Figure 2.8

Some menu commands, like Save All, are represented as buttons on the toolbar.

The Least You Need to Know

◆ You can start Visual Basic .NET from your Windows Start menu.

◆ When Visual Basic .NET first appears, you can choose to start a new project, load any Visual Basic .NET project from your disk drive, or load a project on which you've recently worked.

◆ The Visual Basic .NET toolbox contains the controls you use to put together your program's user interface.

◆ A Visual Basic .NET form represents your program's window.

◆ The Properties window displays the attributes of an object selected in the form.

◆ The Solution Explorer window shows the main objects in your project. Usually, a project has at least one form.

◆ You type your program's commands into the Visual Basic .NET code window.

◆ You can access many Visual Basic .NET commands from the menu bar and the toolbar. Some commands even have hotkeys that enable you to select a command directly from your keyboard.

Chapter 3

Creating Your First Project

In This Chapter

- ◆ Start a new Visual Basic .NET programming project
- ◆ Use controls to build a user interface
- ◆ Write program source code
- ◆ Convert a program into an executable Windows application

Finally, it's time to actually do something with Visual Basic .NET. In this chapter, you'll learn the basic skills you need to create a simple program. This knowledge will be important to you as you explore the language itself in Part 2, "Writing Basic Program Code." This knowledge will also be important to you when you brag to your friends about your programming prowess.

Creating a Program … in a Nutshell

Creating a simple Visual Basic .NET program is easier than goosing a sleeping cat. You need to only complete three steps, after which you'll have a program that can be run outside of the Visual Basic .NET programming environment, just like any other application you may have installed on your computer. The three steps are as follows:

1. Create the program's user interface.

2. Write the program source code that makes the program do what it's supposed to do.

3. Compile the program into an executable file that can be run as a standalone application (that is, the application can be run without being loaded into Visual Basic .NET).

Of course, there are many details involved in each of these three steps (well, except for the last one, which is pretty much automatic), especially if you're writing a lengthy program. As you work, you'll complete these steps in the order in which they're listed above. However, you'll also frequently go back from step 2 to step 1 to fine-tune your user interface. And you may even go back to step 2 from step 3 if you discover problems after compiling your program. Such is the nature of the programming beast.

Step 1: Creating the User Interface

As you learned in Chapter 2, "Cranking Up Visual Basic .NET," a program's user interface enables the user to interact with the program. The user interface comprises any objects that the user manipulates in order to give commands or information to the program. Such objects include buttons, menus, and text boxes, to name just a few.

Visual Basic .NET makes it easy to create a user interface by providing a set of ready-to-go controls in a toolbox. All you have to do to create your user interface is start a new project and position the controls on the form, which is the object that represents the program's main window.

In this section, you'll create only a very simple user interface. You'll learn just enough so you can understand the sample programs in the next section of the book. You won't get into more sophisticated programs until after you learn about the Visual Basic .NET language itself. If you want to speed up this process, you could try using this book as a pillow and hope the information soaks in while you sleep. Probably, though, you'll just have to keep reading.

Getting Started

Go ahead and start Visual Basic .NET (or actually Visual Studio .NET, if you want to be fussy about it). When you do, you see a screen that looks a lot like the one shown in Figure 3.1.

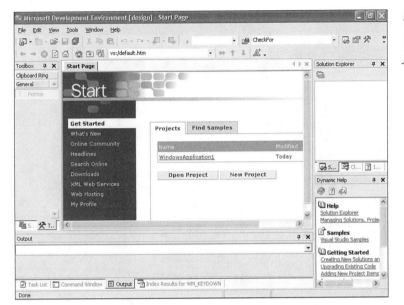

Figure 3.1

Visual Basic .NET when it first appears.

To start creating your first user interface, follow these steps:

1. Click the New Project button in the Visual Studio Home Page.

2. When the New Project dialog box appears, click Visual Basic .NET Projects in the Project Types box, and then click the Windows Application.

3. Next, you must tell Visual Basic .NET the name of the program and where you want it stored on your hard drive. In the Name box type **MyProgram** (after deleting the default name, of course), and in the Location window, type the location you want—or just leave it set to the default, which should be the Visual Studio Projects that was automatically created when you installed Visual Studio .NET, as shown in Figure 3.2.

4. Finally, click the OK button, and Visual Basic .NET will create a Form object for your program's window, as well as display a bunch of goodies in the toolbox, Solution Explorer, and Properties window. Figure 3.3 shows how Visual Basic .NET should look at this point.

Figure 3.2

The Visual Basic .NET New Project dialog box.

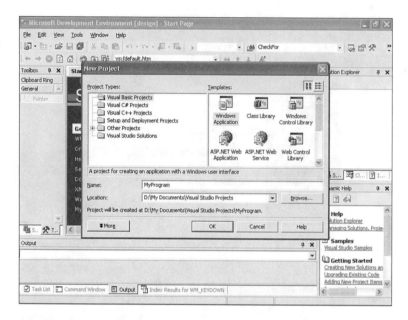

Figure 3.3

Visual Basic .NET with the new MyProgram project ready to go.

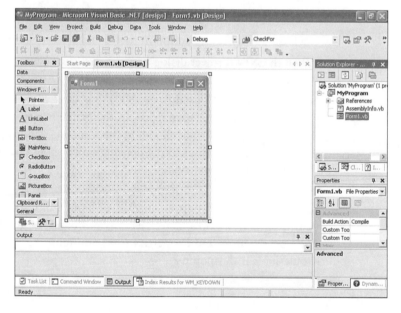

Click the Windows Forms button at the top of the toolbox. Do you see all those icons in the Visual Basic .NET toolbox? Each icon represents one of the controls you can use to build your program's user interface.

This chapter won't go into a lot of detail about each of the controls; you'll learn most of the details in Part 5, "Writing Windows Applications." Your goal right now is to get a general idea of how to create a Visual Basic .NET program. (Or maybe you grabbed this book only because your boss just walked in. In that case, you have an entirely different goal.)

Adding a Button

How about putting a button on your new form? You're not going to believe how easy this is. Just double-click the Button control in the Visual Basic .NET toolbox. When you do, a button magically appears on the form, as shown in Figure 3.4.

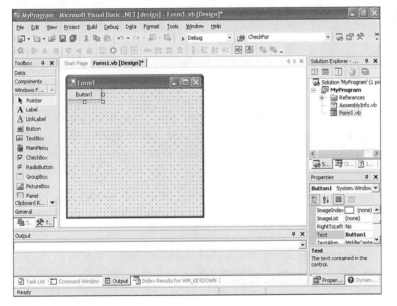

Figure 3.4

When you double-click a control in the toolbox, the control appears on the form.

See the small squares that border the button object? Those are the button's sizing handles. You can change the size of the button by placing your mouse pointer over one of the sizing handles, holding down the left mouse button, and dragging the handle. When you place your mouse pointer over a sizing handle, the mouse pointer changes to a new image that indicates the directions you can drag the handle.

For example, place your mouse pointer over the sizing handle in the center of the button's bottom edge. The mouse pointer changes into a double-headed arrow that points up and down. This arrow means that you can drag the button's bottom edge either up or down. Go ahead and drag the edge down, as shown in Figure 3.5.

Figure 3.5

You can resize most controls by dragging their sizing handles.

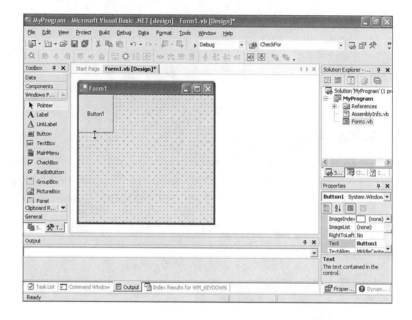

You should notice two things as you drag the button's edge. First, the button's size changes with the mouse pointer wherever you drag it. Second, you're filled with a nice, tingly feeling as you realize that you just got one step closer to conquering Visual Basic .NET.

When the button is the size you want it to be, just release your mouse button. The button then settles down to the new size.

To move the button, place your mouse pointer over the button. The mouse cursor changes into an icon with four arrows. Press and hold your mouse button and drag the button to the center of the form, as shown in Figure 3.6.

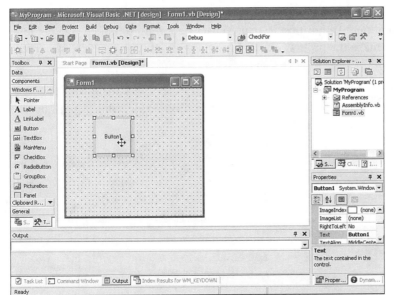

Figure 3.6

Here's the button after it has been resized and moved.

Step 2: Adding the Program Source Code

You now have a button in a form, which is all fine and good except for the fact that the button does nothing. Don't believe it? Click the Start button (the button that looks like a small, blue triangle) on the Visual Basic .NET toolbar (not the toolbox). (When your mouse pointer is over the right button, a little box appears containing the word "Start.") When you click the Start button, Visual Basic .NET runs your modest little program. You'll see a small window, as shown in Figure 3.7.

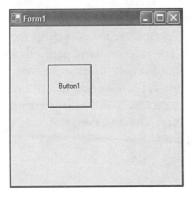

Figure 3.7

Your first Visual Basic .NET program.

Go ahead and click your program's button. Nothing happens, right? OK, so the button looks like it pops in and out. All buttons do that. What's important to notice is that clicking the button doesn't make the program do anything useful. Of course, you're about to fix that little snafu.

Close your program's window, and get back to the Visual Basic .NET main window. Now, double-click your form's Button1 button. Presto! Your project's code window pops up, as shown in Figure 3.8.

Figure 3.8

The code window appears whenever you double-click an object.

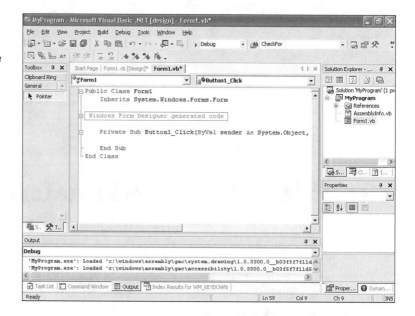

When you double-clicked the Button object, Visual Basic .NET not only displayed the code window, but also started some program source code for you. This piece of source code is called a procedure. To put it simply, whenever the user clicks the Button1 button, Visual Basic .NET goes to the Button1_Click procedure and performs all the commands the procedure contains. You can also think of Button1_Click as an *event*, which is an action that Windows passes to your program for handling. When you ran the program previously, and clicked the button, Visual Basic .NET did exactly what it was supposed to do and went to the Button1_Click procedure. Unfortunately, you hadn't yet placed commands in the procedure, so nothing happened.

You can change that easily, by adding the source code line

```
MessageBox.Show("Visual Basic rocks!")
```

to the `Button1_Click` procedure, as shown in Figure 3.9.

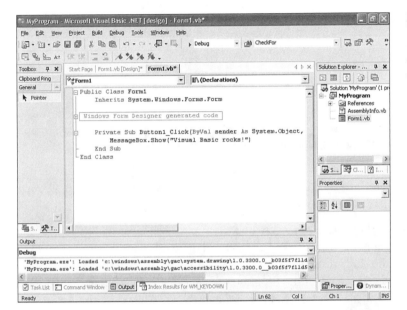

Figure 3.9

You type your own program code between the start and end of a procedure.

Now, run the program again (by clicking the Start button). When you click the button this time, a message box appears with the message "Visual Basic rocks!" as shown in Figure 3.10.

As you may have already guessed, the `MessageBox.Show` command tells Visual Basic .NET to display a message box. The text in the quotes after the `MessageBox.Show` command is the text the message box should display. You'll see the `MessageBox.Show` command a lot throughout this book.

Techno Talk

An **event** is nothing more than something the user or the computer does to interact with your program. For example, when you clicked your program's Button1 button, you caused a Click event. To tell Visual Basic .NET what to do with this event, you must complete the `Button1_Click` event procedure. You'll learn plenty of other events by the time you get to the end of this book.

Figure 3.10

Now your Button1 button actually does something.

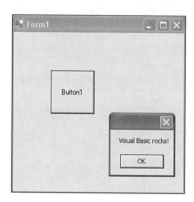

Step 3: Creating Your Program's Executable File

Now, if you're done patting yourself on the back and yelling for the family to come and fuss over your first Visual Basic .NET program, you can take the step that converts your Visual Basic .NET project into a full-fledged, standalone Windows application.

Actually, just by running the program, you created the application's executable. However, this version of the program has a lot of extra data, called debugging information, stored in the executable file. While this information is handy when you're working on a program, it does take up a lot of extra space when the program's done. (You'll learn about debugging when you get to Chapter 17, "Mastering the Art of Bug Extermination.")

> **By the Way**
>
> Not all files on your disk drive represent applications. Many are data files that other programs need to load. Files that end in .exe, however, are *executable files* that you can double-click to run. For example, Visual Studio. NET's executable file is named devenv.exe. If you find this file with Windows Explorer and double-click it with your mouse, you'll start Visual Studio (just like you do when you select Microsoft Visual Studio .NET 7.0 from your Start menu).

If you look next to the button you clicked to start your program (on the toolbar), you'll see a box that contains the word "Debug." This box tells you that you're currently working with the debug version of the program. Click the little arrow to the right of the box, and select Release from the list that appears, as shown in Figure 3.11.

Now, in the Build menu, you'll see a command called Build MyProgram, where MyProgram is the name of the current project as shown in Figure 3.12.

Click the Build MyProgram command. When you do, Visual Basic .NET changes your program into an executable Windows application, which no longer contains the extra debugging information.

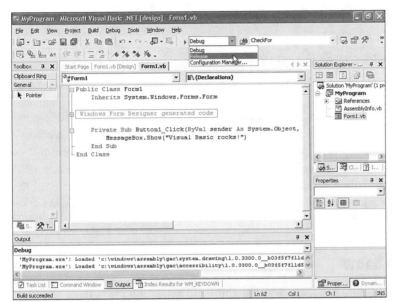

Figure 3.11

The Release configuration creates a smaller executable file that doesn't contain debugging information.

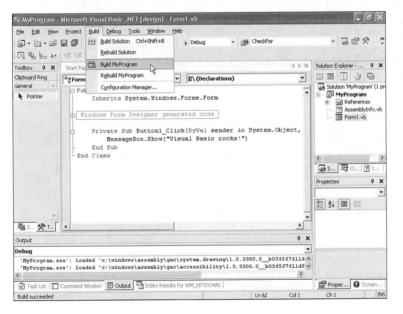

Figure 3.12

The Build MyProgram command changes your program into an executable file.

Now that Visual Basic .NET has converted your program to an executable file, you don't need Visual Basic .NET to run the program. To prove this, first save your program. To save your program, you have three options. You can …

- Click the Save All button in the toolbar (that's the button that looks like a stack of floppy disks, remember?).
- Select the File menu's Save All command.
- Press Ctrl+Shift+S on your keyboard.

Now you can exit from Visual Basic .NET by closing its window. Visual Basic .NET vanishes from your screen and is now closed. The executable program file you just created with the help of Visual Basic .NET, MyProgram.exe, is located in your Visual Studio Projects\MyProject\bin folder (assuming you chose the default location when you started the project). Double-click the file, and your Visual Basic .NET application appears on the screen. Go ahead and click the Command1 button to display the message box. It works! Break out the champagne and cheese fondue!

The Least You Need to Know

- To create a Visual Basic .NET application, you build a user interface, write the program source code, and then compile the program into an executable file.
- You build a user interface by placing controls from the Visual Basic .NET toolbox onto your program's form.
- You can resize controls (and the form) by dragging the control's sizing handles, which appear when the control is selected.
- One way to display the code window is to double-click the object for which you want to write program code.
- When the user clicks a button, Visual Basic .NET generates a Click event. The program code you add to the button's Click event procedure determines what the button does.
- The Build menu's Build (or Rebuild) command converts your Visual Basic .NET program into a standalone Windows application.

Part 2

Writing Basic Program Code

You're probably dying to get started with writing real programs. Good news! This is the part where you do that. Along the way, you learn about things like variables and strings, as well as how computers do math and make decisions. Here, you'll even learn about how to handle disk files, how to send data to a printer, how to deal with programming errors, and a whole bunch more.

Chapter 4

Variables and I/O: Programming Secrets

In This Chapter

- ◆ Understand input and output
- ◆ Learn to use the `DrawString` command
- ◆ Discover variables and how to declare them
- ◆ Use TextBox controls for input
- ◆ Use Label controls to give the user information

A computer wouldn't be of much use if you didn't have a way of getting data in and out of it. For example, let's say you want to type that letter to your congressperson. For this task, you need a word-processing application and an input device that enables you to get the characters that make up the letter into your computer's memory where you can manipulate them. Your input device could be a keyboard that enables you to type your letter, placing it into memory one character at a time. Alternatively, you could also use a microphone in combination with a voice recognition software package and dictate the letter as you would to a secretary.

When you finish typing and editing your letter, you need a way to get it out of the computer's memory so the congressperson can read it. You need another kind of device—an output device—to which you can send the letter to get it into a form that is useful. You probably want to use a printer, but you might also save your letter onto a disk and send the disk to the recipient. (You could also email the letter, of course, but we're talking about output devices here.) Then he could just load the letter into his computer's memory and read it on-screen.

The process of moving data in and out of a computer is called, appropriately enough, input and output (or I/O, for short). There are all kinds of input and output, but you need to know only a couple to get started with Visual Basic .NET. In this chapter, you'll learn to ask a user for data and accept that data from the keyboard. You'll also learn to print the data on your computer's screen or on your printer.

Computer Programs and I/O

The program that is currently running controls most input and output. If you load a program that doesn't use the keyboard, the program will not notice your keystrokes—no matter how much you type. Likewise, if a program wasn't designed to use your printer, you have no way of accessing the printer from that program. Obviously, then, if it's up to a program to control your computer's input and output, every programming language must contain commands for input and output. In fact, a programming language without I/O commands would be about as useful to you as a book of matches would be to a fish. By providing commands for putting data into the computer and getting data back out again, a computer language enables you to create interactive programs.

Interactive programs allow two-way communication between the user and the computer. For example, the computer might output a question to the user by printing the question on-screen. The user might then answer the question by typing on his or her keyboard.

Visual Basic .NET, like any other computer language, features several commands for controlling input and output. Because this is a book about Visual Basic .NET, however, things are a little bit more complicated than they were back in Visual Basic 6. The `DrawString` command, for example, enables you to make text appear on the computer's screen. You might want to do this in order to ask the user a question, or you might print text on the screen to show the user a piece of information he asked for. (By the way, you can also use a Label control to display text on the screen.) But before you can call upon the DrawString command, you must create graphics, font, and brush objects.

When creating a graphics object, you gain access to lots of cool commands, not the least of which is DrawString. You create a graphics object in your program by using this code:

```
Dim g As Graphics = CreateGraphics()
```

A font object tells the program the font you want to use to display the text. The easiest way to create a font object is to borrow the font object that Visual Basic .NET already created for your form. You do that with the following snippet:

```
Dim f As Font = Form1.DefaultFont
```

Finally, the brush object tells Visual Basic .NET the text color you want to use. Because you want your text to appear solid, you must create a solid brush. You create a black, solid brush using the following line of code:

```
Dim b As New SolidBrush(Color.Black)
```

Now, suppose you want to print a simple message on the screen. Try this:

1. Get Visual Basic .NET cranked up, and start a new project called TextProgram. (For details on starting a new project, see Chapter 3, "Creating Your First Project.")

2. Place a Button control at the bottom of the form and double-click the button to display its Click procedure in the code window.

3. Complete the procedure as shown in this code:

```
Private Sub Button1_Click(ByVal sender As System.Object, _
        ByVal e As System.EventArgs) Handles Button1.Click
    Dim g As Graphics = CreateGraphics()
    Dim f As Font = Form1.DefaultFont
    Dim b As New SolidBrush(Color.Black)
    g.DrawString("Here's some text output.", f, b, 20, 10)
    g.DrawString("Here's some more text output.", f, b, 20, 30)
    g.DrawString("And here's still more text output.", f, b, 20, 50)
End Sub
```

When you run the program and click the button, you see the screen shown in Figure 4.1.

Figure 4.1

Windows applications dis-play text in their windows.

As you can see, each `DrawString` command creates a single line of text on-screen, in the form's window. The command prints the text that you place after the open parenthesis. This text, called a *string literal*, must be enclosed in quotation marks. After the text, you list the font and brush objects, as well as the horizontal and vertical position of the text. You separate all these values with commas, and you end the command with a close parenthesis.

What's the g in front of the `DrawString` command? `DrawString` is actually a command that belongs to the graphics object. By placing the name of the object (g, in this case), followed by a dot, in front of the `DrawString` command, Visual Basic .NET knows where to look for the `DrawString` command. If you want to get technical about it, `DrawString` isn't really a command at all, but rather something called a *method*. You'll learn a lot about methods later in this book, especially in Chapter 23, "Properties, Methods, and Events: A Class's Innards." For now, just think of `DrawString` as a command.

> **Techno Talk**
>
> A **string** is a group of text characters. A **string literal** is text that you want the computer to use exactly as you type it. You tell the computer that a line of text is a string literal by enclosing the text in quotation marks. You'll run into strings and string literals a lot as you program with Visual Basic .NET or any other computer language.

Now you know how to use Visual Basic .NET to ask a computer user a question, which is one form of output. But how can you get the user's answer into your program? As you may have guessed, Visual Basic .NET has a way to get typed input from the user. You need to add a TextBox control to your form. But before you can learn about the TextBox control, you need to know about variables.

Introducing Variables

When you input data into a computer, the computer stores that data in its memory. You can think of your computer's memory as millions of little boxes, each holding a single value. Normally, each little box is numbered, starting at 0. The actual number of boxes in your computer depends upon how much memory you have installed. Figure 4.2 illustrates how your computer's memory is organized.

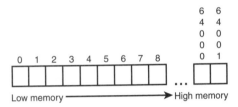

Figure 4.2

Computer memory is a lot like a bunch of numbered boxes where a program can store values.

When you input data into your computer, your computer stuffs the data into one of those little boxes that make up its memory. How does it know in which box the value should be stored, and how can you refer to that box in a way that makes sense within a program? This is where variables come in.

Variables are really just memory boxes with names. Because you, the programmer, supply the names, you can name your variables almost anything you want, making your programs easier to read and understand. Later in your program, you can store values into the memory box, by referring to its name. For example, to keep track of the score in a game, you might have a variable named score. Whenever the player's score changes, you can put the new score value into the variable named score. In this way, you've set aside a little piece of memory that contains data you need in your program.

You must, however, follow certain rules when creating variable names:

1. First, a variable name must be no longer than 255 characters. (If you need more characters than that, I suggest you look up the word "concise" in your dictionary.)

2. Second, the name must start with a letter. The other characters can be letters, numbers, or the underscore character. (You can't use spaces and most kinds of punctuation in a variable name.) Because Visual Basic .NET isn't case sensitive, you can use any combination of upper- or lowercase letters in a variable name—for example, the variable names Score, score, and SCORE all mean the same thing to Visual Basic .NET.

3. Finally, you can't use a Visual Basic .NET keyword as a variable name.

The following list shows examples of valid variable names.

```
Total
Money_Spent
FirstName
name23
AMOUNT
```

And here are some invalid variable names.

```
3456
current.balance
Date Paid
Print
```

Using Variables for Input

To get user input into your Visual Basic .NET programs, you can use something called a TextBox control. Suppose, for example, you're writing a program that needs to know the number of cars in a parking garage. Suppose also that when the user runs the program, the first thing he or she must do is input the current car count.

To solve this problem, try this:

1. Start a new Visual Basic .NET project called CarCount. Then, place a TextBox control and a Button control on the form (see Figure 4.3 for details).

2. Double-click the Button control to display its Click procedure in the Visual Basic .NET code window. Complete the Click procedure using the following code:

```
Private Sub Button1_Click(ByVal sender As System.Object, _
        ByVal e As System.EventArgs) Handles Button1.Click
    Dim g As Graphics = CreateGraphics()
    Dim f As Font = Form1.DefaultFont
    Dim b As New SolidBrush(Color.Black)
    Dim cars As Integer = CInt(TextBox1.Text)
    Dim str As String = "You have " & cars & " cars."
    g.DrawString(str, f, b, 20, 10)
End Sub
```

3. Now, run the program. Type a number into the text box (after deleting the "TextBox1" that's already there), and click the button. When you do, Visual Basic .NET jumps to the button's Click procedure, where the program grabs your input from the text box and prints the results in the window, as shown in Figure 4.3.

What happened here? You already know what the first three lines in the `Button1_Click` procedure do. But look at the following line, which is the fourth line in the procedure:

```
Dim cars As Integer = CInt(TextBox1.Text)
```

This line first tells Visual Basic .NET that you want a variable named `cars` that can hold integer values. (An integer is any whole number.) The equals sign tells Visual Basic .NET that you want to place a value into the variable. The `CInt` command converts the characters you typed into the text box into an integer. Visual Basic .NET then places that integer into the variable `cars`.

To understand how all this works, you first need to know that the TextBox control's name is `TextBox1`. It just so happens that a TextBox control has variables of its own. These special variables—called *properties*— enable the TextBox control to store information about itself. One of these pieces of information is the text the control contains, which the control stores in its `Text` property. As you've just seen, you can copy the text into your own variable by using the equals sign.

The word `cars` is a variable name, which is used to identify the little box in memory where Visual Basic .NET stores the response. Suppose you type the number 8 in response to the program. Your computer's memory might then look similar to Figure 4.4.

Whoops!

> If you type, into the text box, characters that aren't numbers, the program will crash. In Chapter 16, "Catching Runtime Errors," you'll learn to handle these kinds of errors, but for now, make sure you type the right kind of information into the text box.

Figure 4.4

Visual Basic .NET assigns a memory location to a variable.

```
                                  c                 6 6
                                  a                 4 4
                                  r                 0 0
                                  s                 0 0
    0  1  2  3  4  5  s  7  8      0 1
                      8                       ...
```

In this figure, Visual Basic .NET has assigned the variable cars to memory location 6 and has placed the value 8 into that location. Luckily, you don't have to worry about where Visual Basic .NET puts variables in memory; Visual Basic .NET handles all that for you.

This program also has a *string variable*, which is a variable that can hold a line of text. As you can see in the following example, the string variable is named str:

```
Dim str As String = "You have " & cars & " cars."
```

> **By the Way**
>
> Notice that Visual Basic .NET can easily tell the difference between the string literal "cars" and the variable cars. Now you know why the quotation marks are so important. In fact, without the quotation marks, Visual Basic .NET would interpret each word following the Print command as a variable rather than as a string.

Pretty fancy-looking string, wouldn't you say? This shows how powerful Visual Basic .NET strings can be. In this case, the string comprises not only string literals (such as "You have "), but also the value stored in the variable cars. See the ampersand (&) characters? By using ampersands, you can build a line of text from different elements. In the previous string declaration, the line of text comprises three elements: the string literal "You have ", the variable cars, and the string literal " cars.". The ampersands tell the Print command to place each of these elements one after the other on the same line.

Declaring Variables

Variables can exist as many different types. You'll learn about variable types in Chapter 5, "Crunching Numbers: It's Easier Than You Think," but for now you can think of variables as holding either numeric values or text. Technically, only a string variable can hold text, and only a numerical variable can hold numerical values. This may not seem to be the case with Visual Basic .NET, though, because Visual Basic .NET is so smart about figuring out how a program uses its variables. However, this cleverness comes with a price—when Visual Basic .NET has to figure out how to use a variable, it takes longer for Visual Basic .NET to assign a value to the variable. For this reason, you should declare your variables before you use them.

When you declare a variable, you not only tell Visual Basic .NET the variable's name, but also how the variable is to be used. For example, look at the following line from your last program:

```
Dim cars As Integer = CInt(TextBox1.Text)
```

You could have written this line as two lines, like this:

```
Dim cars As Integer
cars = CInt(TextBox1.Text)
```

Now, the first line is nothing more than a *variable declaration*. It tells Visual Basic .NET that you're going to use a variable named cars and that that variable will be used as an integer. The second line assigns a value to the variable.

This is all well and good, but what happens if the user types nonnumerical characters into the TextBox control? For example, what if the user typed "ten" into the box instead of "10"? There's no way that Visual Basic .NET can change the string "ten" into a numerical value, so Visual Basic .NET generates an error as shown in Figure 4.5.

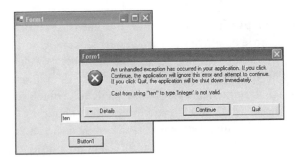

Figure 4.5

Visual Basic .NET displays errors when something goes wrong in your program.

You can never store a string in a numerical variable. For example, the following Visual Basic .NET lines cause an error:

```
' Dont' do this!
Dim value As Integer
value = "This is a string literal"
```

You can, however, create a variable for holding text, by declaring the variable's type to be String. The following example shows a version of the Click procedure that declares cars as a string variable:

```
Private Sub Button1_Click(ByVal sender As System.Object, _
        ByVal e As System.EventArgs) Handles Button1.Click
    Dim g As Graphics = CreateGraphics()
    Dim f As Font = Form1.DefaultFont
    Dim b As New SolidBrush(Color.Black)
    Dim cars As String = TextBox1.Text
    Dim str As String = "You have " & cars & " cars."
    g.Clear(Color.White)
    g.DrawString(str, f, b, 20, 10)
End Sub
```

This version of the procedure works just like the previous one, with a couple of small difference. It doesn't matter whether the user types a string or a number into the text box. In both cases, the result is a string that gets stored into cars. You may find it confusing that the value 10 can be both a numerical value and a text value. But you have to remember that there's a big difference between the text character "1" and the value 1. When numbers are part of a string, Visual Basic .NET treats them just the same as any other character, such as "A" or "?". The downside is that a program cannot perform mathematical operations with numbers that are stored as strings. Numbers in a string are not really numbers at all, anymore than letters are numbers.

Another difference in this example is the use of the command g.Clear(Color.White) to erase the window's drawing area each time you click the button. This command fills the window with the color white.

Here's something else interesting about variables and strings. In some cases, it only takes one memory location (one of those little boxes you learned about) to store a number. However, strings are often made up of more than one character, and only one character can fit in any memory location. This means that string data actually takes up much more space in your computer's memory than numerical values do. Exactly how much space can be hard to predict because Visual Basic .NET stores extra information about the string along with the string. But any string takes up a little more memory than the number of characters in the string. For example, the string "This is a test" takes up a little more than 14 memory locations.

Check This Out

As you write your Visual Basic .NET programs, watch out for misspelled variable names. Spelling a variable name incorrectly creates program bugs that are difficult to find. For example, suppose you have in your program a variable named TotalNumbers. As you type the lines of your program, you accidentally spell this variable as Total_Numbers. To Visual Basic .NET, TotalNumbers and Total_Numbers are different variables, each with their own value.

One way around this problem is to add the line Option Explicit On to all your Visual Basic .NET programs. This line tells Visual Basic .NET that every variable name must be declared before it can be used. Then, if you accidentally misspell a variable name, Visual Basic .NET will recognize the misspelled name as an undeclared variable and generate an error. If you have changed the default setting, place the Option Explicit On line at the very top of the project's code window, outside of any procedures in the program.

Unlike previous versions of Visual Basic, Visual Basic .NET defaults to having the Option Explicit On setting activated automatically—that is, if you haven't changed Visual Studio.NET's default settings, you probably don't need to add Option Explicit On to your source code files to get protection from misspelled variable names.

Labeling Your Text Boxes

A TextBox control without a label is as confusing as a David Lynch film. After all, unless you tell the user what you expect him to enter, how will he know what to do? (This, of course, doesn't apply to programs written for mind readers.) Because you frequently need to prompt for information in programs, Visual Basic .NET provides a special control, called a Label control, for labeling items in a window.

You can easily add a label to the program you've been working on in this chapter. First, place a Label control on the form, dragging it into place above the TextBox control. Then, change the Label control's Text property to **Enter the number of cars: and press Return.** You can make this change by clicking the label to select it, and then changing the value of the Text property in the Properties window, as shown in Figure 4.6.

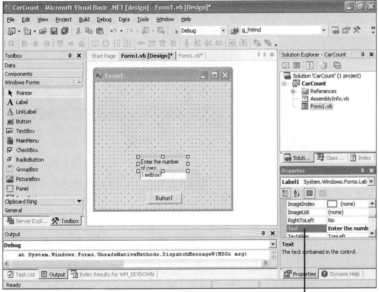

Change the Text Property here

Figure 4.6

You can change the label's text in the Properties window.

(If you like, you can also erase the string "TextBox1" from the text box by deleting the text from the TextBox control's Text property in the Properties window.) Figure 4.7 shows the program in its final form.

Figure 4.7

Now the text box has a label so the user knows what to type.

Having Fun with Input and Output

Now that you've learned a little about Visual Basic .NET input and output, how about finishing up with a program that puts this new knowledge to the test?

1. Start a new Visual Basic .NET project, and place three TextBox controls, two Label controls, and one Button control as shown in Figure 4.8.

Figure 4.8

Position your controls as shown here.

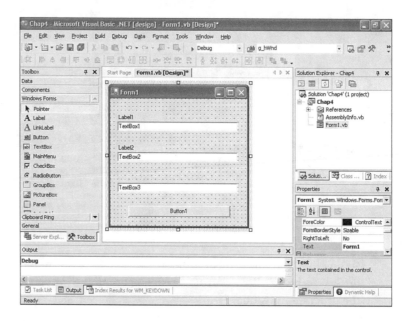

Be sure to place the controls in order from top to bottom so that the TextBox controls are in the order Text1, Text2, and Text3. And remember that you can use the control's handles to resize them.

2. Clear all the text from the TextBox controls' Text properties. Then, change the first label's Text property to **Enter first name:** and the second label's Text property to **Enter last name:.** Finally, double-click the Button control to display its Click procedure, and complete the procedure as follows:

```
Private Sub Button1_Click(ByVal sender As System.Object, _
        ByVal e As System.EventArgs) Handles Button1.Click
    Dim firstName As String
    Dim lastName As String
    firstName = TextBox1.Text
    lastName = TextBox2.Text
    TextBox3.Text = "Hello, " & firstName & " " & lastName
End Sub
```

Whoops!

Novice programmers often don't realize how fussy Visual Basic .NET is about tiny errors, such as missing or incorrect punctuation. Every character in a program is important. Be careful not to overlook any or to mistype any. Such mistakes can cause Visual Basic .NET to display an error or result in unpredictable program bugs. Most big companies can tell you horror stories about how a single missing semicolon or comma caused them thousands of dollars worth of problems.

3. Now, run the program, and type your first and last names into the appropriate text boxes. Click the button, and a personalized greeting appears in the third text box, as shown in Figure 4.9.

Figure 4.9

This chapter's final program says hello.

You should be able to figure out most of what's going on in this program's Click procedure. The first two lines tell Visual Basic .NET that the variables firstName and lastName will be holding text data. The next two lines copy the text from the TextBox controls into your new string variables. The final line is something new. There, rather than copying text from a TextBox control's Text property, the program is copying text *to* a TextBox control's Text property. This action makes the text appear in the control, as you can see in the previous figure. Notice that, when you're displaying text in controls, you don't need to bother with all that graphics object junk. Cool!

The Least You Need to Know

- ◆ Input and output devices transfer data to and from a computer.

- ◆ The DrawString method of the Graphics object prints a line of text in a window.

- ◆ String literals must be enclosed in quotation marks.

- ◆ Your computer's memory can be thought of as a series of little boxes, with each box holding a single value.

- ◆ Variables are named places in memory where a program can store data.

- ◆ Numeric variables can hold only numeric values. String variables can hold only text (or numbers that the computer treats as text).

- ◆ You can use TextBox controls to get input from a program's user. You should use Label controls to label text boxes.

- ◆ A TextBox control's Text property holds the text in the control, whereas a Label control's Text property holds the text displayed in the label.

Crunching Numbers: It's Easier Than You Think

In This Chapter

- ◆ Use variables in mathematical expressions
- ◆ Understand arithmetic operations
- ◆ Discover the order of operations
- ◆ Learn about different data types

You've probably heard that programming a computer requires lots of math. And if you're like most people, all those formulas and equations you learned in high school now look stranger than an ostrich at a square dance. Guess what? Most programs require only simple mathematical calculations—addition, subtraction, multiplication, and division—the same stuff you do every day.

Moreover, when you're writing a program, you won't have to wear down pencils adding long columns of numbers or fry your brain trying to figure out 35,764 divided by 137. The computer can do the calculations for you. If you know how to use the basic arithmetic operations to solve simple problems, you know all the math necessary to write a computer program. (Well, most computer programs, anyway; don't expect to be able to write the next version of *Baldur's Gate* without a college degree in mathematics.) Computer programming is more logical than mathematical. It's just a matter of common sense. So, if you have trouble remembering to come in out of the rain, computer programming may not be for you.

Still, you can't avoid math entirely. Heaven knows, your humble author has tried. Computers, after all, are number-crunching machines that like nothing better than spitting out the results of hundreds, thousands, or even millions of calculations. It's up to you, the wise programmer, to give the computer the commands it needs to perform these calculations. In this chapter, you'll learn to do just that.

Looking at Variables Mathematically

In Chapter 4, "Variables and I/O: Programming Secrets," you learned about variables—the little boxes in memory in which your program stores numbers. A computer program can also use values that never change called literals. Unlike a literal such as the number 3, variables can represent almost any value Variables are extremely valuable entities. Because variables represent numbers, you can use them in mathematical operations. (Variables can also represent text, but in this chapter, we're talking about math and you can't do math with text.)

For example, suppose you run a small video store, and you want to know how many tapes you have. You might think to yourself, "I've got 20 copies of *Naughty Banshees* from Venus, 50 copies of *Dances with Muskrats*, and 10 copies of *Ren and Stimpy's 60-Minute Workout*. So, I've got 80 videotapes." If you want to use the computer to solve this mathematical problem, you could load up a calculator program and type the command 20+50+10. The computer would print the answer 80, as you can see in Figure 5.1.

Just as you would suspect, the ± symbol also means addition in a computer program.

There's a better way, however, to solve the videotape problem—one that works with any number of videotapes. This new method uses variables in mathematical operations. As you've learned, you can name a variable just about anything you like. (Yes, you can even call a variable lateForDinner.) Names such as naughty, dances, and stimpy are completely acceptable. Beginning to see the light?

Figure 5.1

One way to perform calcula-tions on your computer is with a software calculator.

Try this:

1. Start a new Visual Basic .NET project named VideoCount, and place four Label controls, three TextBox controls, and one Button control as shown in Figure 5.2.

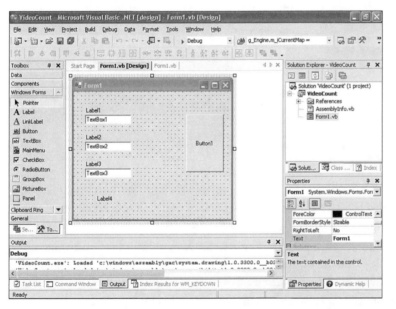

Figure 5.2

Position the controls as shown here.

2. Double-click the Form object, and add the following code to the Form1_Load proce-dure that Visual Basic .NET already started for you:

```
Label1.Text = "Enter # of Naughty Banshees:"
Label2.Text = "Enter # of Dances with Muskrats:"
Label3.Text = "Enter # of Ren and Stimpy:"
Label4.Text = "Total number of video tapes:"
```

```
TextBox1.Text = "0"
TextBox2.Text = "0"
TextBox3.Text = "0"
Button1.Text = "Calculate"
```

Figure 5.3 shows what the Load procedure should look like when you're done.

Figure 5.3

The form's Load procedure.

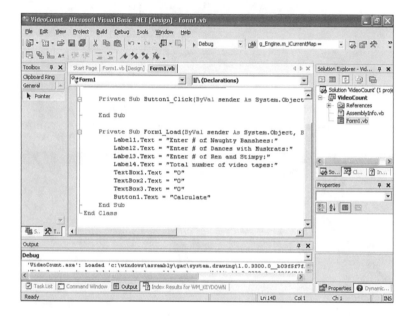

The form's Load procedure sets the various controls' Text properties to the text the controls need to display. Visual Basic .NET jumps to the Load procedure when you run the program, making it a great place to set things up in your program.

3. Now, above the code window, click the Form1.vb [Design] tab to return to the form. Then, double-click the button to go to its Click procedure. Add the following lines to the procedure, as shown in Figure 5.4:

```
Dim naughty As Integer = CInt(TextBox1.Text)
Dim dances As Integer = CInt(TextBox2.Text)
Dim stimpy As Integer = CInt(TextBox3.Text)
Dim tapes As Integer = naughty + dances + stimpy
Label4.Text = "Total number of video tapes: " & tapes
```

The Button1_Click procedure, which Visual Basic .NET jumps to when the user clicks the button, gets the values typed into the text boxes, changes the values to integers, adds the values together, and uses the fourth Label control's Text property to display the result of the calculation.

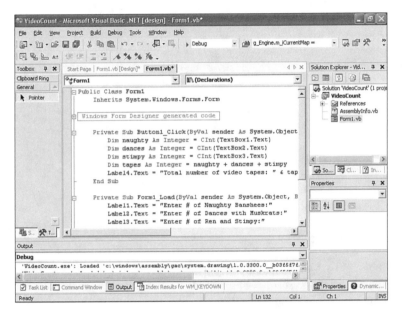

Figure 5.4

Using the button's Click *procedure.*

4. Now run the program and type three values into the text boxes, and click the Calculate button. The computer zaps your entries into the variables naughty, dances, and stimpy (converting the values from strings to integers) Then the program adds the variables and plunks the total into another variable called tapes. Finally, the program uses the fourth Label control's Text property to display the number contained in tapes, as shown in Figure 5.5. (Visual Basic .NET automatically converts the number to text so that it can be displayed in the control.)

Check This Out

If a Label control isn't big enough to hold its text, you can resize the control by clicking it and then dragging the control's sizing handles. You can do the same thing to resize your program's form or any other control. However, you can only do this type of resizing when you're designing the program, not when the program is running.

By using a program similar to this one, you can get a new tape total anytime you like. Just provide your program with new counts for each movie.

Figure 5.5

This program sums the number of videotapes.

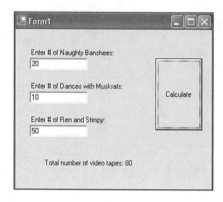

Venturing Beyond Addition

Of course, computers can do more than add. They can perform any basic arithmetic operation. Visual Basic .NET even has functions for figuring out things like square roots and absolute values. If you don't know what a square root or an absolute value is, don't hit the panic button; you still won't have trouble programming your computer. Just don't plan to write an algebra tutorial any time soon.

Let's assume that your videotape store is still thriving, despite its horrible selection and the fact that the local chapter of Citizens Against Painfully Stupid Movies has a contract out on your head. Suppose you now want to find the total value of your inventory as well as the average cost per tape. To find the total value of your inventory, follow these steps:

1. Multiply each title's price by the number of copies you own. Perform this calculation for all titles.

2. Add together the amounts from Step 1 to get the total value.

3. To find the average value per tape, divide the total value by the total number of tapes.

To build this program, follow these steps:

1. Start a new Visual Basic .NET project named VideoValue, and resize the form, place eight Label controls, six TextBox controls, and one Button control as shown in Figure 5.6.

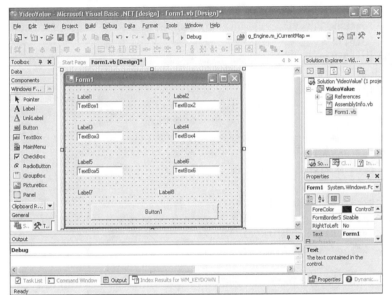

Figure 5.6

Position the controls for the VideoValue project as shown here.

2. Now, double-click the Form object, and type the following code into the Load procedure:

```
Button1.Text = "Calculate"
Label1.Text = "# of Naughty Banshees:"
Label2.Text = "Price each:"
Label3.Text = "# of Dances with Muscrats:"
Label4.Text = "Price each:"
Label5.Text = "# of Ren and Stimpy:"
Label6.Text = "Price each:"
Label7.Text = "Total value:"
Label8.Text = "Average value:"
TextBox1.Text = "0"
TextBox2.Text = "0"
TextBox3.Text = "0"
TextBox4.Text = "0"
TextBox5.Text = "0"
TextBox6.Text = "0"
```

3. Go back to the form (by clicking the Form1.vb [Design] tab), double-click the button, and finish the Button1_Click procedure with these lines:

```
Dim quantity As Integer
Dim totalNumTapes As Integer
Dim price As Single
```

```
Dim totalValue As Single
quantity = CInt(TextBox1.Text)
totalNumTapes = quantity
price = CSng(TextBox2.Text)
totalValue = quantity * price
quantity = CInt(TextBox3.Text)
totalNumTapes = totalNumTapes + quantity
price = CSng(TextBox4.Text)
totalValue = totalValue + quantity * price
quantity = CInt(TextBox5.Text)
totalNumTapes = totalNumTapes + quantity
price = CSng(TextBox6.Text)
totalValue = totalValue + quantity * price
Dim averageValue As Single = totalValue / totalNumTapes
Label7.Text = "Total value: " & totalValue
Label8.Text = "Average value: " & averageValue
```

4. After typing in the code, run the program, and enter appropriate values into each of the text boxes. Then click the Calculate button to see the total value of the video tapes and the average value for a tape, as shown in Figure 5.7.

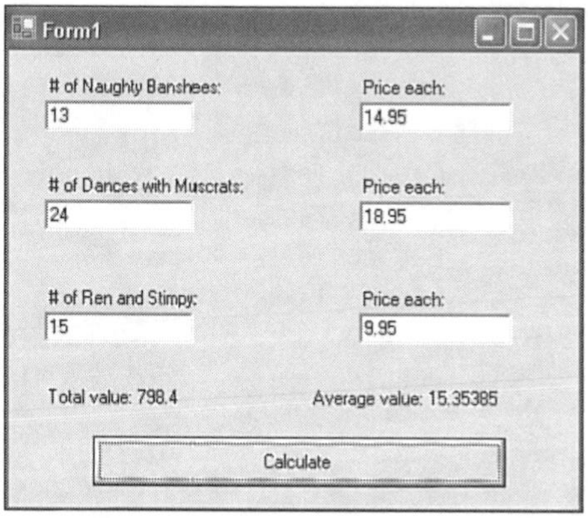

Figure 5.7

This program calculates the total and average values of videotapes.

When you run this program, Visual Basic .NET begins at the form's Load procedure, where it sets the various controls' Text properties. When you click the Calculate button, Visual Basic .NET jumps to the Button1_Click procedure, where the program gets the quantity and price of the first video title. These values are temporarily stored in the variables quantity and price. The quantity is then placed in the variable totalNumTapes. The total value for all tapes with that title is calculated by multiplying the price of the tape by the quantity; that total is stored in the variable totalValue.

Next, the program gets the quantity and price of the second title. After the program retrieves that information, it adds the quantity for the second title to `totalNumTapes` (which already contains the quantity for the first title). This total is the combined quantity for the first two titles. The program calculates the total value for the two titles by multiplying the second tape's price by its quantity and adding that amount to `totalValue`.

The program processes the third tape the same way. Then, the program calculates the average value for all tapes by dividing `totalValue` by `totalNumTapes`. Finally, the program displays the results by setting the Label7 and Label8 `Text` property.

Yes, this program is a bit longer than the first one, but it still uses only basic arithmetic. It's longer because it performs more calculations than the first example.

If you look at the program carefully, you'll see some new ideas. First, the program declares a few of the variables as `Single`, rather than `Integer`. A `Single` value holds a *floating-point* number, which is a number with integer and decimal portions. For example, 26.82 is a floating-point number.

Second, you might have seen something strange about `totalNumTapes`. Specifically, what the heck does the following line do:

```
totalNumTapes = totalNumTapes + quantity
```

How can the same variable be on both sides of an equation? Why do I keep asking these dumb questions?

First, you have to stop thinking that the equals sign (=) always means equals. It doesn't. In Visual Basic .NET arithmetic operations, this symbol actually means "takes the value of," which makes it an assignment operator. (Even in programming, however, the equals sign still can mean "is equal to," as you'll learn in Chapter 7, "If, Else, and ElseIf: Decisions, Decisions, Decisions.")

You also must understand that Visual Basic .NET interprets statements from the right side of the equals sign to left side. So, the program adds `totalNumTapes` and `quantity` first, and then assigns the result of the addition back to `totalNumTapes`—that is, the result is stored in `totalNumTapes`, wiping out the value that was there previously.

Check This Out

Notice how the program reuses the variables **price** and **quantity**. You don't need to save the price and quantity of each tape once you've added them to the running totals, so you can use **price** and **quantity** as input variables for every tape.

By the Way

Visual Basic .NET uses an assignment operator to assign a value to a variable. In Visual Basic .NET, the assignment operator is an equals sign (=), but other computer languages may use different assignment operators. In Pascal, for example, the assignment operator is a colon followed by an equals sign (:=).

Confused? Suppose `totalNumTapes` is equal to 7, and `quantity` is equal to 3. When the program sees this line:

```
totalNumTapes = totalNumTapes + quantity
```

It adds 7 to 3 and pops the value 10 into `totalNumTapes`. Using this method, you can add values to a variable that already holds a value. You'll do this often in your programs.

By the way, a Visual Basic .NET program uses an asterisk (*) to represent multiplication, not a × symbol as you might expect. The forward slash character (/) represents division, because the computer keyboard doesn't have a regular division symbol. You could try painting a division symbol on one of your keys, but you'll still have to use the slash character in your programs.

Table 5.1 shows all of the arithmetic operators Visual Basic .NET.

Table 5.1 Visual Basic .NET Arithmetic Operators

Operator	Name	Use To
+	Addition	Sum values
–	Subtraction	Subtract values
*	Multiplication	Multiply values
/	Division	Divide values
\	Integer division	Determine the whole number result of division
^	Exponentiation	Raise a value to a power
Mod	Modulus	Determine the remainder of division

Table 5.2 shows some examples of mathematical operations using the arithmetic operators.

Table 5.2 Visual Basic .NET Arithmetic Operators in Action

Operation	Result
5+8	13
12–7	5
3*6	18
10/3	3.333333
10\3	3
2^3	8
10 Mod 3	1

Check This Out

When you use regular division, denoted by the forward slash character (/), you are performing the type of division you learned in school. You may end up with a result like 2 (such as in the operation 4/2) or a result like 2.4 (such as in the operation 12/5).

When you use integer division, denoted by the backslash character (\), your answer will always be an integer, because Visual Basic .NET drops any part of the result that lies to the right of the decimal point. This means that, with integer division, the operation 12\5 results in 2, rather than 2.4.

The Mod operator performs division, too, but it only gives you the remainder of the division. For example, 4 goes into 14 three times with a remainder of 2, so the operation 14 Mod 4 yields a result of 2. As a beginning programmer, you probably won't have a lot of use for this operator.

Finally, the exponentiation operator (^) is used to raise numbers to a power. When you raise a number to a power, you multiply the number times itself the number of times indicated by the exponent (the number after the ^ character). For example, 10^2 is the same as 10 * 10, which equals 100. The operation 5^3 is the same as 5 * 5 * 5, which equals 125.

Knowing Your Order of Operations

Another curious line in the previous program is

```
totalValue = totalValue + price * quantity
```

This program line is similar to the line that calculates the total number of tapes, but it contains both an addition and multiplication operation. This brings up the important topic of operator precedence or, as it's more commonly known, the order of operations.

If you were to add totalValue to price and then multiply the sum by quantity, you'd get an incorrect result. Operator precedence dictates that all multiplication must take place before any addition. So in the preceding line, totalValue is calculated by first multiplying price times quantity and then adding that product to totalValue.

As a rule, the order of operations for Visual Basic .NET is exponentiation first; then multiplication, division, integer division, and modulus; and finally, addition and subtraction. Operations of the same precedence are evaluated from left to right. For example, in the expression 3 * 5 / 2,

Whoops!

Don't forget about operator precedence; if you do, your calculations won't be accurate, and your programs won't run correctly.

3 is first multiplied by 5, which gives a result of 15. This result is then divided by 2, giving a result of 7.5. The Visual Basic .NET operator precedence is summarized in Table 5.3.

Table 5.3   Visual Basic .NET Operator Precedence

Order	Operator	Name
1	^	Exponentiation
2	* / \ Mod	Multiplication, division, integer division, and modulus
3	+ –	Addition and subtraction

Check This Out

When writing a program line that contains many arithmetic operations, you may want to use parentheses to more clearly indicate the order of operation. For example, the formula `totalValue = totalValue + (price * quantity)` is easier to read than the original formula `totalValue = totalValue + price * quantity`. Both formulas, however, yield the same result.

You can change operator precedence by using parentheses. For example, suppose you wanted the addition in the following line to be calculated before the multiplication:

```
totalValue = totalValue + price * quantity
```

In this case, you could rewrite the line as

```
totalValue = (totalValue + price) * quantity
```

Any operation enclosed in parentheses is performed first. Consequently, Visual Basic .NET adds `totalValue` and `price` first, and then multiplies the sum by `quantity`.

Using Data Types

You'll be happy to know you're almost finished with the math stuff. You only have to explore one more topic before you move on: data types. You've already had a little experience with data types in Chapter 4, but you probably didn't pay too much attention at the time.

When you used numeric variables and string variables, you were using variables of two different data types. Numeric variables can hold only numbers, and string variables can hold only text strings. What you haven't learned is that numeric variables can be divided into many other data types, including integers, long integers, single-precision, and double-precision.

> ### By the Way
>
> Although numeric variables can hold only numbers and string variables can hold only text strings, that doesn't mean a string variable can't hold a character that represents a number. For example, when assigned to a numeric variable, the number 3 represents a value that can be used in arithmetic operations. However, the character 3 assigned to a string variable is just a text character—no different from any other text character, such as A or Z. Although a string variable can hold number characters, those characters cannot be used directly in mathematical operations.

An integer is any whole number, such as 23, 76, –65, or 1,200. Notice that none of these numbers contain a decimal portion. Notice also that none of them are smaller than –2,147,483,648 or greater than 2,147,483,647. A Visual Basic .NET integer must fall into this range.

What if you need to use a number that doesn't fit into the integer range? For example, what if, for some bizarre reason, you're trying to count all the stars in the universe? You can use a long integer. A long integer resembles an integer in that it can hold only a whole number. However, the range of a long integer is much, much larger: –9,223,372,036,854,775,808 to 9,223,372,036,854,775,807, to be exact. Unless you're trying to calculate the national debt or count the number of times Elizabeth Taylor has been married, you're not likely to need values larger than these. (For you geeks out there, 9,223,372,036,854,775,807 is pronounced, "nine quintillion, 223 quadrillion, 372 trillion, 36 billion, 854 million, 775 thousand, eight hundred and seven." Yikes!)

> ### ⚠ CAUTION
> ### Whoops!
>
> When writing a program, you may be tempted to make all your integer variables long integers and all your floating-point variables double-precision. When you do this, you no longer need to worry about whether your values go out of range. However, this technique has two drawbacks. First, long integers and double-precision floating-point numbers take up more memory space than their smaller counterparts. Second, your computer takes longer to access and manipulate these larger values, so using them can significantly slow down your programs. Use long integers and double-precision values only when you really need them.

Numbers that contain a decimal portion are called floating-point numbers. Like integers, they come in two flavors. A single-precision floating-point number is accurate down to six decimal places (for example, 34.875637). A double-precision floating-point number, on the other hand, is accurate down to 14 decimal places (for example, 657.36497122357638). Floating-point numbers in Visual Basic .NET can be very tiny or incredibly large.

Visual Basic .NET also provides a couple of unusual data types, called `Object` and `Decimal`. An `Object` variable can contain almost any type of data, leaving it to Visual Basic .NET to figure out the best way to store the data. In fact, `Object` is the default Visual Basic .NET data type. When you declare a variable with no data type, Visual Basic .NET makes it an `Object`. For example, the following lines both declare a variable of the `Object` data type:

```
Dim value1
Dim value2 As Object
```

The `Decimal` data type is another floating-point type of number but is even more accurate than the `Double` data type. Let's just say that a `Decimal` value can be almost big enough to hold the value of Bill Gates's net worth!

> **CAUTION**
>
> ### Whoops!
>
> Like a variable, a literal has a data type. The difference is that the data type is implicit. For example, 10 is an integer, 23.7564 is a single-precision real number, and "Alexander" is a string. You can tell what the data type is just by looking at the value, and so can Visual Basic .NET.

Mixing Data Types

If you look back at the previous example program, you may notice this line:

```
totalValue = quantity * price
```

Here, Visual Basic .NET multiplies a floating-point number, `price`, times an integer, `quantity`. Seems like the old case of apples and oranges, doesn't it? In a way, it is. You must be careful when mixing data types in expressions, to be sure you get the result you expect. The data type you'll end up with is the one on the left of the equals sign. In this case, the variable on the left of the equals sign, `totalValue`, is a single-precision floating-point number (the `Single` data type), so the result of the multiplication will be a single-precision floating-point number.

Unless the expression contains only integers, be especially careful when assigning results of a calculation to an integer. You could get an incorrect result. For example, take a look at this line:

```
result = 13.5 * 3.3
```

This operation makes `result` equal to 45, not 44.55 as you might expect. Why? The variable `result` is an integer, so it cannot hold a floating-point number like 44.55. When Visual Basic .NET solves this expression, it first multiplies 13.5 times 3.3 to get the result of 44.55. Visual Basic .NET then rounds this answer to the nearest integer, which is 45, because you've asked it to store the answer as an integer.

Unless you've changed its settings, Visual Basic .NET defaults to `Option Strict On`, a setting that protects you from making the kinds of mistakes described in the previous paragraph. The `Option Strict On` setting won't let you do things like assign floating-point numbers to integers or declare variables without specifying a data type.

The Least You Need to Know

- Computer programming requires more logic than math. However, you can't avoid some mathematical operations in your programs.

- Variables can hold any value you assign to them, whereas literals never change. Because variables can change value in your programs, you can use them to represent numbers whose values you don't know ahead of time.

- You can perform all normal arithmetic operations with Visual Basic .NET, including addition (+), subtraction (-), multiplication (*), and division (/). Other operations available are integer division (\), exponentiation (^), and modulus (`Mod`).

- When used in arithmetic expressions, the equals sign (=) acts as an assignment operator.

- All arithmetic expressions in Visual Basic .NET follow the standard rules of operator precedence (order of operations).

- Variables and literals in a Visual Basic .NET program can be one of many data types, including integer, long integer, single-precision floating-point, double-precision floating-point, and string.

Chapter 6

Strings: A Frank Textual Discussion

In This Chapter

♦ Join strings together

♦ Calculate the length of a string

♦ Manipulate substrings

♦ Convert between strings and numbers

Pictures of bathing beauties (or well-oiled hunks, for you ladies) may be more fun to look at than a screen full of words and numbers. The simple truth, however, is that most information displayed on your computer screen is in text form. This fact separates computer users into two groups: those who would rather hang out at the beach and those who understand that computers were designed to help humans deal with large amounts of information, which most often is presented in text form.

Because text displays are so important in computing, Visual Basic .NET has a number of functions and commands that manipulate text. These functions enable you to join two or more strings into one, find the length of a string, extract a small portion of a string, or convert numbers to strings or strings to numbers. In this chapter, you'll learn to use many of the Visual Basic .NET string-handling functions. The rest of you, follow me.

Joining Strings

You'll often have two or more strings in your programs that you must combine into one. For example, you may have a user's first name and last name in two separate strings. In order to get the user's entire name into a single string, you have to concatenate (join together end-to-end) the two strings. Use the Visual Basic .NET concatenation operator, which is the ampersand (&) character on your keyboard, to handle this string-handling task. To join three strings, for example, type the following:

```
string1 & string2 & string3
```

Simply joining the strings, however, is not a complete program statement; you also must tell Visual Basic .NET where to store the new string. To do this, use the Visual Basic .NET assignment operator, the equals sign (=). The assignment operator for strings works just like the assignment operator for numeric variables. For example, to make the string variable insult equal to the text string "Your breath is strong enough to lift a horse", use the following command:

```
insult = "Your breath is strong enough to lift a horse"
```

To see how all this works, look at the following lines:

```
Dim str1 As String
Dim str2 As String
Dim str3 As String
str1 = "This is "
str2 = "a test."
str3 = str1 & str2
MessageBox.Show(str3)
```

These lines first declare three string variables and assign strings to two of the variables, str1 and str2. Then, the sixth line joins the first two strings together and assigns the result to the third string variable, str3.

Determining the Length of a String

Every string has a length, which is the number of characters contained in that string. For example, the string "Why did the chicken cross the road?" has a length of 35, because it contains 35 characters. (Spaces are characters, too!) The string "Because the farmer was chasing him with a hatchet." has a length of 50.

Check This Out _____

An empty string is a string that contains 0 characters. How can a string contain 0 characters? When you assign a string variable to an empty string, you get a string with a length of 0, as shown in the following example: `string1 = ""`.

Notice that there are no characters between the quotation marks. This creates an empty string. At first, you may think creating an empty string makes about as much sense as drinking from an empty glass. But sometimes you may want to initialize a string variable this way so that you know the string contains no old data.

Sometimes in your program, you may need to know the length of a string. To find the length of a string variable, use the String object's `Length` property, as in the following example:

```
Dim string1 As String
Dim length As Integer
string1 = "VB rocks the house!"
length = string1.Length
```

(Notice that this example refers to a string variable called `string1`. The number is actually part of the variable's name, and is required because `String` is a Visual Basic .NET keyword. For more details, refer to Chapter 4, "Variables and I/O: Programming Secrets," if you need to review the rules of creating variable names.)

The `Length` property returns the length of the string as a numerical value that can be used anywhere you can use a numeric value.

You're now probably asking, "What the heck is a property?" A property is nothing more than an attribute of an object. Just as you, as a human object, have as an attribute the color of your eyes, a String object has as an attribute the number of characters in the string. As you've seen in the previous example, you access an object's properties by following the object's name with a period and the name of the property:

```
length = string1.Length
```

To get a better idea of how the `Length` property works, try this:

1. Start a new Visual Basic .NET project named StringLength, and then place four Label controls, two TextBox controls, and one Button control as shown in Figure 6.1.

Figure 6.1

Position the controls as shown here.

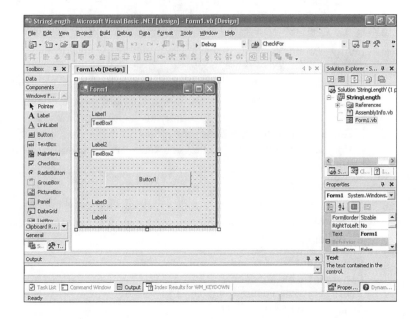

2. Double-click the Form object to display the code window, and then type the following lines into the form's Load procedure (Visual Basic .NET will have already started the Form1_Load procedure for you):

```
Label1.Text = "First name:"
Label2.Text = "Last name:"
Label3.Text = "Full name:"
Label4.Text = "Name length:"
Button1.Text = "Process Names"
TextBox1.Text = ""
TextBox2.Text = ""
```

Figure 6.2 shows you how the finished procedure should look.

3. Click the Form1.vb [Design] tab to get back to the form, and then double-click the button control. Visual Basic .NET brings up the Button1_Click procedure for you. Add the following lines to that procedure:

```
Dim firstName As String
Dim lastName As String
Dim fullName As String
Dim nameLength As Integer
firstName = TextBox1.Text
lastName = TextBox2.Text
fullName = firstName & " " & lastName
nameLength = fullName.Length
Label3.Text = "Full name: " & fullName
Label4.Text = "Name length: " & nameLength
```

Figure 6.3 shows you how the finished procedure should look.

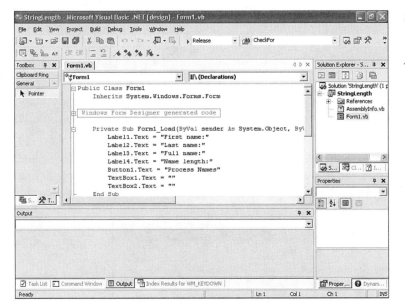

Figure 6.2

The finished Form1_Load *procedure.*

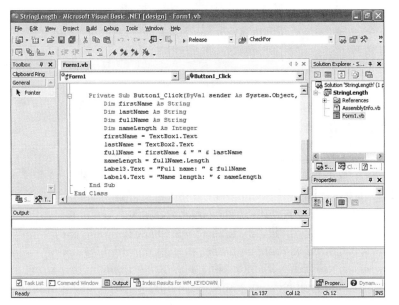

Figure 6.3

The finished Button1_Click *procedure.*

The Form1_Load procedure sets the various controls' Text properties to the text the controls need to display. As you may remember, Visual Basic .NET jumps to the Form1_Load procedure when you run the program, so it's a good place to assign starting values to controls' properties. Finally, the Button1_Click procedure, which Visual Basic .NET jumps to when the user clicks the button, performs the following actions …

◆ It declares the variables needed in the procedure.

◆ It retrieves the names typed into the text boxes.

◆ It joins the names together.

◆ It uses the third and fourth Label controls' Text properties to display the final name and the length of the name.

Try the program yourself. Run the program, and then type a first name and last name into the appropriate boxes. Click the Process Names button, and the program displays the full name and the name's length, as shown in Figure 6.4.

Figure 6.4

This program can count the number of characters in a name.

Extracting a Substring

Just as you can join strings to create a larger string, so too can you separate strings into smaller strings called *substrings*. A Visual Basic .NET String object provides the Substring method especially for extracting whatever portion of a string you need.

The Substring method can return a specified number of characters in a string from a given character to the end of the string. This is similar to what happens when the hatchet-wielding farmer catches up with his runaway chicken—except cutting a substring from another string is a lot less messy than separating a chicken from its head.

Techno Talk

A **substring** is a portion of a larger string. For example, the string "mour Twit" is a substring of "Seymour Twitdum".

To use Substring this way, you might type the following command:

```
string2 = string1.Substring(3)
```

This method call has one argument—the starting character in the string (where the first character number is 0). So, the previous example returns all the characters in `string1` from character 3 to the end. If `string1` was the phrase "Yo ho ho and a bottle of rum", `Substring(3)` would return the string "ho ho and a bottle of rum". The following code snippet shows the lines you would type to create and display this sample substring:

```
Dim string1 As String
Dim string2 As String
string1 = "Yo ho ho and a bottle of rum."
string2 = string1.Substring(3)
MessageBox.Show(string2)
```

You can also use the `Substring` method to extract a substring from anywhere inside the source string. To do this, substring needs not only the starting character but also the number of characters to include. So, the following statement returns an eight-character substring that starts at the seventh character of `string1`:

```
string2 = string1.Substring(7, 8)
```

If `string1` was the phrase "Visual Basic is way cool!", the previous call to `Substring(7, 8)` would return the string "Basic is". The following lines accomplish that task:

```
Dim string1 As String
Dim string2 As String
string1 = "Visual Basic is way Cool!"
string2 = string1.Substring(7, 8)
MessageBox.Show(string2)
```

To get a little practice with substrings, try this:

1. Start a new Visual Basic .NET project named Substrings, and place four Label controls, one TextBox control, and one Button control, as shown in Figure 6.5.

2. Double-click the `Form` object to display the code window, and type the following lines into the `Load` procedure (Visual Basic .NET will have already started the `Form1_Load` procedure for you):

```
Label1.Text = "Enter string:"
Label2.Text = ""
Label3.Text = ""
Label4.Text = ""
TextBox1.Text = "ABCDEFGHIJKLMNOP"
Button1.Text = "Get Substrings"
```

Figure 6.5

Position the controls as shown here.

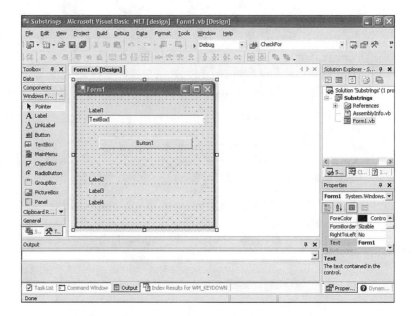

3. Now, click the Form1.vb [Design] tab to get back to the form, and then double-click the button control. Visual Basic .NET brings up the Button1_Click procedure for you. Add the following lines to that procedure:

```
Dim string1 As String
Dim string2 As String
Dim string3 As String
Dim string4 As String
string1 = TextBox1.Text
string2 = string1.Substring(0, 5)
string3 = string1.Substring(string1.Length - 5, 5)
string4 = string1.Substring(3, 5)
Label2.Text = "First five characters are " & _
    "'" & string2 & "'"
Label3.Text = "Last five characters are " & _
    "'" & string3 & "'"
Label4.Text = "Five characters in the middle are " & _
    "'" & string4 & "'"
```

(Notice the underscore character [_]. The underscore tells Visual Basic .NET that the current program line continues onto the next line. By using the underscore character [preceded by a space character], you can divide unusually long program lines into smaller chunks.)

The `Form1_Load` procedure sets the various controls' `Text` properties to the text the controls need to display. Finally, the `Button1_Click` procedure, which Visual Basic .NET jumps to when the user clicks the button, performs the following actions …

- ◆ It declares the variables needed in the procedure.
- ◆ It gets the string typed into the text box.
- ◆ It calls the `Substring` method to extract three substrings from the `string1` string.
- ◆ It uses the remaining Label controls' `Text` properties to display the substrings.

4. Run the program, and then type some text into the text box (make sure it's at least eight characters, or the program will crash). Click the Get Substrings button, and the program displays the results shown in Figure 6.6.

Figure 6.6

This program can extract and display substrings.

Finding Substrings

Now that you know how to extract a substring from a larger string, you may wonder how you can find the exact substring you want. Suppose, for example, that you have a string containing a list of names, and you want to find the name Twitdum. The method `IndexOf` was created for just this task. (Well, actually, it was created to find any string, not just Twitdum.)

Like the method `Substring`, you can use `IndexOf` a couple of ways. For example, the following line finds the position of the substring Twitdum in `string1`:

```
position = string1.IndexOf("Twitdum")
```

When you find the position of the string, simply use `Substring` to extract the actual string. (If `IndexOf` cannot find the requested substring, it returns a value of –1.) In the previous "Twitdum" example, you'd use `Substring` to extract the substring:

```
string2 = string1.Substring(position, 7)
```

After finding the first occurrence of a substring, you may want to search the rest of the string for another occurrence. After all, your name list might contain more than one Twitdum. (It's such a common name, after all.) To continue searching, you use the second form of the IndexOf method. This second form takes as arguments not only the substring for which to search, but also the starting position of the search.

You could use the value returned in position to continue searching the string, as in the following example:

```
position = string1.IndexOf("Twitdum", position + 1)
```

Notice that the starting position, which is the method's second argument, is position + 1, not just position. If you used position, the method would find the same substring it just found. An error like this in your program can be very hard to detect.

The following program demonstrates how all this substring-search stuff works. To build the program, follow these steps:

1. Start a new Visual Basic .NET project named StringSearch.

2. Double-click the form to display the code window.

3. Complete the Form1_Load procedure with the following lines:

```
Dim string1 As String
Dim string2 As String
Dim msg As String
Dim position As Integer
string1 = "SmithTwitdumFreemanTwitdumRothTwitdum"
position = string1.IndexOf("Twitdum")
string2 = string1.Substring(position, 7)
msg = "The first occurrence of " & "'" & string2 & "'"
msg = msg & " is at position " & position
msg = msg & vbCrLf & vbCrLf

position = string1.IndexOf("Twitdum", position + 1)
string2 = string1.Substring(position, 7)
msg = msg & "The second occurrence of " & _
    "'" & string2 & "'"
msg = msg & " is at position " & position
msg = msg & vbCrLf & vbCrLf

position = string1.IndexOf("Twitdum", position + 1)
msg = msg & "The third occurrence of " & _
    "'" & string2 & "'"
msg = msg & " is at position " & position
MessageBox.Show(msg)
End
```

This program requires no input. Just run it and compare the message shown in the message box with the program listing. (Click the message box's OK button to close the message box and end the program.) Figure 6.7 shows the message box the program displays.

Figure 6.7

A message box displays the results of all the fancy string handling.

A few things about this program might have you scratching your head (no, you don't have lice), so it might be a good idea to go through it a little at a time. First, the following lines declare the variables used in the procedure:

```
Dim string1 As String
Dim string2 As String
Dim msg As String
Dim position As Integer
```

The next line in the program sets the source-string variable to its starting value:

```
string1 = "SmithTwitdumFreemanTwitdumRothTwitdum"
```

With the source-string variable ready to go, the program can call the IndexOf method to look for the first occurrence of the name Twitdum, like this:

```
position = string1.IndexOf("Twitdum")
```

Next, the program assigns the located substring to the string2 variable by using, as one of the Substring method's arguments, the position value returned by the IndexOf method:

```
string2 = string1.Substring(position, 7)
```

The next three lines start building the message that the program will display in its message box:

```
msg = "The first occurrence of " & "'" & string2 & "'"
msg = msg & " is at position " & position
msg = msg & vbCrLf & vbCrLf
```

There's some curious stuff going on in these lines. First, notice how the program can build a long string message by continually adding text to the msg string. This technique is similar to the way you learned to add values to an integer value with the following line:

```
value = value + 1
```

Also, see the two instances of vbCrLf? You may be wondering what language that is. The value vbCrLf is a symbol that Visual Basic .NET uses to represent two special characters, a carriage-return and a linefeed. To put it simply, when you add this symbol to a string, you're starting a new line. By using two of these symbols, the program starts a new line twice, which puts a blank line after the preceding text string.

Getting back to the program, most of the rest of the procedure finds the next two occurrences of the name Twitdum and continues to build the msg string, which will be displayed in the message box.

Speaking of message boxes, the following line, found near the end of the procedure, is where the program displays the message box:

```
MessageBox.Show(msg)
```

As you can see, to display a message in a message box, all you need to do is to type the MessageBox.Show command followed by the string you want to display in parentheses.

Finally, the procedure ends appropriately enough with the End command:

```
End
```

This one word is all you need to end the program. Because the End command terminates the program inside the Form1_Load procedure, the form never even appears on the screen. From the user's point of view, the program does nothing more than display a message box and then end.

Check This Out

The MessageBox.Show statement can display a line of text (and other types of data). In the previous example, the line of text was stored in a variable called msg. However, if the line of text you want to display is a string literal rather than the contents of a variable, don't forget that you need to enclose the string in quotes, like this: MessageBox.Show("This is your text.")

Changing Case

As you know, alphabetic characters in Visual Basic .NET can be typed either in uppercase or lowercase letters. Sometimes, you might want your strings to be displayed all in one case or the other. To change all characters in a string to either uppercase or lowercase, use a String object's handy ToUpper and ToLower methods.

There's not a heck of a lot to say about these functions; they just do what they do. For example, look at the following lines:

```
Dim myString As String
Dim lcString As String
Dim ucString As String
```

```
myString = "This Is a Test"
lcString = myString.ToLower
ucString = myString.ToUpper
```

After Visual Basic .NET executes these commands, the `lcString` variable will contain the string "this is a test" and the `ucString` variable will contain the string "THIS IS A TEST". 'Nuff said?

Converting Numbers to Strings

You probably remember that there's a big difference between numerical values and text strings, even if the text string contains numeric characters. Numerical values, such as the number 5 or the integer variable `number`, can be used in mathematical operations. Strings, however, cannot. Luckily, Visual Basic .NET features a handy method, `Int32.Parse`, that enables you to convert number strings into numerical values that can be used in mathematical operations. You can also change numerical values into strings with the `Int32.ToString` method—something you might want to do with the result of a calculation.

To convert a number string into an integer, use the `Int32.Parse` method as shown in the following snippet:

```
number = Int32.Parse(string1)
```

The variable `string1` is the string you want to convert to an integer. Keep in mind that `Int32.Parse` can convert only string characters that represent numbers: digits and minus signs.

Another command enables you to change strings into floating-point values. The following statement makes `number` equal to 3.4:

```
number = Single.Parse("3.4")
```

Converting strings to numerical values is only half the story. You may also need to go the other way and convert a numerical variable into a string. For example, you might want to convert a numerical value to a string so you can add it to a text document. You can do this conversion by calling an object's `ToString` method, which looks like this:

```
string1 = number.ToString()
```

Here, `number` is the numerical value you want to change into string form. For example, the following program statements makes `myString` equal to the string "34.45":

```
Dim myString As String
Dim num As Single = 34.45
myString = num.ToString()
```

The Least You Need to Know

◆ You can use the ampersand operator (&) to join strings together. This process is called concatenation.

◆ The equals sign (=) can be used with strings just as it is used with numerical values. Specifically, you use the assignment operator to set a string variable to a specific string value.

◆ The length of a string is the number of characters contained in the string. An empty string contains no characters and so has a length of 0.

◆ A String object's Length property returns, as a numerical value, the length of a string.

◆ A substring is a portion of a larger string.

◆ The method Substring enables a program to extract substrings from other strings.

◆ The method IndexOf returns the position of a substring within a string.

◆ You can use the String methods ToLower and ToUpper to convert strings to lowercase and uppercase, respectively.

◆ The method Parse converts number strings to numerical values. The method ToString does the opposite, converting numerical values to strings.

If, Else, and ElseIf: Decisions, Decisions, Decisions

In This Chapter

◆ Use branching to change program flow

◆ Learn about If, Else, and ElseIf

◆ Discover relational operators

◆ Work with logical operators

In the previous chapters, you've learned much about the way Visual Basic .NET works. You now know how to type programs, input and output data, perform mathematical operations, and handle strings. But these techniques are merely the building blocks of a program. To work with these building blocks in a useful way, you have to understand how computers make decisions.

In this chapter, you learn how your programs can analyze data in order to decide what parts of your program to execute. Until now, your programs have executed their statements mostly in sequential order, starting with the first line and working, line by line, to the end of the program. Now it's time to learn how you can control your program's flow—the order in which the statements are executed—so that you can do different things based on the data your program receives.

If the idea of computers making decisions based on data seems a little strange, think about how you make decisions. For example, suppose you're expecting an important letter. You go out to your mailbox and look inside. Then you choose one of the following two actions:

◆ If there's mail in the mailbox, you take it into the house.

◆ If there's no mail in the mailbox, you complain about the postal system.

In either case, you've made a decision based on whether or not there is mail in the mailbox.

Computers use this same method to make decisions (except that they never complain, and they don't give a darn how late your mail is). You will see the word "if" used frequently in computer programs. Just as you might say to yourself, "If the mail is in the mailbox, I'll bring it in," so a computer uses "if" to decide what action to take.

Understanding Program Flow and Branching

Program flow is the order in which a program executes its code. Your programs so far in this book have had sequential program flow. Truth is, almost all program code executes sequentially. However, virtually every program reaches a point where a decision must be made about a particular piece of data. The program must then analyze the data, decide what to do about it, and jump to the appropriate section of code. This decision-making process is as important to computer programming as pollen is to a bee. Virtually no useful programs can be written without it.

When a program breaks the sequential flow and jumps to a new section of code, it is called *branching*. When this branching is based on a decision, the program is performing *conditional branching*. When no decision-making is involved and the program always branches when it encounters a branching instruction, the program is performing *unconditional branching*.

To continue with the mailbox example, suppose you went out to the mailbox and found your mail, but decided to complain about the Post Office anyway. Because the poor mail carrier was destined to be the focus of your wrath whether or not the mail was delivered on time, your complaining is unconditional. No matter what, after going to the mailbox, you complain.

Introducing the If...Then Statement

Most conditional branching occurs when the program executes an If…Then statement, which compares data and decides what to do next based on the result of the comparison.

If the comparison works out one way, the program performs the statement following the Then keyword. Otherwise, the program does nothing and drops to the next program line. This gives each comparison two possible outcomes.

For example, in older DOS programs, you've probably seen programs that print menus on the screen. To select a menu item, you often type its selection number. When the program receives your input, it checks the number you entered and decides what to do.

To see what I mean, try this:

1. Start a new Visual Basic .NET project (using the Windows Application template) named Branching, and then place a Label control, a TextBox control, and a Button control on the form. Resize the label so that it's the same length as the TextBox, as shown in Figure 7.1.

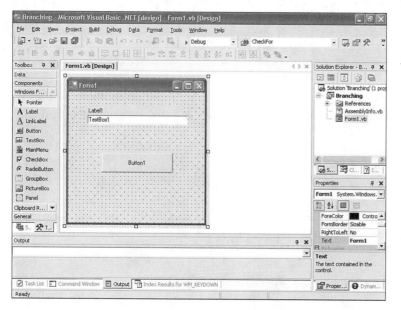

Figure 7.1

Position the controls on your form as shown here.

2. Now, double-click the form to display the code window, and type the following lines into the Load procedure (Visual Basic .NET will have already started the Form1_Load procedure for you):

```
Label1.Text = "1 = Red, 2 = Green, 3 = Blue"
TextBox1.Text = ""
Button1.Text = "Process Selection"
```

Figure 7.2 shows how the finished procedure should look.

Figure 7.2

The finished Form1_Load
procedure.

3. Click the Form1.vb [Design] tab to redisplay the form, and then double-click the button control. When the Button1_Click procedure appears, complete it with the following lines:

```
Dim choice As Integer
Dim entry As String
entry = TextBox1.Text
choice = Int32.Parse(entry)
If choice = 1 Then MessageBox.Show("You chose red.")
If choice = 2 Then MessageBox.Show("You chose green.")
If choice = 3 Then MessageBox.Show("You chose blue.")
```

Figure 7.3 shows how the finished procedure should look.

The Form1_Load procedure sets the Text properties of the various controls to the text the controls need to display. Finally, the Button1_Click procedure, which Visual Basic .NET jumps to when the user clicks the button, performs the following actions:

◆ It declares the variables needed in the procedure.

◆ It retrieves the text typed into the text box.

◆ It converts the text value to an integer.

◆ It uses If...Then statements to determine which message box to display.

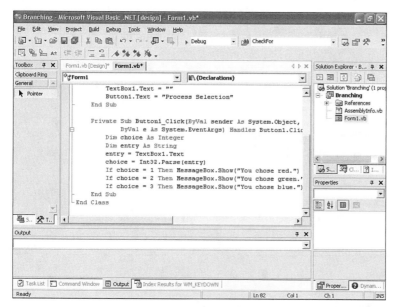

Figure 7.3

The finished Button1_Click *procedure.*

4. Run the program, and then type a value from 1 to 3 into the text box. Click the Process Selection button, and the program displays a message box that tells you the color you selected, as shown in Figure 7.4.

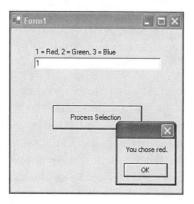

Figure 7.4

This program shows how a program can make decisions.

As you now know, the preceding program shows a menu and enables you to enter a menu selection. The program then uses a series of If...Then statements to compare the value you entered with the acceptable menu choices. See the equals characters (=) in the If...Then statements? These are not assignment operators; they are relational operators, which enable the program to compare two or more values. Look at the first If...Then statement in the program:

```
If choice = 1 Then MessageBox.Show("You chose red.")
```

If this line were written in English, it would read "If the value of the variable choice equals 1, then show 'You chose red.'" The other If…Then statements in the program have similar meanings.

By the Way

Relational operators such as the equals character enable you to compare two pieces of data. By comparing variables to literals, for example, you can check variables for specific values. The most common relational operator is the equals sign (=), which checks whether two expressions are equal. However, there are also relational operators for such relationships as less than (<), greater than (>), and not equal (<>). (You'll see these operators later in this chapter.) When you use relational operators to compare two values, you are writing a Boolean expression, which is an expression that is either true or false.

Simple If…Then Statements

A simple If…Then statement includes the keyword If followed by a Boolean expression. You follow the Boolean expression with the keyword Then and, finally, with the statement that you want executed if the Boolean expression is true.

As I said, a Boolean expression is an expression that evaluates to either true or false. For example, the expression 3 + 4 = 7 is true, whereas the expression 6 + 1 = 9 is false. A Boolean expression usually compares a variable to a constant or to another variable, such as num + 1 = 7 or num1 - 10 = num2.

How do If…Then statements work? Let's say that when you run the previous program, you type the value 1 into the text box. When the program gets to the first If…Then statement, it checks the value of choice. If choice equals 1 (which it does, in this case), the program shows the message "You chose red" and then drops down to the next If…Then statement. This time, the program compares the value of choice with the number 2. Because choice doesn't equal 2, the program ignores the Then part of the statement and drops down to the next program line, which is another If…Then statement. The variable choice doesn't equal 3 either, so the program ignores the Then portion of the third If…Then statement.

By the Way

The conditional expression in an If…Then statement, no matter how complex, always evaluates to either true or false. True and false are actual values: true equals any non-0 value, and false equals 0. Consequently, the statement If 1 Then MessageBox.Show("True!") prints the message "True!"; but the statement If 0 Then MessageBox.Show("False!") does nothing. In the first statement, the value 1 is considered true, so the program executes the Then part of the statement. In the second statement, the 0 is considered false, so the program ignores the Then portion of the statement.

Suppose you enter the number 2 into the text box. When the program gets to the first If...Then statement, it discovers that choice is not equal to 1, so it ignores the Then part of the statement and drops down to the next program line, which is the second If...Then statement. Again, the program checks the value of choice. Because choice equals 2, the program can execute the Then portion of the statement; the message "You chose green" appears. Program execution drops down to the third If...Then statement, which does nothing because choice doesn't equal 3.

Multi-Line If...Then Statements

The previous program demonstrated the simplest If...Then statement. This simple statement usually fits your program's decision-making needs just fine. Sometimes, however, you want to perform more than one command as part of an If...Then statement. To perform more than one command, press Enter after Then, write the commands you want to add to the If...Then statement, and end the block of commands with the End If keywords. The following code shows a revised version of the Button1_Click procedure from the previous program that uses multi-line If...Then statements:

```
Private Sub Button1_Click(ByVal sender As System.Object, _
        ByVal e As System.EventArgs) Handles Button1.Click
    Dim choice As Integer
    Dim entry As String
    entry = TextBox1.Text
    choice = Int32.Parse(entry)

    If choice = 1 Then
        MessageBox.Show("You chose red.")
        Button1.BackColor = Color.Red
    End If

    If choice = 2 Then
        MessageBox.Show("You chose green.")
        Button1.BackColor = Color.Green
    End If

    If choice = 3 Then
        MessageBox.Show("You chose blue.")
        Button1.BackColor = Color.Blue
    End If
End Sub
```

This version of the Button1_Click procedure is similar to the previous one. The primary difference is that the program not only displays the message box, but also changes the button's background color to the selected color. The three If...Then statements compare the user's selection with the possible choices. When an If...Then statement's conditional expression evaluates to true, the program executes the lines between the If and the next End If.

What's happening in this version of the Button1_Click procedure? Suppose you run the program and enter the number 2. When the program gets to the first If...Then statement, it compares the value of choice with the number 1. Because these values don't match (or, as programmers say, the statement doesn't evaluate to true), the program skips over every program line until it finds an End If statement, which marks the end of the block of code that goes with the If.

Check This Out

Notice that some program lines in the most recent Button1_Click procedure are indented. By indenting the lines that go with each If block, you can more easily see the structure of your program. The procedure also uses blank lines to separate blocks of code that go together. The computer doesn't care about the indenting or the blank lines, but these features make your programs easier for you, or another programmer, to read.

By the Way

In the sample program, a message box appears when the user selects a color choice. The button's background color doesn't change until the message box is dismissed because the message box statement comes before the statement that changes the background color. A program's execution can't continue after a message box appears, until the user dismisses the message box.

This brings the program to the second If...Then statement. When the program evaluates the conditional expression, it finds that choice equals 2, and it executes the Then portion of the If...Then statement. This time the Then portion is not just one command, but two. The program displays a message box and, after the user dismisses the message box, changes the button's background color to green (the color selected from the menu). Finally, the program reaches End If, which marks the end of the If...Then statement.

This brings the program to the last If...Then statement, which the program skips over because choice doesn't equal 3.

You might think it's a waste of time for the program to evaluate other If...Then statements after it finds a match for the menu item you chose. You'd be right, too. When you write programs, you should always look for ways to make them run faster; one way to make a program run faster is to avoid all unnecessary processing. But how, you may ask, do you avoid unnecessary processing when you have to compare a variable with more than one value?

One way to keep processing to a minimum is to use the Visual Basic .NET ElseIf clause. Before you learn about ElseIf, however, let's look at the simpler version, Else. This keyword enables you to use a single If...Then statement to choose between two outcomes. When the If...Then statement evaluates to true, the program executes the Then part of the statement. When the If...Then statement evaluates to false, the program executes the

Else portion. When the If…Else statement evaluates to neither true nor false, it's time to get a new computer! The following program demonstrates how Else works. Just replace your current Form1_Load and Button1_Click procedures with the following code. To do this, just delete the existing procedures from the program and put these in their place:

```
Private Sub Form1_Load(ByVal sender As System.Object, _
        ByVal e As System.EventArgs) Handles MyBase.Load
    Label1.Text = "Enter name:"
    TextBox1.Text = ""
    Button1.Text = "Process Selection"
End Sub

Private Sub Button1_Click(ByVal sender As System.Object, _
        ByVal e As System.EventArgs) Handles Button1.Click
    Dim name As String
    name = TextBox1.Text
    name = name.ToUpper()
    If name = "FRED" Then
        MessageBox.Show("Hi, Fred!")
    Else
        MessageBox.Show("Hello, stranger!")
    End If
End Sub
```

Check This Out

You've probably figured out by now that **BackColor** is the property of the Button object that determines the button's background color. By setting this property's value, the program change's the window's color. The **Color.Red**, **Color.Green**, and **Color.Blue** values are color values that Visual Basic .NET has already defined for you. To see other color values, type Color followed by a period inside a procedure, and Visual Basic .NET will display a list of colors from which you can choose.

In these lines, the Form_Load procedure sets the Text properties of the various controls to the text the controls need to display. Finally, the Button1_Click procedure, which Visual Basic .NET jumps to when the user clicks the button, performs these actions:

- ◆ It declares the variable needed in the procedure.
- ◆ It retrieves the text typed into the text box.
- ◆ It changes the text to all uppercase.
- ◆ It uses an If…Then/Else statement to determine which message box to display.

Run the program, and then type a name into the text box. Click the Process Selection button. If you typed "Fred", the program gives you a personalized greeting, as shown in Figure 7.5; otherwise, the program displays the message "Hello, stranger!". Thanks to the ToUpper method, you can type "Fred" with any combination of upper- or lowercase letters, and the program will still recognize the name.

Figure 7.5

This program recognizes the name Fred.

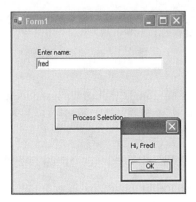

As you can see, the program executes the Else clause only when the If…Then statement is false. If the If…Then statement is true, the program ignores the Else clause.

This program also demonstrates how to compare strings. Strings are compared just as numerical values are: by using the equals character (=), which, in the case of an If…Then statement, is a relational operator. You will compare strings often in your programs, especially programs that require text input from the user. By using string comparisons, you can catch an incorrect response to a prompt and display an error message to inform the user of the incorrect entry.

Simply put, Else provides a default outcome for an If…Then statement. A default outcome doesn't help much, however, in an If…Then statement that must associate program code with more than two possible outcomes. Suppose you want the program to recognize your friends' names, too. No problem. First, get some friends; then use the Visual Basic .NET ElseIf keyword, as shown in this example:

```
Private Sub Button1_Click(ByVal sender As System.Object, _
        ByVal e As System.EventArgs) Handles Button1.Click
    Dim name As String
    name = TextBox1.Text
    name = name.ToUpper
    If name = "FRED" Then
        MessageBox.Show("Hi, Fred!")
    ElseIf name = "SARAH" Then
        MessageBox.Show("How's it going, Sarah?")
```

```
        ElseIf name = "TONY" Then
            MessageBox.Show("Hey! It's my man Tony!")
        Else
            MessageBox.Show("Hello, stranger.")
        End If
End Sub
```

This version of the `Button1_Click` procedure retrieves the user's name from the text box and then changes the name to all uppercase letters. Next, the `If…Then` statement checks for the name "FRED". If the user entered "FRED", the program prints Fred's message. Otherwise, the `ElseIf` clauses check for other names and print an appropriate message if a match is found. If none of the names match the user's input, the program executes the `Else` clause, displaying a generic message in the message box.

Check This Out

When you need to get string input from the user, it's often a good idea to change the input to all upper- or lowercase. This enables the program to recognize a word no matter the case in which the user types it. For example, in the new `Button1_Click` procedure, the program converts the user's input to uppercase before comparing it to the names in the `If` and `ElseIf` clauses. With this method, Fred can type his name any way he likes: Fred, fred, FRED, or even fRed. One of your goals as a programmer should be to make your programs as easy to use as possible. Allowing the user to enter a string in any form is one way to do this.

The following code presents a new `Button1_Click` procedure for the color menu program. This procedure uses `ElseIf` and `Else` clauses. You should now know enough about computer decision-making to figure out how it works.

```
Private Sub Button1_Click(ByVal sender As System.Object, _
        ByVal e As System.EventArgs) Handles Button1.Click
    Dim choice As Integer
    Dim entry As String
    entry = TextBox1.Text
    choice = Int32.Parse(entry)
    If choice = 1 Then
        MessageBox.Show("You chose red.")
        Button1.BackColor = Color.Red
    ElseIf choice = 2 Then
        MessageBox.Show("You chose green.")
        Button1.BackColor = Color.Green
    ElseIf choice = 3 Then
        MessageBox.Show("You chose blue.")
        Button1.BackColor = Color.Blue
```

```
    Else
        MessageBox.Show("Invalid selection.")
    End If
End Sub
```

Note that the `Else` clause ensures that the program catches all results other than the ones for which you specifically wrote `If` or `ElseIf` clauses.

Using Relational Operators

The previous programs in this chapter used only the equals operator to compare values. Often you'll need to compare values in other ways. You might, for example, want to know if a value is less than or greater than another value. Visual Basic .NET features an entire set of relational operators you can use in `If...Then` statements and other types of comparisons. Table 7.1 summarizes the relational operators.

Table 7.1   Relational Operators

Operator	Meaning	Examples
=	Equals	3=(4–1) or "FRED"="FRED"
<>	Not equal	5<>(3+3) or "FRED"<>"SAM"
<	Less than	3<23 or "A"<"B"
>	Greater than	41>39 or "BART">"ADAM"
<=	Less than or equal	5<=6 or "ONE"<="ONE"
>=	Greater than or equal	10>=10 or "THREE">="TWO"

To see how relational operators are used, start with the last Visual Basic .NET program from this chapter and replace the `Form1_Load` and `Button1_Click` procedures with this code:

```
Private Sub Form1_Load(ByVal sender As System.Object, _
        ByVal e As System.EventArgs) Handles MyBase.Load
    Label1.Text = "Enter a number no larger than 50: "
    TextBox1.Text = ""
    Button1.Text = "Process Selection"
End Sub

Private Sub Button1_Click(ByVal sender As System.Object, _
        ByVal e As System.EventArgs) Handles Button1.Click
    Dim Number As Integer
    Dim entry As String
    entry = TextBox1.Text
```

```
    Number = Int32.Parse(entry)
    If Number < 10 Then
        MessageBox.Show("Less than 10.")
    ElseIf Number < 20 Then
        MessageBox.Show("Greater than 9 and less than 20.")
    ElseIf Number < 30 Then
        MessageBox.Show("Greater than 19 and less than 30.")
    ElseIf Number < 40 Then
        MessageBox.Show("Greater than 29 and less than 40.")
    ElseIf Number < 50 Then
        MessageBox.Show("Greater than 39 and less than 50.")
    ElseIf Number = 50 Then
        MessageBox.Show("Your number is 50.")
    Else
        MessageBox.Show("Out of the acceptable range.")
    End If
End Sub
```

This program asks the user to enter a number no greater than 50. After the user types the number, the program uses an If...Then statement with a series of ElseIf clauses to determine the range within which the number falls. For this determination, the program uses the less-than operator (<). If the selected number is less than the specified numerical literal in the If or ElseIf clauses, the program displays an appropriate message to the user. If the number is larger than the specified literal, the program moves on to the next clause and again makes the comparison, this time with a higher numerical literal. Finally, if the number turns out to be larger than the allowed maximum of 50, the program prints an error message.

Go ahead and run the program, and type a value into the text box. After you type the number, the program determines the number's range and prints a message informing you of this range, as shown in Figure 7.6.

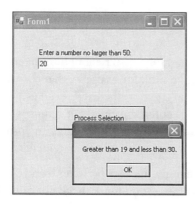

Figure 7.6

This program can analyze and report on the values you enter.

This program doesn't just demonstrate the use of the less-than operator; it keeps you off the streets by having you do a lot of typing! More important, though, the program further illustrates the way a block of `If` and `ElseIf` clauses work.

Suppose when you run the program, you type the number 9. When the program gets to the `If` clause, it compares 9 to 10 and discovers that 9 is less than 10. (And to think you paid hundreds of dollars for a machine to tell you that.) The `If` clause then evaluates to true, and the program prints the message "Less than 10."

Look at the block of `ElseIf` statements that go along with the `If`. Isn't 9 also less than 20? Moreover, isn't 9 also less than 30, 40, and 50? Why then, when you enter the number 9, don't you also see the messages associated with all these `ElseIf` statements, as well as the message associated with the `If`?

The answer has to do with the way the `If…ElseIf` block works. Once an `If` or `ElseIf` evaluates to true, the program skips the rest of the statements in the block—or, as programmers say, the program branches to the next statement after the block. In the case of your new program, there is no statement after the block so the program simply exits the procedure.

By the Way

When using relational operators with strings, the value of each letter in a string is relative to its alphabetic order. In other words, the letter "A" is less than the letter "B," the letter "B" is less than the letter "C," and so on. When comparing lowercase letters and uppercase letters, however, the lowercase letters have a greater value than their uppercase counterparts. Therefore, "a" is greater than "A," and "b" is greater than "B," but "c" is greater than "b." Finally, just as when you organize words into alphabetical order, when a program compares strings, the letters on the left have greater significance than those on the right. For example, Mick is less than Mike to Visual Basic .NET.

Using Logical Operators

A single comparison in an `If…Then` statement often isn't enough to determine whether data matches your criteria. How can you be sure, for example, that the user enters a number within a specific range? You could hold a gun to the user's head as he's typing the data. Although this may ensure that data is entered properly, it requires that you stay by the computer at all times—which is hardly practical. A better way to ensure that data is in the correct range is to use logical operators in your `If…Then` statements.

Let's say your program asks the user to enter a number between 0 and 50, inclusive. To discover whether a number is within this range, you must check not only that the number is greater than or equal to 0, but also that the number is less than or equal to 50. To help handle these situations, Visual Basic .NET features four logical operators—And, Or, Xor (exclusive Or), and Not—that can be used to combine expressions in an If statement.

The And operator requires all expressions to be true in order for the entire expression to be true. For example, the following expression is true because the expressions on both sides of the And are true:

```
(3 + 2 = 5) And (6 + 2 = 8)
```

By contrast, the following expression is false, because the expression on the left of the And is false:

```
(4 + 3 = 9) And (3 + 3 = 6)
```

Remember this when combining expressions with And—if any expression is false, the entire expression is false.

The Or operator requires only one expression to be true in order for the entire expression to be true. For example, the following expressions are both true, because at least one of the expressions being compared is true:

```
(3 + 6 = 2) Or (4 + 4 = 8)
(4 + 1 = 5) Or (7 + 2 = 9)
```

Note that in the second case both expressions being compared are true, which also makes an Or expression true.

The Xor (exclusive Or) operator requires one and only one expression to be true in order for the entire expression to be true. For example, the following expression is true because only the (4 + 4 = 8) expression is true:

```
(3 + 6 = 2) Xor (4 + 4 = 8)
```

By contrast, the next expression is false, because both expressions are true:

```
(4 + 1 = 5) Xor (7 + 2 = 9)
```

Confused yet?

The Not operator reverses the value of (or negates) a logical expression. For example, the following expression is not true:

```
(4 + 3 = 5)
```

However, if you add the Not operator in front of the expression, it reverses the (4 + 3 = 5) expression's false outcome to true:

```
Not (4 + 3 = 5)
```

Take a look at the following expression:

```
(4 + 5 = 9) And Not (3 + 1 = 3)
```

Is this expression true or false? If you said true, you understand the way the logical operators work. The expressions on either side of the And are both true, so the entire expression is true. Table 7.2 summarizes how you use the logical operators.

Table 7.2   Logical Operators

Operator	Meaning
And	True if both sides of the expression are true.
Or	True if one or both sides of the expression are true.
Xor	True if only one side of the expression is true.
Not	Reverses true to false and vice versa.

Of course, you wouldn't write expressions like the following one in your program:

```
(4 + 5 = 9) And Not (3 + 1 = 3)
```

They would serve no purpose because you already know how the expressions evaluate.
However, when you use variables, you have no way of knowing in advance how an expression may evaluate. For example, is the following expression true or false?

```
(num < 9) And (num > 2)
```

You don't know without being told the value of the numerical variable num. By using these
logical operators in your If...Then statements, though, your program can do the evaluation
and based on the result—true or false—take the appropriate action.

The following new Button1_Click procedure demonstrates how logical operators work.
In your Visual Basic .NET program, replace the old procedure with the new one.

```
Private Sub Button1_Click(ByVal sender As System.Object, _
        ByVal e As System.EventArgs) Handles Button1.Click
    Dim Number As Integer
    Dim entry As String
    entry = TextBox1.Text
    Number = Int32.Parse(entry)
    If (Number < 0) Or (Number > 50) Then
        MessageBox.Show("The number " & Number & " is out of range!")
    Else
        MessageBox.Show("The number " & Number & " is in range.")
    End If
End Sub
```

When you run the program, it asks you to enter a number between 0 and 50. (Well, actually, it still asks for a number no greater than 50, but we'll let that little technicality go by.) If you type a number that is out of that range, the program will let you know. Although this version of the `Button1_Click` procedure is similar to the previous one, it works very differently. After the user types a number, the program uses a single `If…Then` statement to determine whether the number is within the acceptable range. If the number is out of range, the program prints an error message, as shown in Figure 7.7.

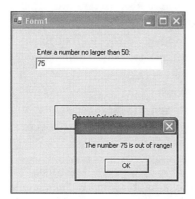

Figure 7.7

This program reports all invalid entries.

Revisting the Infamous GoTo

Most of this chapter has been dedicated to conditional branches. If you recall, however, programmers can also use unconditional branches. This type of branching can be accomplished by using the `GoTo` instruction, which forces program execution to branch to a specific line number or label. Because line numbers in BASIC programs are now obsolete, you don't have to worry about how to use them—you'll probably never need them. You may, however, want to use labels.

Here's a new `Button1_Click` procedure that demonstrates the `GoTo` command:

```
    Private Sub Button1_Click(ByVal sender As System.Object, _
        ByVal e As System.EventArgs) Handles Button1.Click
        Dim Number As Integer
        Dim entry As String
        entry = TextBox1.Text
        Number = Int32.Parse(entry)
        If Number <= 100 Then Goto lessthan
        MessageBox.Show("Your number is greater than 100.")
        Exit Sub
lessthan:
        MessageBox.Show("Your number is less than or equal to 100.")
    End Sub
```

Whoops!

Although the GoTo statement may seem like a handy thing to have around, programmers have misused it so much in the past that most avoid it like nuclear waste. Overuse of GoTo can turn a program into a tangled, unreadable mess. A modern, structured language like Visual Basic .NET has little need for the GoTo instruction. In fact, GoTo used to be inserted only for handling errors, but these days, it isn't even used for that. You'll learn about error handling in Chapter 16, "Catching Runtime Errors."

This procedure uses the GoTo instruction to branch to a specific place in the program. The destination of the branch is marked by the label lessthan.

In this procedure, after getting a number from the user, the If...Then statement checks whether the number is less than or equal to 100. If it is, the program executes the Then portion of the statement, which is a GoTo statement. GoTo sends program execution to the label lessthan, at which point the program prints an appropriate message. If the number the user enters is greater than 100, the If...Then statement's conditional expression evaluates to false. In this case, program execution drops down to the next line, the program displays a message, and the Exit Sub statement ends the procedure before program execution gets to the lessthan program label.

In this program, notice that when the label's name follows the GoTo, it doesn't include a colon; however, the actual label in the program does include a colon.

The Least You Need to Know

♦ Program flow is the order in which a program executes its statements.

♦ When a computer program branches, it jumps to a new location in the code and continues execution from there.

♦ An If...Then statement compares the values of data and decides what statements to execute based on that evaluation.

♦ The Else and ElseIf clauses allow If...Then statements to handle many different outcomes.

♦ The End If keywords mark the end of a multi-line If...Then statement, including multi-line statements with ElseIf and Else clauses.

♦ The relational operators—equals (=), does not equal (<>), less than (<), greater than (>), less than or equal (<=), and greater than or equal (>=)—enable programs to compare data in various ways.

♦ Logical operators—And, Or, Xor, and Not—enable an If...Then statement to evaluate more than one expression, yet they still resolve the expressions to a single true or false.

Select Case: Another Way to Decide

In This Chapter

- ◆ Replace If...Then statements with Select Case statements
- ◆ Use a Select Case statement to make decisions based on the value of variables
- ◆ Discover the Is keyword for examining a variable for a range of values

Thanks to the If...Then statements you just learned in the previous chapter, your computer programs can now make decisions. Go ahead and ask your computer to decide between the fish tie and the Simpsons' tie. Nothing happened? That could be because the computer doesn't care for your taste in ties, or more likely, it's because a computer doesn't usually make those kinds of decisions (which isn't saying that a computer can't, given the right programming). Computer programs usually make much simpler decisions, and another way they can make such decisions is with the Select Case statement.

Introducing the Select Case Statement

The If...Then statement is only one way a computer can make decisions. Using a Select Case statement gives the same results. The best way to learn how to use a `Select Case` statement is to compare it to an `If...Then` statement. For example, in the previous chapter, you wrote a `Button1_Click` procedure that looks like this:

```
Private Sub Button1_Click(ByVal sender As System.Object, _
        ByVal e As System.EventArgs) Handles Button1.Click
    Dim name As String
    name = TextBox1.Text
    name = name.ToUpper
    If name = "FRED" Then
        MessageBox.Show("Hi, Fred!")
    ElseIf name = "SARAH" Then
        MessageBox.Show("How's it going, Sarah?")
    ElseIf name = "TONY" Then
        MessageBox.Show("Hey! It's my man Tony!")
    Else
        MessageBox.Show("Hello, stranger.")
    End If
End Sub
```

You can rewrite this procedure using a `Select Case` statement and get rid of all those `If`'s, `Then`'s, `ElseIf`'s, and `Else`'s. Such a procedure might look like this:

```
Private Sub Button1_Click(ByVal sender As System.Object, _
        ByVal e As System.EventArgs) Handles Button1.Click
    Dim name As String
    name = TextBox1.Text
    name = name.ToUpper
    Select Case name
        Case "FRED"
            MessageBox.Show("Hi, Fred!")
        Case "SARAH"
            MessageBox.Show("How's it going, Sarah?")
        Case "TONY"
            MessageBox.Show("Hey! It's my man Tony!")
        Case Else
            MessageBox.Show("Hello, stranger.")
    End Select
End Sub
```

Check This Out

Because the `Select Case` statement tends to be much more concise than an `If...Then` statement, programmers usually use a `Select Case` statement when the program must decide between many different possible outcomes. For example, if a program must examine a variable for a value between 1 and 20 and execute different program lines for each possible value, a `Select Case` statement sure saves on the typing!

This new procedure is about the same size as the original. However, it's a bit easier to see what's going on, because the decision-making is more concise, using fewer keywords and expressions.

Digging Into the Select Case Statement

Now that you've taken a gander at the Select Case statement, I suppose that you're going to insist on an explanation. Here goes. As you can see, the Select Case starts with the following line:

```
Select Case name
```

The first two words, "Select Case", tell Visual Basic .NET that you're starting a Select Case statement. (Sorry, but sometimes technical books have to state the obvious in order to get to the meatier stuff. Bear with me.) The "name" part of the line tells Visual Basic .NET that the computer will be making a decision based on the contents of the variable named name.

That neatly brings you to the next line, which looks like this:

```
Case "FRED"
```

This is just a quick way of saying

```
If name = "FRED" Then
```

See how a Select Case statement is more concise than an If…Then statement? A line with five keywords, expressions, and operators reduces to one keyword and a value.

Now, if name happens to equal "FRED" (Yay, Fred!), the program executes the line or lines following the Case clause which in this case would be this snippet:

```
MessageBox.Show("Hi, Fred!")
```

If name doesn't equal "FRED", the program drops down to the next Case clause and checks to see whether name equals "SARAH":

```
Case "SARAH"
    MessageBox.Show("How's it going, Sarah?")
```

Our main man, Tony, who's no less important than Fred and Sarah, gets his own Case clause, as well:

```
Case "TONY"
    MessageBox.Show("Hey! It's my man Tony!")
```

If someone other than Fred, Sarah, or Tony types his name into the program's text box, the Case Else clause leaps into action, making sure that everyone gets some sort of greeting:

```
Case Else
    MessageBox.Show("Hello, stranger.")
```

Finally, the program tells Visual Basic .NET that the Select Case statement is over with this line:

```
End Select
```

Digging Even Deeper

You wouldn't have to burn up too much brain fuel to realize that Select Case statements work with more than strings. Sure enough, Select Case statements can also handle other types of data, such as integers and floating-point values. For example, consider the following Button1_Click procedure from Chapter 7, "If, Else, and ElseIf: Decisions, Decisions, Decisions":

```
Private Sub Button1_Click(ByVal sender As System.Object, _
        ByVal e As System.EventArgs) Handles Button1.Click
    Dim choice As Integer
    Dim entry As String
    entry = TextBox1.Text
    choice = Int32.Parse(entry)
    If choice = 1 Then
        MessageBox.Show("You chose red.")
        Button1.BackColor = Color.Red
    ElseIf choice = 2 Then
        MessageBox.Show("You chose green.")
        Button1.BackColor = Color.Green
    ElseIf choice = 3 Then
        MessageBox.Show("You chose blue.")
        Button1.BackColor = Color.Blue
    Else
        MessageBox.Show("Invalid selection.")
    End If
End Sub
```

You may recall that this particular version of the Button1_Click procedure gets a number from a text box and sets the form's background color based on that number. If you don't recall this procedure, you can check back with Chapter 7. If you don't recall even what "Microsoft" means, you should probably take a break and get a snack.

For those of you who aren't heading for the kitchen, you can rewrite the previous Button1_Click procedure using the following code:

```
Private Sub Button1_Click(ByVal sender As System.Object, _
        ByVal e As System.EventArgs) Handles Button1.Click
    Dim choice As Integer
    Dim entry As String
    entry = TextBox1.Text
    choice = Int32.Parse(entry)
    Select Case choice
        Case 1
            MessageBox.Show("You chose red.")
            Button1.BackColor = Color.Red
        Case 2
            MessageBox.Show("You chose green.")
            Button1.BackColor = Color.Green
        Case 3
            MessageBox.Show("You chose blue.")
            Button1.BackColor = Color.Blue
        Case Else
            MessageBox.Show("Invalid selection.")
    End Select
End Sub
```

This procedure not only demonstrates using a Select Case statement with an integer, but also shows how you can have more than one program line associated with each Case clause. Here, except for the Case Else clause, each Case clause shows a message box and then changes the form's background color. You can have as many lines as you want with each Case clause, although you'll probably want to limit the line count to something less than the number of pages in the latest Tom Clancy novel.

Ranges and the Select Case Statement

So far, all your Select Case statements have checked a variable for a specific value. Select Case, though, can be more flexible than that; a program can use a Select Case statement to check for a range of values.

What's that strange feeling? Why, it's a sample program coming on!

1. Start a new Visual Basic .NET project named SelectCase, and place a Label control, a TextBox control, and a Button control on the form, as shown in Figure 8.1.

2. Double-click the form to bring up the code window, and type the following program lines into the Load procedure (which Visual Basic .NET will have already started for you):

```
Label1.Text = "Enter a value from 1 to 10:"
TextBox1.Text = "1"
Button1.Text = "Check Value"
```

Figure 8.1

Position your controls as shown here.

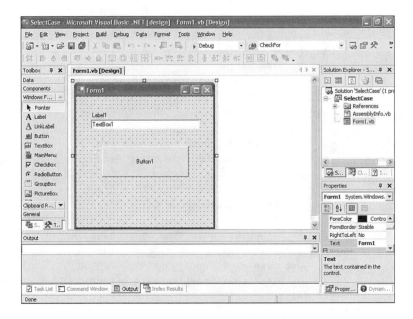

3. Start a `Button1_Click` procedure, and add the following lines to it:

```
Dim value As Integer
value = Int32.Parse(TextBox1.Text)
Select Case value
    Case Is < 4
        MessageBox.Show("Your value is less than 4.")
    Case Is < 8
        MessageBox.Show("Your value is less than 8.")
    Case Is < 11
        MessageBox.Show("Your value is less than 11.")
    Case Else
        MessageBox.Show("Your value is out of range.")
End Select
```

4. Save your work, and then run the program. When the application's window appears, type a number from 1 to 10 into the text box and click the Check Value button. When you do, the program displays a message box describing where your number falls in the 1-to-10 range. Figure 8.2 shows the program after the user has clicked the Check Value button.

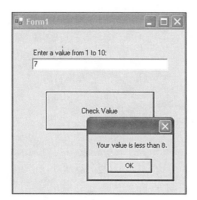

Figure 8.2

This program can check value ranges with a Select Case *statement.*

The only real difference between this Select Case statement and the others you've written is the way each Case clause examines the variable's value:

Case Is < 4

Now, thanks to the Is keyword, the Case clauses can determine whether the value fits some specified criteria. In the case of the previous example, if value is less than 4, the program executes the lines that make up the body of the Case Is < 4 clause, and then skips over the remaining Case clauses. Otherwise, as always, the program moves on to the next Case.

Check This Out

You can use all kinds of relational operators along with a Case clause's Is keyword. For example, the clause Case Is >= 10 works just fine, as does Case Is <> 4. You can even do something strange like Case Is = 10. Why is this strange? Because it's the same as writing Case 10.

The Least You Need to Know

- ◆ A Select Case statement can replace most If…Then statements.
- ◆ A Select Case statement is more concise than its If…Then counterpart.
- ◆ A program can, with a Select Case statement, examine variables containing most any type of data, including strings, integers, and floating-point values.
- ◆ The Select Case statement, with the use of the Is keyword, can examine variables for a range of values.

Chapter **9**

Looping with For...Next: Counting the Computer Way

In This Chapter

◆ Discover program loops

◆ Write a simple For...Next loop

◆ Use the Step clause to count forward by any amount

◆ Learn to make the computer count backward

◆ Use variables in For...Next loops

A computer handles repetitive operations especially well—it never gets bored, and it can perform a task as well the 10,000th time as it did the first. Consider, for example, a disk file containing 10,000 names and addresses. If you tried to type labels for all those people, you'd be seeing spots before your eyes in no time. A computer, on the other hand, can spit out all 10,000 labels tirelessly—and with nary a complaint to the union.

Every computer language must have some form of *looping* command to instruct a computer to perform repetitive tasks. Visual Basic .NET features three types of looping: For…Next loops, Do…While loops, and Do…Until loops. In this chapter, you learn to use the first of these powerful programming techniques. In Chapter 10, "Looping with Do, While, and Until," I'll discuss the other two.

Techno Talk

In computer programs, **looping** is the process of executing a block of statements repeatedly. Starting at the top of the block, the statements are executed until the program reaches the end of the block, at which point the program goes back to the top and starts over. The statements in the block may be repeated any number of times, from once to forever.

Introducing the For…Next Loop

Probably the most often used loop in Visual Basic .NET is the For…Next loop, which instructs a program to perform a block of code a specified number of times. You could, for example, use a For…Next loop to instruct your computer to print those 10,000 address labels. Because you don't currently have an address file, however, let's say you want to print your name on the screen ten times. To see one way to accomplish that task, follow these steps:

1. Start a new Visual Basic .NET project named ForNext, and place a Label, TextBox, and Button controls on the form as shown in Figure 9.1.

Figure 9.1

Position the controls as shown in this figure.

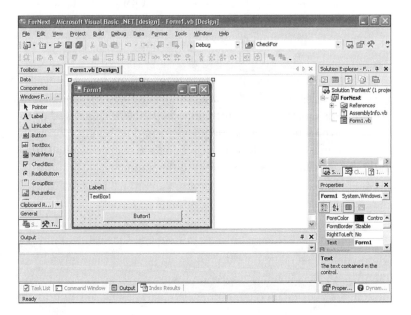

2. Double-click the form to start the Form1_Load procedure, and add the following lines to complete that procedure:

```
Label1.Text = "Enter name:"
TextBox1.Text = ""
Button1.Text = "Display Name"
```

3. Click the Form1.vb [Design] tab to return to the form, double-click the button control to start the Button1_Click procedure, and complete it with these lines:

```
Dim g As Graphics = CreateGraphics()
Dim f As Font = Button1.Font
Dim b As New SolidBrush(Color.Black)
Dim name As String
name = TextBox1.Text
g.DrawString(name, f, b, 20, 10)
g.DrawString(name, f, b, 20, 25)
g.DrawString(name, f, b, 20, 40)
g.DrawString(name, f, b, 20, 55)
g.DrawString(name, f, b, 20, 70)
g.DrawString(name, f, b, 20, 85)
g.DrawString(name, f, b, 20, 100)
g.DrawString(name, f, b, 20, 115)
g.DrawString(name, f, b, 20, 130)
g.DrawString(name, f, b, 20, 145)
```

4. Now run the program. Type a name into the text box, and then click the Display Name button. When you do, the program prints the name 10 times in the form's window, as shown in Figure 9.2.

Figure 9.2

Any name you enter appears 10 times in the window.

Look at the program listing. See all those DrawString commands? As a computer programmer, whenever you see program code containing many identical instructions, a little bell should go off in your head. When you hear this little bell, you should say to yourself, "Hmmmm. This looks like a good place for a loop."

Having many lines in your program containing identical instructions makes your program longer than necessary and wastes memory. It also shows poor programming style. Unless you want your programming friends to snicker behind your back, learn to replace redundant program code with program loops.

The previous program's Button1_Click procedure can be streamlined easily by using a For…Next loop as shown in this example:

```
Private Sub Button1_Click(ByVal sender As System.Object, _
        ByVal e As System.EventArgs) Handles Button1.Click
    Dim g As Graphics = CreateGraphics()
    Dim f As Font = Button1.Font
    Dim b As New SolidBrush(Color.Black)
    Dim name As String = TextBox1.Text
    Dim position As Integer = 10
    Dim x As Integer
    For x = 1 To 10
        g.DrawString(name, f, b, 20, position)
        position = position + 15
    Next x
End Sub
```

All you have to do is replace the previous program's Button1_Click procedure with this new one. When you run the program, the output will be identical to the first program's output, but now the program is shorter and contains no redundant code.

Look at the program line beginning with the keyword For. The loop starts with this line. The word For tells Visual Basic .NET that you're starting a For…Next loop. After the word For, you'll see the loop-control variable x. The loop-control variable, which can have any legal numerical variable name, is where Visual Basic .NET stores the current loop count. See the number after the equals sign? Visual Basic .NET uses this number to begin the loop count. The number after the keyword To is the last value of x in the loop. That is, as the loop runs, x will take on values from 1 to 10, as you'll see in the following paragraphs.

In the new Button1_Click, when the For loop begins, Visual Basic .NET places the number 1 in the variable x. The program then drops down to the next line, which prints the user's name, after which the program adds 15 to the position variable, so the next line printed will appear below the previous one. The following line …

```
Next x
```

... tells Visual Basic .NET to *increment* (or increase) the loop-control variable and start again at the top of the loop. So, x becomes 2, and the program returns to the For line. The program then compares the value in x with the number following the keyword To. If the loop count (in x) is less than or equal to the number following To, the program executes the loop again. In the case of the Button1_Click procedure, this process continues until x is greater than 10.

Whew! Got all that? If you just woke up, rub the fuzzies from your eyes and read the previous paragraph a couple times to make sure it sinks in. If you still can't stay awake, take a nap.

Suppose you want to modify the program to print your name only five times. What would you change? If you answered, "I'd change the 10 in the For line to 5," you win the Programmer of the Week award. If you answered, "I'd change my socks," start reading this chapter from the beginning.

Techno Talk

In computer programs, variables are often incremented and decremented. When you **increment a variable,** you add some value to it. When you **decrement a variable,** you subtract some value from it. If the value of the increment or decrement is not explicit, it's assumed that the value is 1. For example, the statement "The program increments the variable **num** by 5" means that **num** is increased in value by 5. On the other hand, the statement "The program increments **num**" usually means that **num** is increased by 1.

Adding the Step Clause

The previous example of a For...Next loop increments the loop counter by 1. But suppose you want a For...Next loop that counts from 5 to 40 by fives? You can do this by adding a Step clause to your For...Next loop, as shown in this example:

```
Private Sub Button1_Click(ByVal sender As System.Object, _
      ByVal e As System.EventArgs) Handles Button1.Click
   Dim g As Graphics = CreateGraphics()
   Dim f As Font = Button1.Font
   Dim b As New SolidBrush(Color.Black)
   Dim name As String = TextBox1.Text
   Dim position As Integer = 10
   Dim x As Integer
   For x = 5 To 40 Step 5
      g.DrawString(name & " -- Loop counter value: " & x, _
         f, b, 20, position)
      position = position + 15
   Next x
End Sub
```

Replace your previous `Button1_Click` procedure with this one, and then run the program. When you enter a name and click the button, you see a window similar to the one shown in Figure 9.3.

Figure 9.3

This program displays both a name and the value of the loop counter.

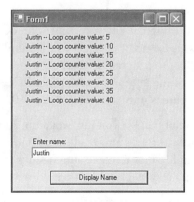

As you can see, the program prints both your name and the current value of the loop variable eight times.

Look closely at the new `Button1_Click` procedure. Unlike the previous programs, this loop doesn't start counting at 1. Rather, the loop variable begins with a value of 5. Then, thanks to the `Step 5` clause, Visual Basic .NET increments the loop variable by 5 each time through the loop. So, x goes from 5 to 10, from 10 to 15, and so on up to 40, resulting in eight loops.

Can you think of a way to use the `Step` clause to get rid of the `position` variable? How about making the loop start at 10 and then use a `Step 15`? Then you can use the loop variable x as the position for the next line to print, like this:

```
Private Sub Button1_Click(ByVal sender As System.Object, _
      ByVal e As System.EventArgs) Handles Button1.Click
   Dim g As Graphics = CreateGraphics()
   Dim f As Font = Button1.Font
   Dim b As New SolidBrush(Color.Black)
   Dim name As String = TextBox1.Text
   Dim x As Integer
   For x = 10 To 145 Step 15
       g.DrawString(name & " -- Loop counter value: " & x, _
           f, b, 20, x)
   Next x
End Sub
```

Replace your current `Button1_Click` procedure with this new one, and then run the program again. This time, you see the window, shown in Figure 9.4.

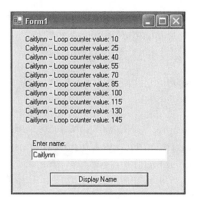

Figure 9.4

The ForNext *program refined yet again.*

The following code shows how you can use the Step clause to count backward:

```
Private Sub Button1_Click(ByVal sender As System.Object, _
        ByVal e As System.EventArgs) Handles Button1.Click
    Dim g As Graphics = CreateGraphics()
    Dim f As Font = Button1.Font
    Dim b As New SolidBrush(Color.Black)
    Dim name As String = TextBox1.Text
    Dim position As Integer = 10
    Dim x As Integer
    For x = 40 To 5 Step -5
        g.DrawString(name & " -- Loop counter value: " & x, _
            f, b, 20, position)
        position = position + 15
    Next x
End Sub
```

Figure 9.5 shows what a program run looks like when you replace the previous Button1_Click procedure with this new one.

Figure 9.5

Now the program counts in reverse.

Notice in the program that the loop limits are in reverse order; that is, the higher value comes first. Notice also that the Step clause specifies a negative value, which causes the loop count to be decremented (decreased) rather than incremented.

Using Variables in Loops

Just as with most numerical values in a program, you can substitute variables for the literals you've used so far in your For...Next loops. In fact, you'll probably use variables in your loop limits as often as you use literals, if not more. To see how this works, follow these steps:

1. Start a new Visual Basic .NET project named ForNext2, and place two Label controls, two TextBox controls, and a Button control on the form as shown in Figure 9.6.

Figure 9.6

Position the controls as shown in this figure.

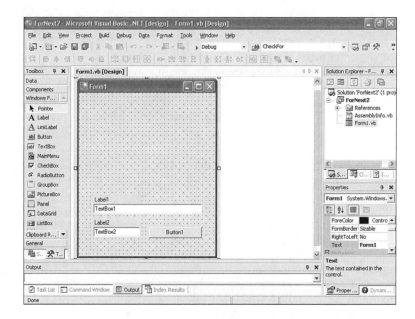

2. Double-click the form to bring up the code window. Type the following program lines into the Load procedure (which Visual Basic .NET will have already started for you):

```
Label1.Text = "Enter name:"
Label2.Text = "Enter loop count:"
TextBox1.Text = ""
TextBox2.Text = ""
Button1.Text = "Display Name"
```

3. Next, click the Form1.vb [Design] tab and double-click the button control to start the `Button1_Click` procedure, and then add the following lines to complete the procedure:

```
Dim g As Graphics = CreateGraphics()
Dim f As Font = Button1.Font
Dim b As New SolidBrush(Color.Black)
Dim position As Integer = 10
Dim name As String = TextBox1.Text
Dim count As Integer = Int32.Parse(TextBox2.Text)
Dim x As Integer
For x = 1 To count
    g.DrawString(name & " -- Loop counter value: " & x, _
        f, b, 20, position)
    position = position + 15
Next x
```

4. Run this program, and enter—in the appropriate text boxes—your name and the number of times you want your name printed. When you click the button, the program prints your name the requested number of times. As you can see in the listing, you can have the program print your name any number of times (up to the maximum number for an integer), because the loop's upper limit is contained in the variable count; count gets its value from you at the start of each program run. Figure 9.7 shows what the program looks like after it's run.

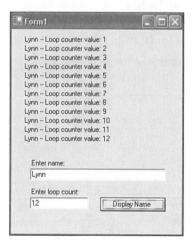

Figure 9.7

Print your name as many times as you'd like.

Using variables in For...Next loops makes your programs more flexible and produces a powerful programming construct. As you'll see in Chapter 10, you can use variables with other types of loops, too. In fact, you can use a numerical variable in a program in most places a numerical value is required. You can even use numerical variables in salads, but they taste bitter and leave a nasty film on your tongue.

By the Way

The loop-control variable in a **For...Next** loop (for example, the x in **For x = 1 To 10**) is nothing special; it's just a typical variable. The only difference between this variable and the other variables you've been using is that Visual Basic .NET knows that it can use the loop-control variable for its own purpose, which is to keep track of the loop count. Because the loop-control variable is a plain ol' variable, you can even assign values to it yourself. However, the practice of directly changing a loop-control variable's value is greatly discouraged.

The Least You Need to Know

- Repetitive operations in a computer program can be handled efficiently by program loops, including For...Next loops, Do...While loops, and Do...Until loops.
- A For...Next loop instructs a program to execute a block of commands a given number of times.
- In the For...Next loop For x = num1 To num2, the variable x is the loop's control variable. The loop limits are the values of num1 and num2.
- By adding a Step clause to a For...Next loop, you can make the loop-control variable count up or down in any increment or decrement. For example, the loop For x = 20 to 10 Step -2 counts backward by 2s, from 20 to 10.
- You can use a numeric variable for either of the two loop limits in a For...Next loop.

Looping with Do, While, and Until

In This Chapter

♦ Learn about Do While loops

♦ Discover how to use Do Until loops

♦ Program Do…Loop While and Do…Loop Until loops

In the previous chapter, I introduced you to program loops. Specifically, you learned about For…Next loops, which enable a program to perform a set of actions a certain number of times. Visual Basic .NET, however, provides four other types of looping techniques, including Do While, Do Until, Do…Loop While, and Do…Loop Until loops. (And you hoped that you were finished with this looping nonsense!) In the following pages, you'll learn how these types of loops can beef up your Visual Basic .NET programs. Or, for the health conscious, "fish" up your Visual Basic .NET programs.

Introducing the Do While Loop

Unlike a For…Next loop, which loops the number of times given in the loop limits, a Do While loop continues executing as long as its control expression is true. The control expression is a Boolean expression much like the Boolean expressions you used with `If` statements. In other words, any expression that evaluates to true or false can be used as a control expression for a `Do While` loop.

To see a `Do While` loop in action, follow these steps:

1. Start a new Visual Basic .NET project named DoWhile, and then place two Label controls, one TextBox control, and one Button control on the form, as shown in Figure 10.1.

Figure 10.1

Position the controls as shown in this figure.

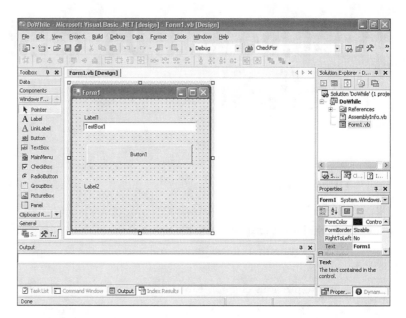

2. Double-click the form to bring up the code window and type the following program lines into the `Load` procedure (Visual Basic .NET will have already started the `Form1_Load` procedure for you):

```
Label1.Text = "Loop-control variable value:"
Label2.Text = "Current variable value: "
TextBox1.Text = "5"
Button1.Text = "Start Loop"
```

3. Double-click the button control to start its `Click` procedure. Complete the procedure with the following lines:

```
Dim control As Integer
Dim isButtonWhite As Boolean
On Error Resume Next
control = Int32.Parse(TextBox1.Text)
```

```
Button1.BackColor = Color.White
isButtonWhite = True
Do While control <> 0
    control = Int32.Parse(TextBox1.Text)
    Label2.Text = _
        "Current variable value: " & control
    If isButtonWhite Then
        Button1.BackColor = Color.Red
    Else
        Button1.BackColor = Color.White
    End If
    isButtonWhite = Not isButtonWhite
    Application.DoEvents()
Loop
MessageBox.Show("looping complete")
```

4. Run the program, and click the Start Loop button to start the Do While loop located in the Button1_Click procedure.

   This Do While loop continually changes the button's background color as well as retrieves the value currently entered into the application's text box. Enter any value you like in the text box. The program loads the value into the control variable and updates the Label control at the bottom of the window to show the current value of control. The Do While loop continues until you enter the value 0 into the text box, as shown in Figure 10.2.

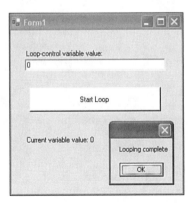

Figure 10.2

A value of 0 stops the loop and displays a message box.

To fully understand this program's Button1_Click procedure, you need to stop staring at the running program with that stunned expression (yeah, the program is kind of cool) and examine the procedure line by line.

The line

```
Dim control As integer
```

declares the variable control as an integer.

Next, the line

```
Dim isButtonWhite As Boolean
```

declares a Boolean variable that the program will use to remember whether the button is white or not. Then, the line

```
On Error Resume Next
```

tells Visual Basic .NET to keep running even if a runtime error occurs. This line is important because the Do While loop is constantly grabbing the contents of the text box and converting the contents to a numerical value. If you backspace to get rid of the current value in the text box, for a couple of seconds the text box will be empty, which means when the program tries to grab and convert the contents, Visual Basic .NET will generate an error. The On Error Resume Next Button ensures that you never even know that an error occurred. (You'll learn more about this error stuff in Chapter 16, "Catching Runtime Errors.")

Next, the line

```
control = Int32.Parse(TextBox1.Text)
```

sets the control variable's starting value, which, by default, is 5, the value that the text box starts with.

Next, the line

```
Button1.BackColor = Color.White
```

sets the button's background color to white, after which the line

```
isButtonWhite = True
```

sets the Boolean variable to indicate that the button is currently white. Now, the line

```
Do While control <> 0
```

starts the loop, because control doesn't equal 0. If the program started with the value 0 entered into the text box, the loop would never start. If you were to read the previous line in English, you would say, "do while control doesn't equal 0."

The lines between the Do While and the Loop lines are the lines that the program executes every time the loop repeats. Inside the loop, the line

```
control = Int32.Parse(TextBox1.Text)
```

gets a new value for the control variable, after which the line

```
Label2.Text = _
    "Current variable value: " & control
```

displays the control variable's current value in the program's second Label control.

After setting the caption, the loop decides whether to set the button's background color to white or red, as shown in the following snippet:

```
If isButtonWhite Then
    Button1.BackColor = Color.Red
Else
    Button1.BackColor = Color.White
End If
```

After the If statement, the line

```
isButtonWhite = Not isButtonWhite
```

reverses the value of the isButtonWhite variable, making it true if it was false or vice versa.

As long as the loop runs, this If…Then statement keeps changing the button's background color between white and red, so that you can actually see the loop running.

This line

```
Application.DoEvents
```

is essential to the program's operation. If this line were missing, you would never be able to enter a value into the text box, because the Do While loop runs so fast that no other input is possible—for any program, not just the example program! This problem occurs because Windows, in order to manage running applications, relies on a series of messages being passed back and forth between Windows and currently running programs. The Application.DoEvents command tells the Do While loop to wait a little while so that other Windows messages can get through. If you take the Application.DoEvents line out of the program, the program will seem to die and sit idle on the screen. In fact, you'll have to press Ctrl+Alt+Delete to end the program, because even Visual Basic .NET loses all control of the system.

At the end of the loop, the line

```
Loop
```

tells Visual Basic .NET that it has reached the end of the Do While loop. At this point, Visual Basic .NET goes back to the Do While line to take another look at the value of control. If control still doesn't equal 0, the loop runs again. On the other hand, if control does equal 0, the Do While loop ends, and the program jumps to the next line after the loop:

```
MessageBox.Show("looping complete")
```

Techno Talk

Initializing a variable means setting it to its starting value. In Visual Basic .NET, all numeric variables are automatically initialized to 0. If you need a variable to start at a different value, you must initialize it yourself.

This line simply displays a message box, letting you know that the loop has stopped.

Notice how the program sets the variable control to a value before the Do While loop starts. This is important because it ensures that the value in control starts at a value other than 0. If control did happen to start at 0, the program would never get to the statements within the Do While loop, because the loop's control expression would immediately evaluate to false. Mistakes like this make programmers growl and answer the phone with, "What do you want, butthead?"

The Do Until Loop

Visual Basic .NET also features another type of loop, called a Do Until loop, which is very similar to a Do While loop. For example, the previous program's Button1_Click procedure could have been rewritten with a Do Until loop, as shown in this example:

```
Dim control As Integer
Dim isButtonWhite As Boolean
On Error Resume Next
control = Int32.Parse(TextBox1.Text)
Button1.BackColor = Color.White
isButtonWhite = True
Do Until control = 0
    control = Int32.Parse(TextBox1.Text)
    Label2.Text = _
        "Current variable value: " & control
    If isButtonWhite Then
        Button1.BackColor = Color.Red
```

```
    Else
        Button1.BackColor = Color.White
    End If
    isButtonWhite = Not isButtonWhite
    Application.DoEvents()
Loop
MessageBox.Show("Looping complete")
```

Do you see the difference between the original Do While loop and the Do Until loop? The Do While loop continues while the control expression is true, whereas the Do Until loop continues as long as its control expression is false. This is why the control expressions in the two loop types have reverse logic.

The Do...Loop While Loop

In both cases, the Do While and Do Until loops check their control expression before the loop runs for even the first time. This means that both these loop types may not loop at all. If the control expression starts off true in a Do Until loop, the entire loop gets skipped. What if you want to write a Do While–type of loop, but want to be sure it executes at least once? Then you could use a Do...Loop While loop.

The only real difference between a Do While loop and a Do...Loop While loop is that, in the latter case, the loop checks its control expression after the loop runs instead of before. For example, the following code shows the familiar Button1_Click procedure, rewritten with a Do...Loop While loop:

```
Dim control As Integer
Dim isButtonWhite As Boolean
On Error Resume Next
control = Int32.Parse(TextBox1.Text)
Button1.BackColor = Color.White
isButtonWhite = True
Do
    control = Int32.Parse(TextBox1.Text)
    Label2.Text = _
        "Current variable value: " & control
    If isButtonWhite Then
        Button1.BackColor = Color.Red
    Else
        Button1.BackColor = Color.White
    End If
    isButtonWhite = Not isButtonWhite
    Application.DoEvents()
Loop While control <> 0
MessageBox.Show("Looping complete")
```

The Do...Loop Until Loop

As you may have guessed, Do...Loop While has a cousin called Do...Loop Until. These two types of loops are just as similar as their counterparts (second cousins?) Do While and Do Until. The only difference is that these loops check their control expressions at the end of the loop rather than at the start. The following example presents yet another version of the Button1_Click procedure, this time using the Do...Loop Until loop:

```
Dim control As Integer
Dim isButtonWhite As Boolean
On Error Resume Next
control = Int32.Parse(TextBox1.Text)
Button1.BackColor = Color.White
isButtonWhite = True
Do
    control = Int32.Parse(TextBox1.Text)
    Label2.Text = _
        "Current variable value: " & control
    If isButtonWhite Then
        Button1.BackColor = Color.Red
    Else
        Button1.BackColor = Color.White
    End If
    isButtonWhite = Not isButtonWhite
    Application.DoEvents()
Loop Until control = 0
MessageBox.Show("Looping complete")
```

Check This Out

Different looping methods work best in different programming situations. Although experience is the best teacher, you should keep some things in mind when selecting a looping construct. When you want a loop to run a specific number of times, the For...Next loop is usually the best choice. When you want a loop to run until a certain condition is met, the **Do While** or **Do Until** loops work best. Finally, if you want to be sure that the loop runs at least once, you should use the **Do...Loop While** or Do...Loop Until loop.

New programmers are infamous for creating loops that never end. For example, if you write a Do While loop whose control expression can never become true, your loop will loop forever. When this happens, it'll look to you as though your program has "locked up" your machine (your computer has stopped dead in its tracks and will accept no input). But, really, your program is looping frantically, with no hope of ever moving on. Often, the only way out of this predicament is to type Ctrl+Alt+Delete to terminate the program.

The Least You Need to Know

◆ A Do While loop continues to run until its control expression becomes false. Because this type of loop checks the control expression before running the loop, a Do While loop can run 0 or more times.

◆ A Do Until loop continues to run until its control expression becomes true and checks the control expression before running the loop. A Do Until loop can run 0 or more times.

◆ A Do...Loop While loop runs until its control expression becomes false, but it checks the control expression at the end of the loop instead of at the beginning. This difference means that a Do...Loop While loop always executes its statements at least once.

◆ A Do...Loop Until loop runs until its control expression becomes true. This type of loop also always executes its statements at least once.

Arrays: Tricky Problems with Clever Solutions

In This Chapter

- ◆ Learn to create arrays
- ◆ Use arrays with loops
- ◆ Understand numerical and string arrays

As you've learned by now, using variables makes your programs flexible. Thanks to variables, you can conveniently store data in your programs and retrieve it by name. You can also get and store input from your program's user. The best thing about variables is that they can constantly change value. They're called variables, after all, because they're variable!

Until now, you've learned about various types of numerical variables, including integers, long integers, single-precision variables, and double-precision variables. You also know about string variables, which can hold text. Now that you have a good understanding of these data types, it's time to explore one last data type—a handy data structure called an array.

Introducing Arrays

Often in your programs, you'll want to store many values that are related in some way. Suppose you manage a bowling league, and you want to keep track of each player's average. One way to do this is to give each player a variable in your program. The following program shows how to accomplish this task.

To build the program, follow these steps:

1. Start a new Visual Basic .NET project named Bowling, and position four Label controls, four TextBox controls, and one Button control. Make the Label controls the same length as the TextBox controls, as shown in Figure 11.1.

Figure 11.1

Position the controls as shown in this figure.

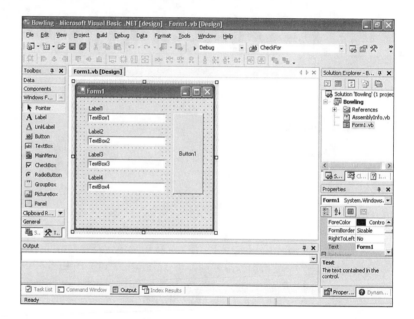

2. Double-click the form to bring up the code window and then type the following program lines into the Load procedure (Visual Basic .NET will have already started the Form1_Load procedure for you):

```
Label1.Text = "Enter Fred's average:"
Label2.Text = "Enter Mary's average:"
Label3.Text = "Enter Thomas's average:"
Label4.Text = "Enter Alice's average:"
TextBox1.Text = "0"
TextBox2.Text = "0"
TextBox3.Text = "0"
TextBox4.Text = "0"
Button1.Text = "Show Scores"
```

3. Double-click the button control to start its Click procedure. Complete the procedure with the following code:

```
Dim avg1 As Integer = Int32.Parse(TextBox1.Text)
Dim avg2 As Integer = Int32.Parse(TextBox2.Text)
Dim avg3 As Integer = Int32.Parse(TextBox3.Text)
Dim avg4 As Integer = Int32.Parse(TextBox4.Text)
MessageBox.Show("Fred's Score:  " & avg1)
MessageBox.Show("Mary's Score:  " & avg2)
MessageBox.Show("Thomas's Score: " & avg3)
MessageBox.Show("Alice's Score:  " & avg4)
```

4. Run the program, and enter bowling scores into the four text boxes. Then click the Show Scores button to display the scores, one at a time, in a message box.

As you can see from the program's Button1_Click procedure, when you click the button, the program does nothing more than retrieve the scores from the text boxes and display them in a message box, as shown in Figure 11.2.

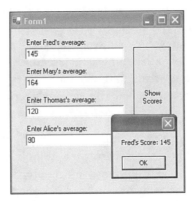

Figure 11.2

The message box formats and displays the scores you enter.

Nothing too tricky going on here, right?

Remember when you learned to keep an eye out for repetitive program code? (Well, I wouldn't suggest actually keeping an eye out. Eyeballs tend to dry out quickly and are easily knocked off your desk.) How about all those repetitive statements in the Button1_Click procedure? The procedure declares four very similar variables as well as gets the values for those variables in a very similar way. Moreover, the program displays the values of all four scores in almost exactly the same way. If you could find some way to make a loop out of this code, you'd need only one line to input all the data and only one line to display the averages for all four bowlers. You could, in fact, use a For…Next loop that counts from 1 to 4.

But how can you use a loop when you're stuck with four different variables? The answer is an array. An array is a variable that can hold more than one value. When you first studied variables, you learned that a variable is like a box in memory that holds a single value. Now, if you take a bunch of these boxes and put them together, what do you have? (No, the answer isn't "a bunch of variables smooshed together.") You'd have an array. For example, to store the bowling averages for your four bowlers, you'd need an array that can hold four values. You could call this array avg. You could also call this array TheseAreTheBowlersAverages, but who wants to do all that typing?

Check This Out

The number 0 is insanely important to computers, as you'll discover as you do more and more programming. Computers don't consider 1 to be the first positive whole number, but rather 0. This is why the first value in an array is stored at a subscript of 0.

By the Way

The little memory boxes that make up an array are called *elements* of the array. For example, in an array named numbers, numbers(0) is the first element of the array, numbers(1) is the second element, and so on.

Now you have an array called avg that can hold four bowling averages. But how can you retrieve each individual average from the array? You could run out on your front lawn in your skivvies, wave a plucked chicken over your head, and shout praises to the gods of computing. However, an easier way—and one that doesn't amuse the neighbors quite so much—is to add something called a *subscript* to the array's name.

A subscript is a number that identifies the box in which an array value is stored. For example, to refer to the first average in your avg array, you'd write avg(0). The subscript is the number in parentheses. In this case, you're referring to the first average in the array. To refer to the second average, you'd write avg(1). The third and fourth averages are avg(2) and avg(3).

If you're a little confused, look at Figure 11.3, which shows how the avg array might look in memory. In this case, the four bowling averages are 145, 192, 160, and 203. The value of avg(0) is 145, the value of avg(1) is 192, the value of avg(2) is 160, and the value of avg(3) is 203.

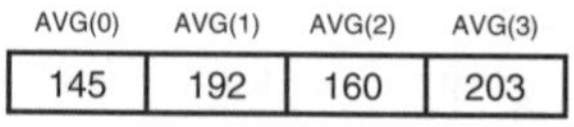

Figure 11.3

An array looks something like this in memory.

AVG(0)	AVG(1)	AVG(2)	AVG(3)
145	192	160	203

Using a Variable As a Subscript

As you've learned, most numerical constants in a Visual Basic .NET program can be replaced by numerical variables. Suppose, then, you were to use the variable x as the subscript for the array avg. Then (based on the averages in the previous figure), if the value of x were 1, the value of avg(x) would be 192. If the value of x were 3, the value of avg(x) would be 203.

Now take one last gigantic intuitive leap (c'mon, you can do it), and think about using your subscript variable x as both the control variable in a For...Next loop and the subscript for the avg array. If you use a For...Next loop that counts from 0 to 3, you can use a single line (not including the For and Next lines) to show all four players' averages. The following new version of your Button1_Click procedure shows how this is done:

```
Dim avg(3) As Integer
avg(0) = Int32.Parse(TextBox1.Text)
avg(1) = Int32.Parse(TextBox2.Text)
avg(2) = Int32.Parse(TextBox3.Text)
avg(3) = Int32.Parse(TextBox4.Text)
Dim x As Integer
For x = 0 To 3
    MessageBox.Show("Bowler's Score: " & avg(x))
Next x
```

This version of Button1_Click first declares an array that can hold four values (subscripts 0 through 3), which in programmer speak is a *four-element array*. The procedure then loads the array from the values entered into the text boxes. Finally, the For...Next loop displays the averages one by one, using the variable x as the array's subscript (sometimes called an *index*).

Whoops!

When you declare your arrays, make sure you have enough room for the data you need to store. Once you declare an array, Visual Basic .NET will not allow you to store or retrieve values beyond the end of the array (except by using the `Redim` command, which we don't cover here). For example, if you declare an array as `numbers(10)` and then try to access `numbers(11)`, your program will come to a crashing halt and give you a subscript-out-of-range error.

Do you understand how the program works? In the For...Next loop, the variable x starts with a value of 0. So, the first message box displays the value of avg(0). The next time through the loop, x equals 1, so the message box displays the value in avg(1). This continues until x becomes 4, and the For...Next loop ends.

Working with String Arrays

The previous program shows how handy arrays can be, but there's something missing from the program. First, there's no built-in Mario game, so using this program for long periods of time is downright boring. More to the point, though, the bowlers' names are missing when the program displays the scores. You can get around this problem easily, by creating an array to hold strings. (You can get over the Mario problem by taking a Nintendo break.) Replace the previous program's Button1_Click procedure with the following lines:

```
Private Sub Button1_Click(ByVal sender As System.Object, _
        ByVal e As System.EventArgs) Handles Button1.Click
    Dim avg(3) As Integer
    avg(0) = Int32.Parse(TextBox1.Text)
    avg(1) = Int32.Parse(TextBox2.Text)
    avg(2) = Int32.Parse(TextBox3.Text)
    avg(3) = Int32.Parse(TextBox4.Text)
    Dim names(3) As String
    names(0) = "Fred"
    names(1) = "Mary"
    names(2) = "Thomas"
    names(3) = "Alice"
    Dim x As Integer
    For x = 0 To 3
        MessageBox.Show(names(x) & "'s Score: " & avg(x))
    Next x
End Sub
```

When you run the program now, it looks and acts almost the same. However, now most of the program's data is handled in arrays. Look closely at the Button1_Click procedure. The procedure declares a string array that can hold four strings, like this:

```
Dim names(3) As String
```

Next, the procedure loads the array with the bowler's names:

```
names(0) = "Fred"
names(1) = "Mary"
names(2) = "Thomas"
names(3) = "Alice"
```

The new For...Next loop now accesses the names array to get the name that's associated with the current score, which enables the message box to show both the name and the score:

```
For x = 0 To 3
    MessageBox.Show(names(x) & "'s Score: " & avg(x))
Next x
```

Figure 11.4 shows how the new message boxes look.

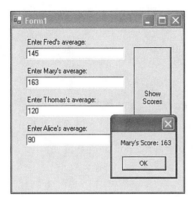

Figure 11.4

The message boxes now display both the name and the score.

The Least You Need to Know

◆ Arrays enable you to store many values under a single variable name.

◆ An array's subscript (or index), which is a number within parentheses appended to the array's name, identifies each element of the array.

◆ By using a numerical variable for an array's subscript, you can easily access each element of the array within a loop.

◆ To tell Visual Basic .NET how large an array should be, you declare the array with a `Dim` statement.

File Handling: The Ol' Data I/O Shuffle

In This Chapter

◆ Open and close files

◆ Save data to a file

◆ Load data from a file

◆ Add data to an existing file

As you've used your computer, you've no doubt noticed that most applications save and load data to and from your hard disk. The applications you write with Visual Basic .NET don't have to be any different; they, too, can save information to a disk file. If you've been trying to save data from your Visual Basic .NET programs by photographing the screen, you're going to love this chapter!

Three Steps to Access a File

Simple file handling is actually an easy process, once you get the hang of it. There are, however, three steps that you need to perform to be sure that your program's data gets properly tucked away in that binary home called a file:

1. Open the file.
2. Send data to the file or read data from the file.
3. Close the file.

In the following sections, you'll cover each of these steps in detail.

Opening a File

Probably the most complicated part of managing file I/O (input/output, remember?) is opening the file in the proper mode. You see, not only can files be used to save and load data, but they also can be used to save and load specific kinds of data in specific ways. For example, there's a big difference between opening a file to read a line of text or opening a file to read a database record, even though a file must be opened in both cases. Specifically, you can open a file in one of five different ways, called modes. These modes are ...

♦ Append
♦ Binary
♦ Input
♦ Output
♦ Random-access

Before you reach for the Valium, let me assure you that these mode thingies are not as confusing as they may seem to be. First, because you're just starting out, you can forget about binary and random-access files. You'll leave those puppies to a more advanced book that covers things like databases, records, and binary files. Feeling better already, right?

The remaining modes are easy to understand. To prove that claim, you're about to open a file in output mode, which makes good sense. You can't, after all, load data from a file until you've saved data to the file. Here are the Visual Basic .NET statements that create and open a file in the output mode:

```
Dim sWriter As IO.StreamWriter
sWriter = IO.File.CreateText("c:\MyFile.txt")
```

The first thing to notice here is the variable sWriter, which is something called an IO.StreamWriter. Sounds really techie, but it really isn't. A *stream* is just a flow of data, in the same way that a real-world stream, like a brook, is a flow of water. A StreamWriter, then, simply writes a stream of data to a file. Easy!

The second line creates the StreamWriter and associates it with a file named "MyFile.txt." In this case, the file is located in the root directory of drive C. If you leave off the file path (the "c:\", in this case, although a path can be longer, such as "c:\My Documents\ WorkStuff"), the file will be opened in the current directory, which is usually the one from which you run the program.

The output mode enables a program to save data to the disk file. In this case, the file is MyFile.txt. If the file doesn't already exist, Visual Basic .NET creates it. If the file does exist, Visual Basic .NET gets the file ready to accept output from your program, which includes erasing the current contents of the file.

Examine that last sentence carefully! Yes, the sentence includes 16 E's, which is the most commonly used letter in the English language. (Bet you now have an uncontrollable urge to count them yourself.) However, you didn't really need to examine the sentence *that* closely. What you do need to notice is the phrase "which includes erasing the current contents of the file." To state the point again, *if you use the output mode to open an existing file, Visual Basic .NET erases the previous contents of the file.*

That's all there is to opening a file. Now, you can refer to the file using the sWriter StreamWriter variable. Every time your program opens a file, the program needs a way to refer to the file. The same way your friends may refer to you as Mack, Sarah, Willie, or "Hey, Einstein," your Visual Basic .NET program must refer to the open file with its StreamWriter variable.

Saving Data to the File

Your file is now open, sitting there patiently on your disk drive like a kitten waiting for a scratch behind the ears. The file, however, will sit there waiting patiently for attention long after the kitten has wondered away in boredom. I wouldn't suggest that you try to scratch your file behind the ears, but it might be a good idea at this point to put some data into the file. You can do this the following Visual Basic .NET command, for example:

```
sWriter.WriteLine("Everyone knows that files have no ears.")
```

As you undoubtedly realize, the command WriteLine tells Visual Basic .NET that you want to print data to a file. Visual Basic .NET knows you're printing to a file thanks to the fact that the sWriter variable is one of those StreamWriter thingies and that that thingy is associated with a file.

 Check This Out _____

When you're typing program lines, make sure you get all the punctuation right. Leaving out something as simple as a comma can bring your program to a crashing halt. For example, don't forget the quotes around a file name, which is really a string literal.

After the `WriteLine` command, you place the data (surrounded by quotes if it's a string) you want to save to the file. In this case, the data is the string "Everyone knows that files have no ears." After Visual Basic .NET has performed this command, your file will contain the string, no fuss or muss.

Closing the File

When you put a bird in a cage, you finish the task by closing the cage door. A file and its data are similar. After you place data into the file, you must close the file; otherwise, you may wind up losing data. Data doesn't have wings like a bird, of course, but it can still fly away into the great unknown. Take it from someone who's lost enough data to fill an encyclopedia.

To close a file, you call upon the ever-trusty `Close` command:

```
sWriter.Close()
```

Techno Talk

Closing files in a Visual Basic .NET program (and most programs written in other languages, as well) is important because not all the data you've sent to the file has necessarily arrived there before you close the file. The reason for this anomaly is something called **buffering**. Because disk drives are so slow compared with computer memory, Visual Basic .NET doesn't actually send data directly to the disk file. Instead, it saves up the data in your computer's memory until it has enough data to be worth taking the time to access the disk drive. The `Close` command tells Visual Basic .NET not only to close the file, but also to be sure to send all the data from the buffer first.

Trying It Out

It's time now to see all this file stuff put to work. To do this, follow these steps:

1. Start a new Visual Basic .NET project (using the Windows Application template) named FileIO, and place Label, TextBox, and Button controls on the form, as shown in Figure 12.1.

2. Double-click the form to bring up the code window, and type the following program lines into the `Load` procedure (Visual Basic .NET will have already started the `Form1_Load` procedure for you):

```
Label1.Text = "Enter the text to file:"
TextBox1.Text = "Default text"
Button1.Text = "Save Text"
```

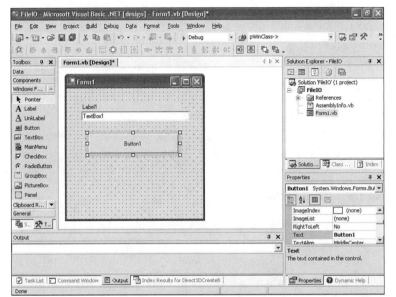

Figure 12.1

Position your controls as shown in this figure.

3. Double-click the Button control, and type the following program lines into the Click procedure (Visual Basic .NET will have already started the Button1_Click procedure for you):

```
Dim data As String = TextBox1.Text
Dim sWriter As IO.StreamWriter
sWriter = IO.File.CreateText("c:\MyFile.txt")
sWriter.WriteLine(data)
sWriter.Close()
MessageBox.Show("Text saved.")
```

4. Save your work, and run the program. When you do, the application's main window appears, as shown in Figure 12.2.

Figure 12.2

This application saves the contents of the text box to a file.

5. Type whatever text you want into the text box (or just leave the default text as is), and click the Save Text button.

Visual Basic .NET saves the contents of the text box to a file named MyFile.txt. This happens in the `Button1_Click` procedure, the first line of which declares a string variable and sets the variable to the text in the text box control:

```
Dim data As String = TextBox1.Text
```

Next comes the old familiar `StreamWriter` variable, which opens the file for output:

```
Dim sWriter As IO.StreamWriter
sWriter = IO.File.CreateText("c:\MyFile.txt")
```

With the file open, the program can save the contents of the variable `data` to the file:

```
sWriter.WriteLine(data)
```

Finally, the program closes the file and displays a message box that informs the user that the text was saved:

```
sWriter.Close()
MessageBox.Show("Text saved.")
```

The thing to notice about this program is that, rather than having the `WriteLine` command save a string literal as was done previously, this `WriteLine` command saves the contents of a string variable. Visual Basic .NET can save a string to the file either way, without the slightest bit of whining.

Loading Data from a File

Your file now has data in it. What that data actually is depends on what you typed into the text box before clicking the Save Text button. Data in a file, however, is about as useful as a clock to a goldfish if you have no way of getting the data out again. That's where the `ReadLine` command comes in handy. Luckily, you're about to see how that works.

1. Go back to that program you just worked on and add another Button control, as shown in Figure 12.3.

2. Add the following line to the `Form1_Load` procedure (it can go anywhere in the procedure):

   ```
   Button2.Text = "Load Text"
   ```

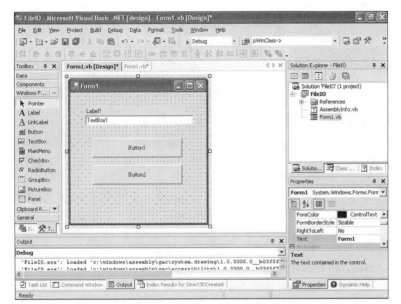

Figure 12.3

Add a button to the program's form.

3. Double-click the new button to display the `Button2_Click` procedure, and complete the procedure with the following lines:

```
Dim data As String
Dim sReader As IO.StreamReader
sReader = IO.File.OpenText("c:\MyFile.txt")
data = sReader.ReadLine()
sReader.Close()
TextBox1.Text = data
```

4. Save your work and run the program. When the program's window appears, clear all the text from the text box, and then click the Load Text button.

   When you do, the program gets the text you saved to the file and displays it in the text box. For example, if you previously saved the text line "You ain't nothin' but a hound dog", your program's window will look similar to Figure 12.4 after you click the Load Text button.

How does this program work? When you click the Load Text button, Visual Basic .NET jumps to the `Button2_Click` procedure, the first line of which declares the following string variable:

```
Dim data As String
```

Figure 12.4

*Now the program can
load text, too.*

After declaring the variable, the program opens the file for input:

```
Dim sReader As IO.StreamReader
sReader = IO.File.OpenText("c:\MyFile.txt")
```

Notice that this time the program creates a `StreamReader` rather than a `StreamWriter`. This makes perfect sense because you want the program to read the contents of the file. With the file open, the program can load the text from the file and into the string variable `data`:

```
data = sReader.ReadLine()
```

Finally, the program closes the file and displays the loaded text in the text box:

```
sReader.Close()
TextBox1.Text = data
```

Appending Data to a File

Every time you click that Save Text button, and the program opens the MyFile.txt file for output, the previous contents of the file get erased like a teacher's chalkboard at the end of the day. This is all fine and dandy if you want to start a new file, but what if you want to *add* something to the file? Easy! You open the file in append mode.

To check this out, follow these steps:

1. Add yet another Button control to your program, as shown in Figure 12.5.

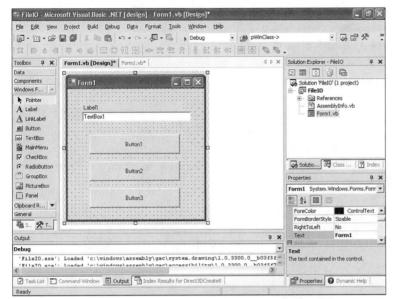

Figure 12.5

Add a third button to the program's form.

2. Add the following line to the Form1_Load procedure (it can go anywhere in the procedure):

```
Button3.Text = "Append Text"
```

3. Double-click the new button to display the Button3_Click procedure. Add the following lines to the procedure:

```
Dim data As String = TextBox1.Text
Dim sWriter As IO.StreamWriter
sWriter = IO.File.AppendText("c:\MyFile.txt")
sWriter.WriteLine(data)
sWriter.Close()
MessageBox.Show("Text appended.")
```

This procedure is almost exactly like the Button1_Click procedure, except that, thanks to the AppendText command, it opens the file in append mode, rather than in output mode.

4. Because your file will have more than one line of text in it after the append, the program needs to change the way it inputs data from the file. Specifically, the program needs to keep loading text strings until it gets to the end of the file. To do this, replace the contents of the current Button2_Click procedure with this snippet:

```
Dim sReader As IO.StreamReader = IO.File.OpenText("c:\MyFile.txt")
Dim data As String = sReader.ReadLine()
```

```
Do While data <> ""
    MessageBox.Show(data)
    data = sReader.ReadLine()
Loop
sReader.Close()
```

5. Save your work and run the program. When the main window appears, type some text into the text box, and then click the Append Text button.

   Visual Basic .NET saves the text immediately after the text that's already in the file. You can save as many text strings as you like by continuing to change the text in the text box and clicking the Append Text button.

When you click the Load Text button, the program no longer displays the text in the text box, because there is more than one line of text in the file. Instead, the program loads a line of text and displays it in a message box, as shown in Figure 12.6.

Figure 12.6

The program now displays text in a text box.

Each time you dismiss the message box, another one appears with the next line of text. This process continues until the program reaches the end of the file.

How does the program know when it's reached the end of the file? The secret to that little mystery lies in the revised `Button2_Click` procedure. The procedure opens the file for input as you'd expect, but then it starts a `Do While` loop, the first line of which looks like this:

```
Do While data <> ""
```

You already know what a `Do While` loop is, and you know what the `<>` operator means, but what's that `""`? Remember when you learned about strings, you discovered something called an empty string? An empty string is what you get back from the `ReadLine` procedure when the program has read all the text from the file.

Inside the loop, the program displays and loads a line of text with this code:

```
MessageBox.Show(data)
data = sReader.ReadLine()
```

Then the Loop keyword sends Visual Basic .NET back to the beginning of the loop, where the program again checks for the end of the file. If the program hasn't reached the end of the file yet, the loop loads another line of text; otherwise, the loop ends.

The Least You Need to Know

◆ Accessing a file requires three steps: opening the file, saving or loading data to or from the file, and closing the file.

◆ You can open a file in one of five modes: append, binary, input, output, and random-access (read and write).

◆ To read from a text file, you must first use the IO.File.OpenText command to create a StreamReader.

◆ To create and write to a text file, you must first use the IO.File.CreateText command to create a StreamWriter.

◆ To append to a text file, you must first use the IO.File.AppendText command to create a StreamWriter.

◆ The WriteLine command stores data in an open file.

◆ The ReadLine command loads data from an open file.

◆ When a program finishes with a file, it must close the file with the Close command. Failure to close the file properly could result in lost data.

◆ The output file mode creates the file if it doesn't exist or opens and erases the file if it does exist.

◆ The input file mode enables a program to read data from an existing file.

◆ The append file mode enables a program to add data to an already existing file.

User-Defined Data Types: Data Your Way!

In This Chapter

♦ Declare custom data types known as structures

♦ Create variables from your structures

♦ Access values in a structure

♦ Pass structures as arguments to procedures

Visual Basic .NET provides all kinds of data types, certainly every kind you'd ever need for the programs you're likely to write. (If you work for NASA, maybe you should consider a fancier programming language.) Still, there are times when it'd be darn handy to be able to put together a custom data type, something that'll help keep track of all those variables you end up with. Luckily, there is a way. In this chapter, you'll discover user-defined data types, and you'll learn to use them to make programming life oh so much easier.

Declaring a Structure

Suppose you're writing a program that keeps track of various types of office supplies—you know, stuff like paperclips, printer paper, pens, and the pillows you rest your head on when the boss isn't looking. Suppose further that you have three sizes of paperclips, two sizes of paper, three colors of pens, and a selection of comfy pillows ranging from the too-small-to-be-comfy-but-hides-quickly type to the man-I-could-spend-my-entire-life-with-my-head-buried-in-this-puppy type.

As you know, when you want to keep track of a piece of data, you must assign to it a variable. If you have three sizes of paperclips, for example, and you want to keep track of them all, you need to create three variables, which might look something like this:

```
Dim ClipsSmall As Integer
Dim ClipsMedium As Integer
Dim ClipsLarge As Integer
```

Now add to those paperclip variables the other stuff you need to keep track of, and you end up with the following list of variables:

```
Dim ClipsSmall As Integer
Dim ClipsMedium As Integer
Dim ClipsLarge As Integer
Dim PaperLetter As Integer
Dim PaperLegal As Integer
Dim PenBlack As Integer
Dim PenBlue As Integer
Dim PenRed As Integer
Dim PillowYuck As Integer
Dim PillowOK As Integer
Dim PillowWakeMeUpAt5 As Integer
```

This is a perfectly acceptable way to handle variables for your office supplies. If you use a list of variables like this, no one will snicker, cut your pay, or paste an "I'm a Sucky Programmer" sign on your back. Still, there is a way to organize all these variables such that they're logically grouped and more convenient to use—it's known as a structure.

A *structure* is a form of user-defined data type, where you assign a name to the structure along with the variables that make up the data within the structure. From then on, you can do things like make sure David Letterman gets a better schedule than Jay Leno, renew *Roswell* for a new season, and cancel shows like *The World's Most Amazing Feather Dusters* and *When Wild Goldfish Attack*. No, wait. That's *TV* programming.

How, you might ask, can you use structures to organize your list of office supplies? You might write something like this:

```
Structure Clips
    Dim Small As Integer
    Dim Medium As Integer
    Dim Large As Integer
End Structure
```

```
Structure Paper
    Dim Letter As Integer
    Dim Legal As Integer
End Structure

Structure Pens
    Dim Black As Integer
    Dim Blue As Integer
    Dim Red As Integer
End Structure

Structure Pillows
    Dim Yuck As Integer
    Dim OK As Integer
    Dim WakeMeUpAt5 As Integer
End Structure
```

As you can see, to create a structure, you start with the `Structure` keyword, followed by the structure's name. Then, you list the variables that you want contained in the structure. Finally, you end the structure with the `End Structure` line.

Declaring a Variable from a Structure

Okay, it's true that it takes more lines of source code to set up the variables this way than it does just to list them all separately. After all, now you've got to write the structure's beginning and ending lines. The extra work pays off, though, as you'll see shortly, after you've learned more about structures.

When you declared your set of office-supply structures, you created new data types. But a data type isn't the same thing as a variable. A data type is only a type of data that you can use for a variable. For example, think about the `Integer` data type. You don't have to declare this data type, because Visual Basic .NET already knows what an integer looks like. But an integer isn't a variable, right? To create an integer variable, you have to provide both a name and the data type:

```
Dim PillowWakeMeUpAt5 As Integer
```

The same is true of your custom data types `Clips`, `Paper`, `Pens`, and `Pillows`. To create variables of these types, you must supply both a name and the data type:

```
Dim MyClips As Clips
Dim MyPaper As Paper
Dim MyPens As Pens
Dim MyPillows As Pillows
```

The Real Advantage

You in the back! Don't think I can't hear you grumbling! Yes, this is a bit of extra work. But look at it this way: Suppose you invent a new snack food named Mustard Crunchies. Mustard Crunchies, then, are a type of food, right? You're not limited to one measly bag of Mustard Crunchies. You can make as many as you want. You can have Larry's Mustard Crunchies, Beth's Mustard Crunchies, Felix's Mustard Crunchies, and you can even make a bag for that freakin' dog down the street that always chews psychedelic designs into your butt every time you walk by. Just *maybe* the crunchies are so good that you can turn that mutt into a friend.

What's true for a food type like Mustard Crunchies is also true for a data type. (Well, you'll never tame a dog with a handful of floating-point numbers, but you get what I mean.) Once you have a data type, you can make as many variables of that type as you like. For example, you can have as many integer variables in a program as you want, right? You can also have as many `Pillow` variables as you want. Ah. The light! Now, we're getting somewhere. You're not the only one in your office with supplies. The other folks have stuff, too; maybe even pillows. This wonderful concept should lead you to an idea about variables that looks something like this:

```
Dim MyClips As Clips
Dim MyPaper As Paper
Dim MyPens As Pens
Dim MyPillows As Pillows
Dim BarrysClips As Clips
Dim BarrysPaper As Paper
Dim BarrysPens As Pens
Dim MarthasClips As Clips
Dim MarthasPaper As Paper
Dim MarthasPens As Pens
```

These 10 lines have created the equivalent of 27 separate variables! You can see how you'll start saving a lot of time and effort as you keep track of supplies for more and more people.

Using Structures Inside Structures

Now, here's something *really* cool. You can make structures that are made of other structures. Suppose, for example, that you, Barry, and Martha run a successful business that has three office locations, and you need to keep track of your supplies at all three places. You could write something like this:

```
Structure Office
    Dim MyClips As Clips
    Dim MyPaper As Paper
```

```
        Dim MyPens As Pens
        Dim MyPillows As Pillows
        Dim BarrysClips As Clips
        Dim BarrysPaper As Paper
        Dim BarrysPens As Pens
        Dim MarthasClips As Clips
        Dim MarthasPaper As Paper
        Dim MarthasPens As Pens
    End Structure

    Dim HomeOffice As Office
    Dim CityOffice As Office
    Dim UndergroundOffice As Office
```

> **By the Way**
>
> For the variables that are part of a structure, you can use any data type that Visual Basic .NET knows about—even the ones you define yourself. Moreover, each variable in a structure doesn't have to have the same data type. They can all be different if that suits your purpose.

Whoa! We just declared the equivalent of 81 variables. Are you dizzy, too? I think I'm freakin' out!

How did I get 81? Well, the `Office` structure holds 10 variables, right? But each of these 10 variables is actually a structure itself. For example, the `MyClips` variable is a `Clips` structure, which itself holds three variables. When you total all these structures (`Clips`, `Paper`, `Pens`, and `Pillows`) up, you discover that the `Office` structure actually represents 27 variables. So, HomeOffice, CityOffice, and UndergroundOffice represent 27 variables each and 3×27 = 81. Here's a summary of all this confusion:

Clips structure = 3 variables

Paper structure = 2 variables

Pens structure = 3 variables

Pillows structure = 3 variables

So

Office structure = 3 Clips, 3 Paper, 3 Pens, and 1 Pillows

Or

Office structure = (3×3)+(3×2)+(3×3)+(1×3) = 27 variables

So

HomeOffice = Office = 27 variables

CityOffice = Office = 27 variables

UndergroundOffice = Office = 27 variables

So

27+27+27 = 81 variables

Accessing Structures

You've got all these cool data types and variables of those types. What the heck do you do with them now? Before a variable is any good, it needs to have a value. This is true of integers, and it's equally true of `Pillows`. For the sake of simplicity, let's go back to the first structure you defined, which looks like this:

```
Structure Clips
    Dim Small As Integer
    Dim Medium As Integer
    Dim Large As Integer
End Structure
```

Now, let's declare a variable of the `Clips` data type:

```
Dim MyClips As Clips
```

Suppose that you have five boxes of small clips, eight boxes of medium clips, and two boxes of large clips. To get this inventory into your program, you'd write this snippet:

```
MyClips.Small = 5
MyClips.Medium = 8
MyClips.Large = 2
```

Looking at this example, you can see that to refer to a value inside a structure, you write the name of the variable you defined for the structure, followed by a dot, and the name of the structure variable you want to access.

How about a more complicated example? Remember the following structure and variable?

```
Structure Office
    Dim MyClips As Clips
    Dim MyPaper As Paper
    Dim MyPens As Pens
    Dim MyPillows As Pillows
    Dim BarrysClips As Clips
    Dim BarrysPaper As Paper
    Dim BarrysPens As Pens
    Dim MarthasClips As Clips
    Dim MarthasPaper As Paper
    Dim MarthasPens As Pens
End Structure

Dim HomeOffice As Office
```

How do you think you could set the starting values for your paperclips in the home office?

Think.

Do I smell wood burning?

Here's the answer:

```
HomeOffice.MyClips.Small = 5
HomeOffice.MyClips.Medium = 8
HomeOffice.MyClips.Large = 2
```

Look how logical this makes your office-supply variables. The names read like a map.

Passing Structures As Arguments

Another advantage of structures shows up when you need to pass variables as arguments to procedures. Which of the following two snippets would you rather write?

```
Function TotalMyClips(ByVal Office1MyClipsSmall As Integer, _
        ByVal Office1MyClipsMedium As Integer, ByVal Office1MyClipsLarge As
Integer, _
        ByVal Office2MyClipsSmall As Integer, ByVal Office2MyClipsMedium As
Integer, _
        ByVal Office2MyClipsLarge As Integer, ByVal Office3MyClipsSmall As
Integer, _
        ByVal Office3MyClipsMedium As Integer, ByVal Office3MyClipsLarge As
Integer) As Integer
    '
    ' Add up clips here.
    '
End Function
```

or

```
    Function TotalMyClips2(ByVal Office1 As Office, _
            ByVal Office2 As Office, ByVal Office3 As Office) As Integer
        '
        ' Add up clips here.
        '
    End Function
```

Before you make up your mind, imagine that you have to write a similar function that adds up *all* the paperclips for *all* the people at *all three* offices. That's a lot of variables to pass.

Now, before I dismiss class, please turn in the answer to that last question. If you liked the first version of the function better, please go stand in the corner and repeat the phrase "I'm a sucky programmer" 100 times. I also have a sign for your back.

The Least You Need to Know

- Visual Basic .NET provides structures to enable you to create user-defined data types.
- A structure is a data type from which you can create variables.
- You access a value in a structure by giving the structure name followed by a dot and the name of the value you want to access.
- Structures simplify some types of programs by providing a shortcut for creating many values simultaneously.
- Structures also provide a shortcut method to send many values as arguments to a procedure.

Chapter 14

Procedures and Functions: Breaking Things Down

In This Chapter

◆ Organize programs into small parts

◆ Write your own procedures

◆ Learn to write functions

◆ Discover variable scope

◆ Find out how to pass arguments to procedures and functions

Until now, your programs have been pretty short, each designed to demonstrate a single programming technique. When you start writing real programs, however, you'll quickly discover that they can grow to many pages of code. When programs get long, they also get harder to organize and read. To overcome this problem, professional programmers developed something called modular programming, which is the topic of this chapter.

The Top-Down Approach to Programming

Long programs are hard to organize and read. A full-length program might contain twenty or more pages of code, and trying to find a specific part of the program in all that code can be tough. To solve this problem, you can use modular programming techniques. Using these techniques, you break a long program into individual subprograms, each of which performs a specific task.

To understand how modular programming works, consider how you might organize the cleaning of a house. (The only reasonable way to clean my house is to douse it with gasoline and throw in a lighted match, but we won't get into that now.) The main task might be called "clean house." Thinking about cleaning an entire house, however, can be overwhelming—just ask my wife. So, to make the task easier, you can break it down into a number of smaller steps, for example:

1. Clean living room.
2. Clean bedroom.
3. Clean kitchen.
4. Clean bathroom.

After breaking the housecleaning task down into room-by-room steps, you have a better idea of what to do. But cleaning a room is also a pretty big task—especially if it hasn't been done in a while or if you have cats coughing up fur balls all over the place. So why not break down the task of cleaning each room into steps as well? For example, cleaning the living room could be broken down into:

1. Pick up room.
2. Dust and polish.
3. Clean furniture.
4. Vacuum rug.

After breaking down each room's cleaning into steps, your housecleaning job is organized much like a pyramid, with the general task on the top. As you work your way down the pyramid, from the main task to the room-by-room list, and finally to the tasks for each room, the tasks become more and more specific.

Check This Out _____

You should break programs up into small subprograms in order to make program code easier to understand. To this end, each subprogram in a program should perform only a single main task, so it stays short and to the point. When you try to cram too much functionality into a subprogram, it loses its identity. If you can't state a subprogram's purpose in two or three words, it's probably doing too much.

Breaking programming tasks down into steps is called modular programming. And when you break your program's modules down into even smaller subprograms—as I did with the task of cleaning a house—you're using a top-down approach to program design. By using top-down programming techniques, you can write any program as a series of small, easy-to-handle tasks.

Visual Basic .NET provides two types of subprograms that you can use when writing programs:

♦ Procedures, which are covered in the next section

♦ Functions, which are covered later in this chapter

Using Procedures

One type of subprogram is a procedure. A procedure is like a small program within your main program. If you were writing a housecleaning program, the procedures in the main module might be called `CleanLivingRoom`, `CleanBedroom`, `CleanKitchen`, and `CleanBathroom`. The `CleanLivingRoom` procedure would contain all the steps needed to clean the living room, the `CleanBedroom` procedure would contain all the steps needed to clean a bedroom, and so on.

Of course, it takes an extremely talented programmer to get a computer to clean a house. If you manage that trick, contact me immediately. For now, you need a more computer-oriented example. Suppose you want to write a program that draws a moving arrow on-screen. (Don't ask why.) The following program shows how to do this.

1. Start a new Visual Basic .NET project named Arrow, and place Label and Button controls on the form, as shown in Figure 14.1.

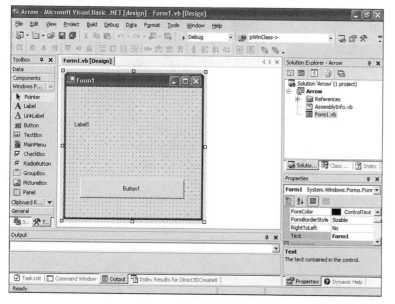

Figure 14.1

Position your controls as shown here.

2. Double-click the form to bring up the Visual Basic .NET code window, and type the following program lines into the Load procedure (Visual Basic .NET will have already started the Form1_Load procedure for you):

```
Label1.Text = ">>--->"
Button1.Text = "Fire Arrow"
```

3. Return to the form design and double-click the Button control, and type the following program lines into the Click procedure (Visual Basic .NET will have already started the Button1_Click procedure for you):

```
Dim x As Integer
For x = 20 To 250
    Call Arrow(x)
Next x
```

4. Type the following procedure right after the Button1_Click procedure's End Sub statement:

```
Sub Arrow(ByVal x As Integer)
    Dim delay As Integer
    Label1.Left = x
    For delay = 1 To 100000
    Next delay
End Sub
```

5. Save your work and run the program. When you do, you see the window shown in Figure 14.2.

Figure 14.2

Your new application fires an arrow.

6. Click the Fire Arrow button and then duck! Your new program fires the arrow across the application's window.

Now for the hundred-million dollar question: How does this program work? The program is divided into three procedures. Two of these procedures, `Form1_Load` and `Button1_Click`, are already good friends. The third procedure is named `Arrow` and is run (called) by the `Button1_Click` procedure. The For…Next loop in the `Button1_Click` calls the `Arrow` procedure each time through the loop.

When the `Button1_Click` procedure calls the `Arrow` procedure, the program lines in `Arrow` execute. In other words, the program branches to the first line of `Arrow` and executes all the statements until it gets to the `End Sub` line. When it reaches the `End Sub` line, the program branches back to `Button1_Click`, to the next line following the procedure call. Because the line following the procedure call is the end of the For…Next loop, the program goes back to the top of the loop, increments x, and calls `Arrow` yet again. This continues until the loop runs out, which is when x grows larger than 250. Figure 14.3 illustrates the process of calling the `Arrow` procedure in the For…Next loop.

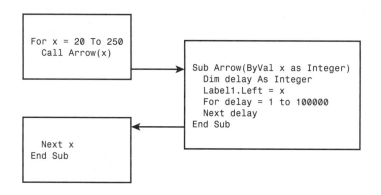

Figure 14.3

Program execution branches from the `Button1_Click` *procedure to* `Arrow` *and back again.*

Take a look at the call to the `Arrow` procedure, which looks like this:

```
Call Arrow(x)
```

See the x in the parentheses? This is a *procedure argument*. Arguments in procedures work just like the arguments you used when calling the built-in Visual Basic .NET functions. You use arguments to pass into procedures the values those procedures need to do their job. You need to give `Arrow` this argument because `Arrow` needs to know the current value of the loop-control variable. This value determines where the arrow is drawn, as you can see when you look at the program lines in the `Arrow` procedure.

The first line declares the procedure and its arguments:

```
Sub Arrow(ByVal x As Integer)
```

The Sub keyword stands for "subroutine" and is followed by the procedure's name. (The rules for naming procedures are the same as those for naming variables.) After the procedure's name come the procedure's arguments in parentheses. Notice that the argument's type is included, just as with a Dim statement. (Don't worry about the ByVal keyword right now.)

The next line declares an integer variable called delay:

```
Dim delay As Integer
```

Because the arrow is just text in a Label control, the program can move the arrow by moving the label. It does this by setting the position of the label's left edge to the value passed into the procedure by Button1_Click:

```
Label1.Left = x
```

Setting the label's Left property causes Visual Basic .NET to move the label to the new location.

Because computers process information faster than Bill Gates amasses dollars, a For…Next loop in the Arrow procedure forces the computer to count from 1 to 100,000 in order to slow down the speed of the arrow:

```
For delay = 1 To 100000
Next delay
```

You can change the 100,000 in this loop to some other value if you want to change how fast the arrow moves. The smaller the loop's limit, the faster the arrow moves.

By the Way

For all practical purposes, a procedure can have as many arguments as you like. But you must be sure that the arguments you specify in the procedure's call exactly match the type and order of the arguments in the procedure's Sub line.

To use more than one argument in a procedure, separate the arguments with commas. For example, to add the argument y to the Arrow call, you'd type Call Arrow(x, y). Then, so the arguments match, you must change the first line of Arrow to Sub Arrow(ByVal x As Integer, ByVal y As Integer).

You can use different variable names in the Sub line as long as they are the same type. In other words, using the arrow example, you can also type Sub Arrow(col As Integer, length As Integer). In the procedure, you'd then use the variable names col and length rather than the original x and y.

Procedures don't have to have arguments. To call a procedure that has no arguments, you wouldn't need any values in the parentheses. For example: Call Arrow().

That wasn't too tough, was it? Unfortunately, using procedures is a little more complicated than it may appear from the previous discussion. If you jump right in and try to write your own procedures at this point, you'll run into trouble faster than a dog catches fleas in the springtime. Before you can write good procedures, you must at least learn about something called variable scope.

Introducing Variable Scope

Now that you know a little about procedures, you should know how Visual Basic .NET organizes variables between procedures. You may wonder, for example, why x must be an argument in the call to Arrow. Why couldn't you just use the variable x in the procedure? After all, they're part of the same program, right?

> ### By the Way
> You can pass one or more arguments to procedures. However, keep in mind that the arguments are passed to the procedure in the order in which they appear in the procedure call. The procedure's `Sub` line should list the arguments in the same order they are listed in the procedure call.

You need arguments in your procedures because of something called *variable scope*, which determines whether program procedures can "see" a specific variable. For example, if you were to change the program so that `Button1_Click` did not pass x as an argument to `Arrow`, you'd get an error when the program tried to execute `Arrow`.

Here's why: A variable in one procedure is not accessible in another. So, when you don't explicitly pass x as an argument, the `Arrow` procedure can't access it. When the procedure tries to access the variable anyway, Visual Basic .NET doesn't recognize it and generates an error.

In the case of the `Arrow` procedure, the x is *local* to `Arrow`. Just as the x of the `Button1_Click` procedure cannot be seen in any other procedure (it's local to `Button1_Click`), the x of the `Arrow` procedure cannot be seen in any procedure except `Arrow`. This may seem at first like a crazy way to do things, but when you think about it, it makes a lot of sense.

By not allowing a variable to be seen outside of the procedure in which it is declared, you never have to worry about some other procedure accidentally changing that variable's value. Moreover, local variables make procedures self-contained, as if everything the procedure needs were put together in a little box. If the value of a variable used in a procedure is giving your program trouble, you know exactly which module to check. You don't need to search your entire program to find the problem any more than you need to search your entire house to find a quart of milk. Figure 14.4 illustrates the concept of global and local variables.

Figure 14.4

Global variables, represented here by `GlobalA` *and* `GlobalB`, *are available in any procedure.*

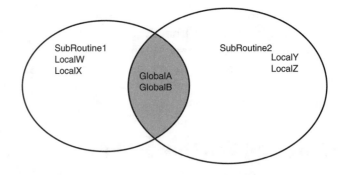

The opposite of a local variable is a *global* variable. You can use global variables in any procedure anywhere in your program. The following code shows a new version of your arrow program, which makes x a global variable. Because x is now a global variable, it need not be passed as an argument to the Arrow procedure.

```
Dim x As Integer

Private Sub Form1_Load(ByVal sender As System.Object, _
        ByVal e As System.EventArgs) Handles MyBase.Load
    Label1.Text = ">>--->"
    Button1.Text = "Fire Arrow"
End Sub

Private Sub Button1_Click(ByVal sender As System.Object, _
        ByVal e As System.EventArgs) Handles Button1.Click
    For x = 20 To 250
        Call Arrow()
    Next x
End Sub

Sub Arrow()
    Dim delay As Integer
    Label1.Left = x
    For delay = 1 To 100000
    Next delay
End Sub
```

Near the top of the program, the line

```
Dim x As Integer
```

is the statement that makes x a global variable. This variable becomes global because the program declares the variable outside of all the other procedures.

> **Whoops!**
>
> As a novice programmer, you may think that using global variables is a great programming shortcut. After all, if you make all your variables global, you'll never have to worry about passing arguments to procedures. However, a program with a lot of global variables is a poorly designed program—hard to read and hard to debug. You should write your programs to include as few global variables as possible.

Using Functions

Functions are another way you can break up your programs into small parts. But unlike procedures, functions return a value to the procedure that calls them. You write functions much like procedures. However, function calls must assign the function's return value to a variable. Suppose you have a function named `GetNum` that gets a number from the user and returns it to your program. A call to the function might look something like `num = GetNum()`.

To get some experience with functions, follow these steps:

1. Start a new Visual Basic .NET project named Function, and place Label, TextBox, and Button controls on the form, as shown in Figure 14.5.

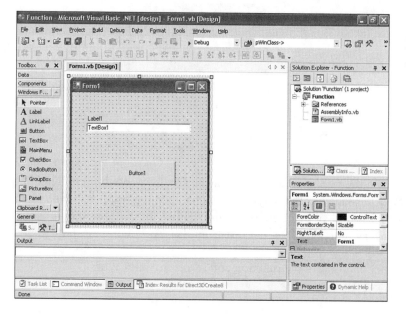

Figure 14.5

Position your controls as shown here.

2. Double-click the form to bring up the Visual Basic .NET code window, and type the following program lines into the Load procedure (Visual Basic .NET will have already started the Form1_Load procedure for you):

```
Label1.Text = "Type a response:"
TextBox1.Text = "Default response"
Button1.Text = "Get Response"
```

3. Double-click the Button control, and type the following program lines into the Click procedure (Visual Basic .NET will have already started the Button1_Click procedure for you):

```
Dim msg As String = GetResponse()
MessageBox.Show(msg)
```

4. Type the following procedure right after the Button1_Click procedure's End Sub statement:

```
Function GetResponse() As String
    Return TextBox1.Text
End Function
```

5. Save your work and run the program. When you do, you see the window shown in Figure 14.6.

Figure 14.6

This program calls a function when you click the button.

6. Type something into the text box, and then click the Get Response button. The program displays a message box that contains the text from the text box. This wouldn't be such a big deal all by itself, except for the fact that the program is using your own GetResponse function to get the text from the text box.

The first line of the function declares the function and its return-value type:

```
Function GetResponse() As String
```

The keyword `Function`, of course, tells Visual Basic .NET that you're declaring a function. The name of the function and a set of parentheses follow the `Function` keyword. If this function required arguments, you'd have to declare them in the parentheses, just as you did with a procedure. The `As String` part of the line tells Visual Basic .NET that this function returns a string value to the calling procedure.

The next line of the function is the line that tells Visual Basic .NET what value to return from the function:

```
Return Text1.Text
```

In this case, the function returns the string the user entered into the `Text1` text box. Notice that, to return a value from a function, you use the `Return` keyword. Makes sense, right?

Finally, the function's last line tells Visual Basic .NET that it has reached the end of the function:

```
End Function
```

The Least You Need to Know

♦ Modular programming means breaking a program up into a series of simple tasks.

♦ Top-down programming means organizing procedures in a hierarchy, with general-purpose procedures at the top that call specific-purpose procedures lower in the hierarchy.

♦ Procedures and functions are the two types of subprograms you can use when writing a Visual Basic .NET program. Functions must return values while procedures do not.

♦ A function declaration includes not only the keyword `Function` and the function name, but also the clause As *type*, which tells Visual Basic .NET the type of value the function returns. In this case, *type* is a data type such as `Integer` or `String`.

♦ A program returns a value from a function by using the `Return` keyword followed by the value to return.

♦ Procedures and functions may or may not receive values called arguments, which are sent to the subprogram by the calling procedure.

♦ Local variables are accessible only within the subprogram in which they appear. Global variables, which are declared outside of any subprogram, are accessible anywhere in a program.

Printing: Your Own Edition of Hard Copy

In This Chapter

- ◆ Discover the Visual Basic .NET PrintDocument control
- ◆ Print text on a page
- ◆ Print multiple pages of text
- ◆ Position text on the page

Since you started studying Visual Basic .NET, you've learned quite a lot about I/O. You now know how to get data from the user, how to give information back to the user, and even how to save and load data to and from a hard disk. There's only one more trick you need to know: How to get your data from the computer onto a piece of paper. That's where the Visual Basic .NET PrintDocument control comes in. Using the PrintDocument control is a heck of a lot easier than copying data off the screen with a pencil and pad!

Introducing the PrintDocument Control

Visual Basic .NET provides a special control called PrintDocument that gives a program access to the user's printer. Using the PrintDocument control, you can do all sorts of printing tasks like printing text and images. Using the PrintDocument control is a snap. In fact, it takes only a few Visual Basic .NET program lines to print a line of text or a graphical shape on the printer. To see how it works, follow these steps:

1. Add a PrintDocument control (found in the Toolbox) to your form. When you do, the control appears on the screen below your form, as shown in Figure 15.1.

Figure 15.1

Adding a PrintDocument control to a form.

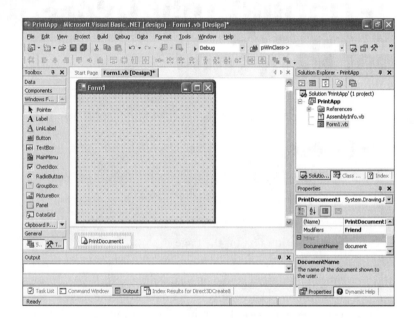

2. Double-click the PrintDocument control in order to bring up the code window and start the control's default event handler, PrintPage, as shown in Figure 15.2.

Inside the PrintPage event handler is where you send stuff to the printer. Remember how you used the Graphics object to draw text and shapes in a window? You draw to the printer in exactly the same way, except you don't have to create a Graphics object first, because the Graphics object is created for you and passed to the PrintPage event handler. Here's how a PrintPage handler that sends a line of text to the printer might look:

```
Private Sub PrintDocument1_PrintPage(ByVal sender As System.Object, _
        ByVal e As System.Drawing.Printing.PrintPageEventArgs) _
        Handles PrintDocument1.PrintPage
```

```
      Dim f As Font = New Font("Arial", 12, FontStyle.Bold)
      e.Graphics.DrawString("This is a test", f, Brushes.Black, 150, 125)
End Sub
```

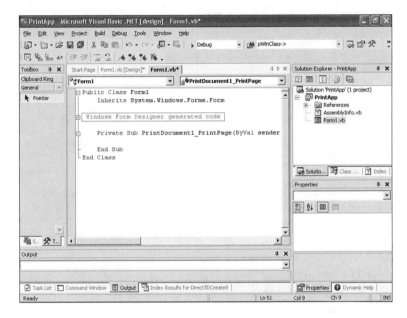

Figure 15.2

Creating the PrintPage *event handler.*

The second argument, named e, is the one that holds the Graphics object you need to draw to the printer. In this PrintPage event handler, the program creates a font for the text, and then calls the Graphics object's DrawString method to print the text.

But how, I hear you ask, do you get the whole printing process started? Easy! Just call the PrintDocument control's Print method. You'd probably do this when the user chooses a print command from a menu, but you can do it anywhere in your program that you like. When you call the PrintDocument control's Print method, it generates the event that causes the program to jump to the PrintPage event handler.

To try printing yourself (well, you won't be printing yourself; threading yourself through the printer's rollers can be a nasty business), follow these steps:

1. Start a new Visual Basic .NET project (a Windows Application, as always) named PrintTest, and place PrintDocument, Label, TextBox, and Button controls on the form, as shown in Figure 15.3.

Figure 15.3

Position the controls as shown in this figure.

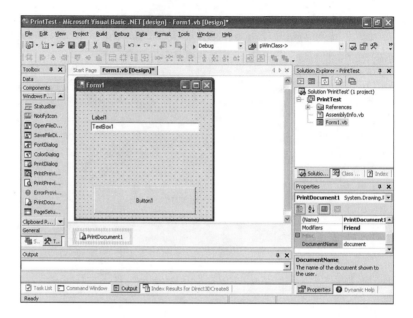

2. Double-click the PrintDocument control. When you do, Visual Basic .NET brings up the code window and starts the `PrintPage` event procedure for you. Complete the procedure with these lines:

```
Dim f As Font = New Font("TimesRoman", 12, FontStyle.Bold)
Dim msg As String = TextBox1.Text
e.Graphics.DrawString(msg, f, Brushes.Black, 50, 50)
```

3. Double-click the Button control and type the following line into the `Click` procedure (Visual Basic .NET will have already started the `Button1_Click` procedure for you):

```
PrintDocument1.Print()
```

4. Double-click the form, and type the following lines into the `Form1_Load` procedure Visual Basic .NET starts for you:

```
Label1.Text = "Line #1:"
TextBox1.Text = "Default line #1"
Button1.Text = "Print Text"
```

5. Save your work and run the program. When you do, you'll see the window shown in Figure 15.4.

6. Type some text into the text box (or stick with the default text), and click the Print Text button. The program then grabs the text from the text box and sends it to your printer.

Figure 15.4

This program sends the contents of a text box to a printer.

When your newly printed page drops into your printer's hopper, whoop with delight and then quickly assure the rest of the family that you're really just fine. (Spouses and children often become alarmed when Mom or Dad starts yelling "Whoop, whoop, whooooop!" for no apparent reason.)

Now that you've gotten all that whooping out of your system, take a look at the program's source-code lines. When you clicked the Print Text button, Visual Basic .NET jumped to the `Button1_Click` procedure, where a single line started the printing process:

Check This Out

Although the print example program printed only a single line of text, printing multiple lines is a simple matter of calling the Graphics object's **DrawString** method once for each line you want to print.

```
PrintDocument1.Print()
```

Calling the `Print` method causes an event that sends program execution to the `PrintPage` event handler. There, the program creates a font:

```
Dim f As Font = New Font("TimesRoman", 12, FontStyle.Bold)
```

gets the text from the TextBox control:

```
Dim msg As String = TextBox1.Text
```

and then sends the text to the printer:

```
e.Graphics.DrawString(msg, f, Brushes.Black, 50, 50)
```

That was easy, eh? What? You say that your documents are more than one page? No problem. Read on.

Printing Multiple Pages

In the previous section, you learned about the PrintDocument control's `PrintPage` event handler, which prints a page of the current document. You also learned that the `PrintPage` argument named e contains the `Graphics` object you need to draw to the printer. Something else the e argument contains is a property named `HasMorePages`. If you set `HasMorePages` to `True`, the PrintDocument control will call the `PrintPage` event handler again. So, to print more than one page, just keep setting `HasMorePages` to `True` until you print your past page, at which point you set `HasMorePages` to `False`.

To try out this bit of printing coolness, follow these steps:

1. Add two Label and two TextBox controls to the previous program, as shown in Figure 15.5.

Figure 15.5

Position the new labels and text boxes as shown in this figure.

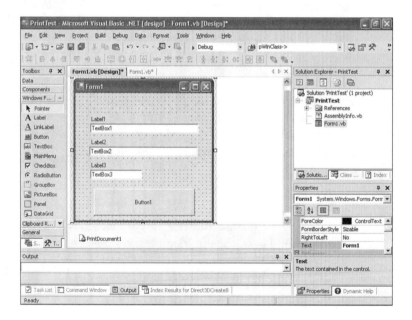

2. Double-click the form to bring up the code window, and replace the lines in the current Form1_Load procedure with these:

```
Label1.Text = "Starting Line Text:"
TextBox1.Text = "Default line #1"
Label2.Text = "Last Line Text:"
TextBox2.Text = "Default line #2"
Label3.Text = "Pages to Print:"
TextBox3.Text = "2"
Button1.Text = "Print Text"
```

3. Add the following line to the existing `Button1_Click` procedure, *before* the call to `PrintDocument1.Print`:

```
numPages = Integer.Parse(TextBox3.Text)
```

4. Replace all the code in the `PrintPage` event handler with this stuff:

```
Static page As Integer = 0
Dim f As Font = New Font("TimesRoman", 12, FontStyle.Bold)
Dim msg As String
page = page + 1
If page < numPages Then
    e.HasMorePages = True
    msg = TextBox1.Text & " --> Page #" & page
Else
    e.HasMorePages = False
    msg = TextBox2.Text & " --> Page #" & page
End If
e.Graphics.DrawString(msg, f, Brushes.Black, 20, 20)
```

5. Finally, right after the box that says "Windows Form Designer generated code", declare this variable:

```
Dim numPages As Integer
```

6. Make sure that your complete program looks like this (long lines in this listing have been broken into a series of shorter lines; your program won't have these line breaks):

```
Public Class Form1
    Inherits System.Windows.Forms.Form


    ''''''''''''''''''''''''''''''''''''''''''
    'Windows Form Designer generated code'
    ''''''''''''''''''''''''''''''''''''''''''


    Dim numPages As Integer

    Private Sub Button1_Click(ByVal sender As System.Object, _
            ByVal e As System.EventArgs) Handles Button1.Click
        numPages = Integer.Parse(TextBox3.Text)
        PrintDocument1.Print()
    End Sub

    Private Sub PrintDocument1_PrintPage(ByVal sender As System.Object, _
            ByVal e As System.Drawing.Printing.PrintPageEventArgs) _
            Handles PrintDocument1.PrintPage
```

```
        Static page As Integer = 0
        Dim f As Font = New Font("TimesRoman", 12, FontStyle.Bold)
        Dim msg As String
        page = page + 1
        If page < numPages Then
            e.HasMorePages = True
            msg = TextBox1.Text & " --> Page #" & page
        Else
            e.HasMorePages = False
            msg = TextBox2.Text & " --> Page #" & page
        End If
        e.Graphics.DrawString(msg, f, Brushes.Black, 20, 20)
    End Sub

    Private Sub Form1_Load(ByVal sender As System.Object, _
            ByVal e As System.EventArgs) Handles MyBase.Load
        Label1.Text = "Starting Line Text:"
        TextBox1.Text = "Default line #1"
        Label2.Text = "Last Line Text:"
        TextBox2.Text = "Default line #2"
        Label3.Text = "Pages to Print:"
        TextBox3.Text = "2"
        Button1.Text = "Print Text"
    End Sub
End Class
```

7. Save your work, and run the program. When you do, you'll see the window shown in Figure 15.6.

Figure 15.6

This program prints two pages of text.

8. Type some text into both text boxes (or stick with the default text), put the number of pages to print into the Pages to Print box, and click the Print Text button.

The program then prints the line from the first text box on every page of the document except the last page, which gets the text from the second text box. The program also adds a page number to each page.

Go ahead now and frighten your family again with those ghastly whoop sounds. You've earned it!

You should be able to figure out on your own how this program works. However, the following program line needs some extra explanation:

```
Static page As Integer = 0
```

This variable definition appears in the PrintPage event handler. See the Static keyword? Normally, a variable that's declared inside a procedure loses its value when the procedure is over. However, by adding the Static keyword, the variable remembers its last value from one call to the procedure to the next. You could have defined page as a global variable near the top of the program with the numPages variable and the program would've still run fine. However, only the PrintPage event handler needs to use the page variable, so its definition belongs in that procedure. The Static keyword makes this possible.

> **Check This Out** _____
>
> Once you get the hang of the PrintPage event handler, printing headers and footers on a page is pretty easy. Print your header text at the beginning of PrintPage, and print your footer at the end of PrintPage. In the section "Positioning Text" you'll see how to position text anywhere you want on the page, which will help you get your headers and footers in the right place.

Positioning Text

It takes a lot of work to print out a sophisticated document like Microsoft Word prints. You'll have to do some serious studying to get that far with your printing skills. However, another pretty easy trick you can use to flex your printing muscles is to position text or images on the page. By setting the last two arguments of the DrawString method, for example, you can determine where on a page data gets printed. Other graphics methods have similar positioning arguments. Moreover, you can determine the size of a page by getting the values of the PageBounds.Height and PageBounds.Width properties of the e argument sent to the PrintPage event handler.

To try this trick on your own, follow these steps:

1. Start a new Visual Basic .NET project named PrinterTest2 (a Windows Application), and place Label, TextBox, Button, and PrintDocument controls on the form, as shown in Figure 15.7.

Figure 15.7

Position the controls as shown in this figure.

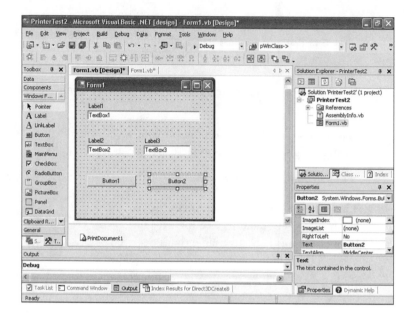

2. Double-click the PrintDocument control. When you do, Visual Basic .NET brings up the code window and starts the `PrintPage` event procedure for you. Complete the procedure with these lines:

```
If testPrint Then
    TextBox2.Text = e.PageBounds.Width
    TextBox3.Text = e.PageBounds.Height
    e.Cancel = True
Else
    Dim printX As Integer = Integer.Parse(TextBox2.Text)
    Dim printY As Integer = Integer.Parse(TextBox3.Text)
    Dim f As Font = New Font("TimesRoman", 12, FontStyle.Bold)
    Dim msg As String = TextBox1.Text
    e.Graphics.DrawString(msg, f, Brushes.Black, printX, printY)
End If
```

3. Double-click the `Button1` control and type the following lines into its `Click` procedure (Visual Basic .NET will have already started the `Button1_Click` procedure for you):

```
testPrint = True
PrintDocument1.Print()
testPrint = False
```

4. Double-click the `Button2` control and type the following line into its `Click` procedure:

```
PrintDocument1.Print()
```

5. Double-click the form, and type the following lines into the `Load` procedure that Visual Basic .NET starts for you:

```
Label1.Text = "Text to Print:"
Label2.Text = "X Position:"
Label3.Text = "Y Position:"
TextBox1.Text = "Default text to print"
TextBox2.Text = 0
TextBox3.Text = 0
Button1.Text = "Test Printer"
Button2.Text = "Print Document"
```

6. Right after the box that says "Windows Form Designer generated code," declare the following variable:

```
Dim testPrint As Boolean = False
```

7. Save your work, and run the program. When you do, you'll see the window shown in Figure 15.8.

Figure 15.8

This program can position text anywhere on the page.

This application's window gives you a place to type the text you want to print, as well as places to type the text's X (horizontal) and Y (vertical) positions on the page. To help you choose the right X and Y values, the window also displays the current page's width and height. The position 0,0 is the page's upper left corner. When you use the highest X and Y values, you're positioning the start of the text in the page's lower-right corner.

8. To fill in the text boxes with the page's maximum coordinates, click the Test Printer button.

9. Type some text into the first text box, type the horizontal and vertical positions for the text in the remaining text boxes, and then click the Print Document button.

The program then retrieves the text from the text box and sends it to your printer, right at the location you specified. Whooooop!

The `PrintPage` event handler is the only place in this program you'll stumble across unfamiliar programming stuff. Here's a line-by-line explanation, starting with the `If` statement:

1 If `testPrint` is `True`, do everything up to the `Else`.

2 Get the page's width and plug it into `TextBox2`.

3 Get the page's height and plug it into `TextBox3`.

4 Set the `Cancel` property to `True` so that `PrintPage` doesn't actually print a page.

5 If `testPrint` is `False`, do the stuff in the `Else`.

6 Get the requested horizontal position for the text.

7 Get the requested vertical position for the text.

8 Create a font for the text.

9 Get from `TextBox1` the text to print.

10 Print the text with the new font, in black, at the selected location.

The Least You Need to Know

◆ The Visual Basic .NET PrintDocument control provides a program quick and easy access to the printer on a system.

◆ The `PrintPage` event handler of your program's PrintDocument control is where the program sends text and graphics to the printer.

◆ The PrintDocument control's `Print` method starts the printing process.

◆ To print multiple-page documents, set the `HasMorePages` property of the `PrintPage` method's second argument to `False` until you've printed the last page.

◆ The `PageBounds.Width` and `PageBounds.Height` properties of the `PrintPage` method's second argument hold the width and height of a page.

◆ Setting the `Cancel` property of the `PrintPage` method's second argument to `False` cancels the printing of the current page.

Chapter 16

Catching Runtime Errors

In This Chapter

- ◆ Understand exceptions
- ◆ Catch exceptions
- ◆ Display information about exceptions
- ◆ Deal with multiple exceptions

I'm willing to bet a pile of dough (the kind you spend, not the kind you bake) that as you've been programming with Visual Basic .NET, you've run into problems where your program stopped unexpectedly and gave you a nasty error message. This type of problem is called a runtime error (as well as other names that can't be used in mixed company), and in this chapter, you'll discover how to stop them from bringing your program down around your ears.

Understanding Runtime Errors

When you're working on a program, you can make all kinds of mistakes, not the least of which is forgetting to spend time with your significant other. But that's your problem. The kind of mistakes I'm talking about are programming errors, of which there are two kinds:

- ◆ Logic errors
- ◆ Runtime errors

Logic errors happen when you loan a friend money and expect to get it back. Logic errors also happen when you write a line of source code that doesn't do what you think it does. Maybe you're adding the wrong variables, printing the wrong text, or displaying a picture of yourself when you first get up in the morning. (Love that hairdo!) But this chapter is about runtime errors, which are much worse, because if they're not handled properly, they can leave your program's user staring at bizarre error messages. Worse, the program can stop running and maybe make the user lose all his work.

The problem with runtime errors is that they force you, as the programmer, to be able to look into the future. That is, when you write a line of program code, you need to ask yourself, "Will Scully and Mulder actually get married?" You also need to ask yourself whether the line of code you're writing might cause an error in the program.

For example, suppose you write a program line that's supposed to open a file, but—thanks to little Eddie, who likes to delete files from the computer when you're not looking—the file no longer exists. When Visual Basic .NET tries to open that file, you'll get a file-not-found runtime error. If you forgot to look into the future and anticipate this error, your program drops deader than a donkey at the bottom of the ocean.

Another example is when something goes horribly wrong with your math, and the computer ends up trying to divide a number by zero. As everyone knows, division by zero is a horrendous crime against the cosmos that, if it happens too often, could actually bring an end to the universe as we know it. It also can, and does, make your program act a lot like that donkey we were just chatting about.

And these are only a couple of examples of runtime errors. There are actually more possible runtime errors than there are drops of water in Lake Erie—137 more to be exact, but who's counting? In any case, if you want to keep your programs running, you have to be prepared for them all. Luckily, there's a way to do this without even knowing what all the errors are.

Learning to Catch Exceptions

When your program causes a runtime error, Visual Basic .NET springs into action and throws something called an *exception*. This thing the computer throws is called an exception not because the computer takes exception to the error, but because the error is an exceptional situation, as in something that doesn't happen too often (you hope). In general, you can think of an exception as nothing fancier than a runtime error.

When your computer throws an exception, someone has to catch it. If you don't believe me, just check out page 5, paragraph 4 of the *Programmers Who Follow the Rules* rulebook. It's right there. Really. Okay, it's not, but it's still a rule. If your program doesn't catch the exception, Visual Basic .NET does, and when Visual Basic .NET is forced to catch exceptions that it also had to throw, it gets mighty ornery. In fact, to pay you back, it displays those nasty error messages and stops your program dead in its tracks. When you think about it, though, this is actually a logical thing to do. I mean, if you tell the computer to open the file, and the file doesn't exist, someone has to tell the computer what to do next. If you don't, the program must end.

The way you tell the computer what to do next is to catch the exception and then provide the computer with new instructions. For example, if your program tries to open a nonexistent file, you can catch the error and then show a message box that tells the user that the file is missing.

However, before you can catch an error, you have to tell the computer that you *want* to catch the error. Yeah, I know. Details, details. Don't blame me. I'm not the one who made computers so stupid. The way you tell the computer that you want to catch an error is by enclosing program lines that might cause a problem inside a `try` program block. Then, inside a `catch` program block, you tell the computer what to do in the event of an error. For example, look at these program lines:

```
Dim zero As Integer = 0
Dim num As Integer
Try
    num = num / zero
Catch
    MessageBox.Show("We're closer to the end of the universe now!")
End Try
```

I'm sure you can see the major no-no in this bit of programming foolishness. The program sets the variable `zero` to 0 and then tries to divide the variable `num` with it. Ouch! Visual Basic .NET groans, complains about the idiots it has to deal with, and immediately thereafter reaches into its bag of exceptions, pulls out a divide-by-zero error, and throws it at your program like Hank Aaron trying to strike out Micky Mantle. (If that's a dumb sports simile, I'll admit right now that I know next to nothing about baseball players.) Figure 16.1 shows the message box you'd see in this particular case.

Figure 16.1

An exception being handled by a message box.

But I'm smarter than the computer. Yes, I am. I've enclosed the offending program statement inside a `try` block. Moreover, I added a `catch` block that grabs the error and tells the computer to display a message box instead of crashing our program.

The cool thing about this `catch` block is that it'll catch any runtime error that the computer throws at it, not just divide-by-zero. Everything between the `try` and the `catch` is fully protected against vindictive computer operating systems that are so bent on making, lives miserable for programmers.

I Want *That* Exception!

But how can your program handle the error cleverly if the program doesn't even know what the error is? I mean, what are you going to do? Will you always display an error message that says something like, "Yep, this program fouled up your computer's memory yet again, and the powers-that-be have absolutely no idea what went wrong. And, frankly, they don't care. Live with it!"? Rather than insult your program's user, you can add the following details to the `catch` statement:

```
Try
    Dim sReader As IO.StreamReader
    sReader = IO.File.OpenText("c:\MyFile2.txt")
Catch ex As Exception
    MessageBox.Show(ex.Message)
End Try
```

When Visual Basic .NET throws an exception, it literally throws something—a little piece of data known as an *exception object*. In this example, you can see the exception object after the `catch` keyword. In this case, `ex` is the name you've given the object and `Exception` is the object's data type.

Now, if you look at the program line inside the `catch` block, you'll see that the message box displays something called `ex.Message`. This is the text message that Visual Basic .NET supplied when it created and threw the exception object. You can display this message in a message box, as shown in Figure 16.2.

Figure 16.2

Displaying the exception's message.

Okay, I agree with you. This particular error message helps the user a bit, but it doesn't really enable you as the programmer to do much about the error. Your program needs to know what happened, too.

The trick is to catch a more specific kind of exception. Exceptions of the `Exception` type can be any kind of exception, but you can also have exception types like

DivideByZeroException, IndexOutOfRangeException, and FileNotFoundException. See the light? How about you modify your try/catch stuff like this:

```
Try
    Dim sReader As IO.StreamReader
    sReader = IO.File.OpenText("c:\MyFile.txt")
Catch ex As System.IO.FileNotFoundException
    MessageBox.Show("An important file is missing." & _
        Microsoft.VisualBasic.ControlChars.CrLf & _
        "Please reinstall the application.")
End Try
```

Now, if the application can't find the file, the user gets the message shown in Figure 16.3.

Figure 16.3

A more useful exception message.

One side effect of catching a specific exception is that now that's the *only* exception the program catches. If an exception other than FileNotFoundException gets thrown, your program is back in crash city, population 1.

However, as you may have guessed, Visual Basic .NET has a fix for this problem, too. All you have to do is put another catch block in the program, this one looking for any other kind of exception:

```
Try
    Dim sReader As IO.StreamReader
    sReader = IO.File.OpenText("c:\MyFile.txt")
Catch ex As System.IO.FileNotFoundException
    MessageBox.Show("An important file is missing." & _
        Microsoft.VisualBasic.ControlChars.CrLf & _
        "Please reinstall the application.")
Catch ex As Exception
    MessageBox.Show(ex.Source & " : " & _
        ex.Message)
End Try
```

You should notice three things about this example:

1. You can have more than one catch block.

2. The second catch block displays not only a message named Message, but also one named Source.

3. Things are getting a little complicated.

As far as item #1 goes, the example is fairly self-explanatory, showing you how to add an extra catch block. As far as item #2 goes, this shows you that exception items carry with them other baggage besides the Message text. Another example of exception baggage is the Source text, which holds the name of the program that sent the exception. If an exception other than FileNotFoundException occurs in this example, you'll see the message box shown in Figure 16.4, assuming that the name of your program is CoolApp.

Figure 16.4

Another exception message.

Catching Even More Exceptions

One last thing: What if you want to catch more than one specific exception, as well as all the leftover ones? Just add another catch block. In fact, you can add as many catch blocks as you need to catch the exceptions that might occur. Here's another example:

```
Try
    Dim sReader As IO.StreamReader
    sReader = IO.File.OpenText("c:\MyFile.txt")
Catch ex As System.IO.FileNotFoundException
    MessageBox.Show("An important file is missing." & _
        Microsoft.VisualBasic.ControlChars.CrLf & _
        "Please reinstall the application.")
Catch ex As System.IO.FileLoadException
    MessageBox.Show("The file failed to load.")
Catch ex As System.IO.EndOfStreamException
    MessageBox.Show("File data ended unexpectedly.")
Catch ex As Exception
    MessageBox.Show(ex.Source & " : " & _
        ex.Message)
End Try
```

By the Way
You can find a list of exception types in your Visual Basic .NET online help. Just do a search on the word exceptions.

You ought to be a baseball player, because now you're really covering all the bases! (Yes, I at least know that they use bases in baseball. The players have to hit the ball with *something*.)

The Example Program

To try this exception stuff out for real, follow these steps:

1. Start a new Visual Basic .NET project (a Windows Application) named Exceptions, and add the controls shown in Figure 16.5.

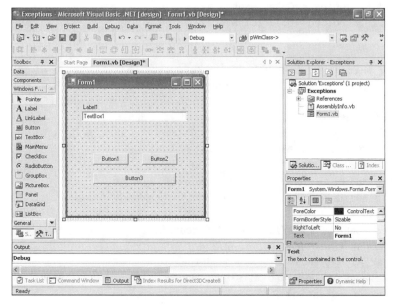

Figure 16.5

Place controls as shown here.

2. Type the following program. Remember to create the event handlers by double-clicking the form and its controls, so you don't have to type everything. You actually need to type only the lines inside each event handler and the one global variable definition. The rest Visual Basic .NET creates for you. By the way, long lines in this listing have been broken into two shorter lines; your program won't have these line breaks:

```
Public Class Form1
    Inherits System.Windows.Forms.Form

    ''''''''''''''''''''''''''''''''''''''''''
    'Windows Form Designer generated code'
    ''''''''''''''''''''''''''''''''''''''''''

    Dim isErrorOn As Boolean = False
```

```
Private Sub Form1_Load(ByVal sender As System.Object, _
        ByVal e As System.EventArgs) Handles MyBase.Load
    Label1.Text = "File Name:"
    TextBox1.Text = ""
    Button1.Text = "Open File"
    Button2.Text = "Create File"
    Button3.Text = "Turn On Error"
    Button1.BackColor = Color.LightGray
    Button2.BackColor = Color.LightGray
End Sub

Private Sub Button1_Click(ByVal sender As System.Object, _
        ByVal e As System.EventArgs) Handles Button1.Click
    Try
        If isErrorOn Then
            Dim z As Integer = 0
            Dim num As Integer = 100 / z
        End If
        Dim fname As String = TextBox1.Text
        Dim sReader As IO.StreamReader
        sReader = IO.File.OpenText(fname)
        MessageBox.Show("File opened successfully.")
        sReader.Close()
    Catch ex As System.IO.FileNotFoundException
        MessageBox.Show("The file you requested is not available.")
    Catch ex As Exception
        MessageBox.Show(ex.Source & " : " & _
            ex.Message)
    End Try
End Sub

Private Sub Button2_Click(ByVal sender As System.Object, _
        ByVal e As System.EventArgs) Handles Button2.Click
    Try
        Dim fname As String = TextBox1.Text
        Dim sWriter As IO.StreamWriter
        sWriter = IO.File.CreateText(fname)
        MessageBox.Show("File created successfully.")
        sWriter.Close()
    Catch ex As Exception
        MessageBox.Show(ex.Source & " : " & _
            ex.Message)
    End Try
End Sub
```

```
Private Sub Button3_Click(ByVal sender As System.Object, _
        ByVal e As System.EventArgs) Handles Button3.Click
    If isErrorOn Then
        isErrorOn = False
        Button3.Text = "Turn On Error"
        Button1.BackColor = Color.LightGray
    Else
        isErrorOn = True
        Button3.Text = "Turn Off Error"
        Button1.BackColor = Color.Red
    End If
End Sub

End Class
```

3. Save your work, and run the program. When you do, you see the window shown in Figure 16.6.

Figure 16.6

The Exceptions application in action …

4. Type a file name into the text box, and click the Create File button. If you typed a legal file name, the program creates the file and tells you that the file was created successfully, as shown in Figure 16.7.

Figure 16.7

… after creating a file …

If you typed an illegal file name, the police will come to your door with a warrant. No, wait! That's disturbing the peace. If you typed a bad file name, the program can't create the file, and it catches the resultant error, as shown in Figure 16.8.

Figure 16.8

... after failing to create the file ...

5. If the file was created okay, click the Open File button, and you'll get the message shown in Figure 16.9.

   If the file wasn't created successfully, you won't be able to open the file, and you'll get an error message.

Figure 16.9

... and after opening the file successfully.

6. If you want the Open File button to create an error other than file-not-found or that weird empty-path error that comes up when you leave the text box empty, click the Turn On Error button. When you do, the Open File button turns red, and no matter what file name you type into the text box, the button will still generate an error. This shows how you can generate your own errors. You might, for example, want to generate an error if the file the user is trying to open doesn't contain the right kind of data. Clicking the error button (which is now called "Turn Off Error") puts everything back to normal.

Spend a little time looking this program over. You should be able to understand everything. If you don't, come on over to my house, and we'll pop open a couple of brewskies and talk about what a pain in the butt this programming stuff is. Whoops! I forgot that I have a glass-eating class. I guess you'll just have to figure the program out yourself.

The Least You Need to Know

- ◆ If runtime errors aren't handled properly, they can result in bizarre error messages and stop the program unexpectedly.

- ◆ When your program causes a runtime error, Visual Basic .NET throws an exception.

- ◆ If your program doesn't catch an exception, Visual Basic .NET does, and it displays an error message of its own.

- ◆ The way you tell the computer that you want to catch an error is by enclosing program lines that might cause a problem inside a `try` program block.

- ◆ A `catch` program block tells the computer what to do in the event of an error.

- ◆ When Visual Basic .NET throws an exception, it creates an exception object and sends it to your program.

- ◆ To catch a specific exception, you specify a more specific exception type, such as `DivideByZeroException`, `IndexOutOfRangeException`, and `FileNotFoundException`.

- ◆ You can have as many `catch` blocks as you need to catch the exceptions that might occur.

Chapter 17

Mastering the Art of Bug Extermination

In This Chapter

- ◆ Examine the Debug menu
- ◆ Step through a program line by line
- ◆ Toggle breakpoints on and off
- ◆ Peek at the values of variables while a program runs

A problem you'll discover when writing full-length programs is finding and fixing programming errors. When a program is only a few lines long, you can easily examine each line of code and locate problems. But when a program grows to hundreds or even thousands of lines, you won't want to look at every line in the program (unless you're the type of person who likes to read phone books from cover to cover). Instead, you'll want to isolate the problem to a specific part of the program so you can find your error more quickly. The Visual Basic .NET built-in debugger, which you'll study in this chapter, can help you find these errors.

Debugging Programs

As your programs get longer, you'll discover that finding errors can be difficult and confusing. Often, something will go wrong with your program, and you'll have no idea where to look for the problem. This can lead to sleepless nights, a bad disposition, and the inability to eat pizza for breakfast. Luckily, Visual Basic .NET includes a simple debugger that can help you locate programming errors. You'll find the commands that control the debugger in the Debug menu, shown in Figure 17.1.

Figure 17.1

The Debug menu will help you find programming errors.

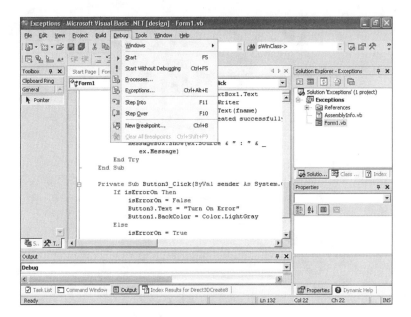

Check This Out

There are two types of programming errors that may crop up in your programs. The first is a *runtime error*, which usually causes the program to crash and display an error message. The other type of error, a *logic error*, is much more insidious and hard to find. A logic error occurs when you think you've written the program to do one thing, but it's really doing something else entirely. Such errors cause programmers to scream, "Don't do what I say; do what I want!"

Stepping Through a Program

The first command you'll explore in the Debug menu is Step Into, which allows you to step through your program one line at a time. Each time you select this command (the easiest way is to press F11), your program executes a single line of code and then pauses for your next command.

To see how this works, follow these steps:

1. Start a new Visual Basic .NET project named DebugTest, and place Label, TextBox, and Button controls on the form, as shown in Figure 17.2.

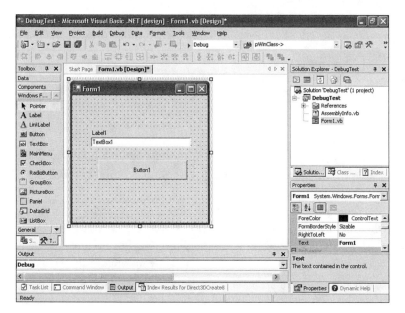

Figure 17.2

Position the controls as shown in this figure.

2. Double-click the form to bring up the code window, and type the following program lines into the Load procedure (Visual Basic .NET will have already started the Form1_Load procedure for you):

```
Label1.Text = "Enter text here:"
TextBox1.Text = "Default text"
Button1.Text = "Click Me"
```

3. Now you can run the program. However, rather than starting the program with the Start command, use the Step Into command. To do this, select the Step Into command from the Debug menu, or just press F11 on your keyboard. When you do, Visual Basic .NET starts running the program, but pauses on the first program line, as shown in Figure 17.3.

   The highlighted line is the next line the computer will execute. No, you didn't write all this code while you were in some sort of wonderful trance. Visual Basic .NET supplied all this stuff automatically when you started your new project.

Figure 17.3

The Step Into command pauses the program on each line.

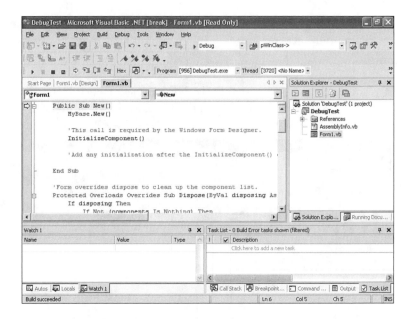

4. To get to your `Form1_Load` procedure, first place the cursor on the `Form1_Load` procedure's first line (the one that starts with the keyword `Private`). Then, to add a breakpoint, press Ctrl+B. You'll see the New Breakpoint dialog box. (A breakpoint is a place in your program where program execution will pause automatically.)

5. Select the File tab and click OK, and your screen will look similar to Figure 17.4.

Figure 17.4

A breakpoint in the program.

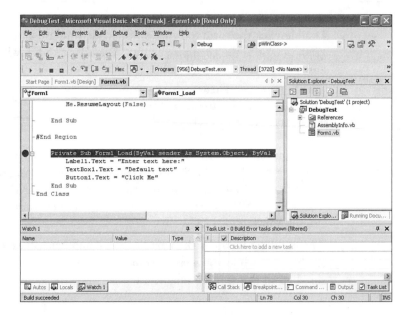

That red line that appears is called a breakpoint, and it tells Visual Basic .NET where you want the program to pause next. When your program runs, and Visual Basic .NET gets to a breakpoint, it performs the following actions:

- ◆ Jumps into debug mode.
- ◆ Displays the code window.
- ◆ Highlights the next line to execute.
- ◆ Waits for your next command.

6. Take another look at the New Breakpoint dialog box, shown in Figure 17.5.

   In the File box is the name of the source code file you're currently working on whereas in the Line box is the number for the line of code on which you want to set a breakpoint. As you can see by the dialog box's buttons, you can even set conditions and counters for the breakpoint, but that's advanced stuff, and I won't cover it here.

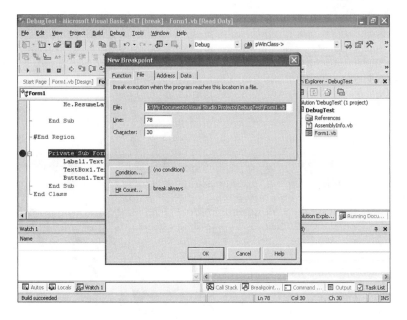

Figure 17.5

The New Breakpoint dialog box.

7. Select the Start command from the Debug menu, or just press F5, to select the Start command, and the program runs until it comes to your breakpoint on the Form1_Load procedure. The next line to execute in your program is highlighted, as shown in Figure 17.6.

8. Go ahead and press F11 again. Visual Basic .NET executes the highlighted line, entering the Form1_Load procedure. Press F11 again, and the program sets the Label1 control's text, and highlights the next line, as shown in Figure 17.7.

9. Press F11 three more times, watching as Visual Basic .NET steps through your program. When there are no more lines to execute, the program's window appears on the screen.

Figure 17.6

The program stopped on the breakpoint.

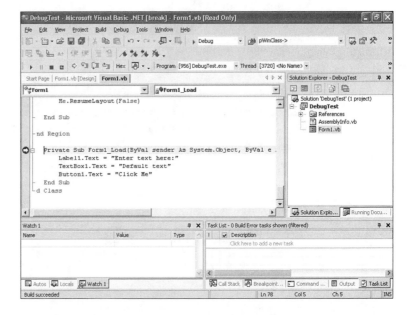

Figure 17.7

The program stopped on the third line.

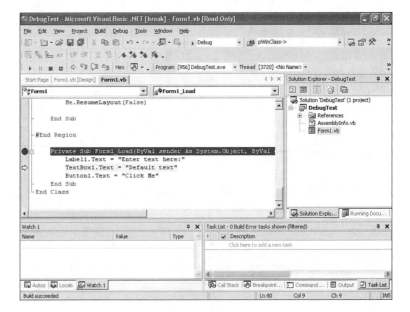

As you can see, the Step Into command enables you to watch how Visual Basic .NET executes each program line. To get a better idea of how this works, let's make things a little more complicated, by following these steps:

1. Close the running program, and then replace the contents of your current
   Form1_Load procedure with this line:

   ```
   Call InitControls()
   ```

2. Also, add this procedure to the program, right below the end of the Form1_Load
   procedure:

   ```
   Sub InitControls()
       Label1.Text = "Enter text here:"
       TextBox1.Text = "Default text"
       Button1.Text = "Click Me"
   End Sub
   ```

   In this version of the program, Form1_Load calls the InitControls procedure, which
   handles the task of setting the controls' text. This little change will dramatically
   affect the way the Step Into command works.

3. Run the new version of the program by pressing F5 to select the Start command.
   Thanks to your breakpoint, Visual Basic .NET runs the program and stops on the
   Form1_Load line. Press F11, and Visual Basic .NET enters the Form1_Load procedure
   and stops on the Call line, as shown in Figure 17.8.

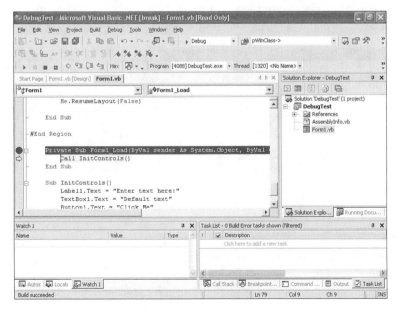

Figure 17.8

Visual Basic .NET is about ready to step into the InitControls *procedure.*

Now, you're about to see why Visual Basic .NET names this command Step Into rather than just Step. Press F11, and Visual Basic .NET "steps into" the InitControls procedure, as shown in Figure 17.9.

Figure 17.9

Visual Basic .NET is now ready to execute the InitControls *procedure.*

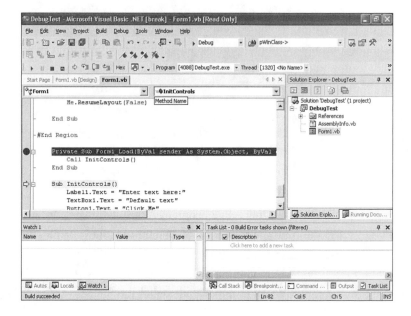

4. Press F11 five times, and watch Visual Basic .NET execute each of the lines in the InitControls procedure. The program then returns to the Form1_Load procedure, as shown in Figure 17.10.

Figure 17.10

Visual Basic .NET is now back to the Form_Load *procedure.*

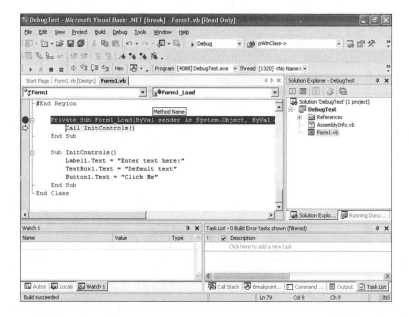

Another handy Visual Basic .NET debugging command is Step Over, which you can select from the Debug menu or by pressing F10. The Step Over command enables you to skip over procedure and function calls, without stepping through them line by line. The skipped-over procedure or function still executes normally; you just don't see it.

To see the Step Over command in action, follow these steps:

1. Restart the program by selecting the Restart command from the debug menu, or by pressing Ctrl+Shift+F5.

2. Press F5 to get to your breakpoint, and press F11 to highlight the `Call InitControls` line.

3. Now press F10. Visual Basic .NET executes the `InitControls` procedure without stepping through it line by line.

The Step Over command can save you a lot of time when you don't care about what's happening inside a procedure.

Techno Talk _____

The Visual Basic .NET debugger is actually very easy to use, especially when compared with the powerhouse debuggers that used to come with languages like Visual C++. The Visual Basic .NET debugger, though, has a lot more power than you'll learn about in this chapter. With the Visual Basic .NET debugger, you can do wild and crazy things like look at the contents of the computer's memory, view the program's instructions as assembly language, and even examine special memory areas called **registers** that hold all kinds of insanely important technical information about the currently running program. If you saw one of these debug windows up on your screen, you'd probably faint or start speaking in tongues.

Watching Variables

When you're stepping through a program, you can do more than just watch the program flow. You can also check the values of variables by following these steps:

1. Select the Debug menu's Stop Debugging command to close your running program.

2. Select the Form1.vb [Design] tab to view the form, and then double-click your form's Button control to start the `Button1_Click` procedure.

3. Complete the `Button1_Click` procedure with these lines:

```
Dim txt As String = TextBox1.Text
MessageBox.Show(txt)
```

4. Save your work, and then place the text cursor in the code window on the following line:

```
Dim txt As String = TextBox1.Text
```

5. Press Ctrl+B, select the File tab in the New Breakpoint dialog box, and press OK. Visual Basic .NET highlights the program line in red, as shown in Figure 17.11.

Figure 17.11

Visual Basic .NET sets a second breakpoint.

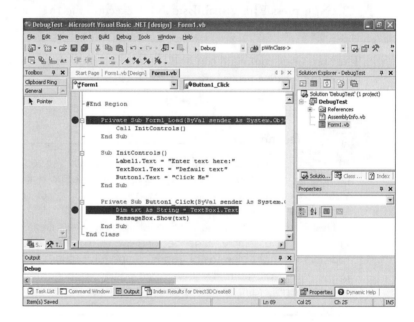

Check This Out

You can have more than one breakpoint set at a time. In fact, you can pretty much have as many breakpoints set as you want. For example, you might set breakpoints at the beginning of several functions so that you can step through those functions when they're called. If you have a lot of breakpoints, you can turn them off all at once with the Clear All Breakpoints command. You can select this command from the Debug menu or by pressing Ctrl+Shift+F9 on your keyboard.

6. Run the program using the Start command (F5). The program stops on the first breakpoint. Because you're not interested in the Form1 Load procedure anymore, press F5 to get the program running again, which causes the program's form to appear.

7. Click the Click Me button. When you do, Visual Basic .NET starts executing the Button1_Click procedure, but before it gets too far, it hits the breakpoint and stops.

8. Position your mouse pointer over the variable txt in the highlighted line. (You don't need to click the variable; just place the pointer over it.) Visual Basic .NET displays a small box with the message txt=Nothing, as shown in Figure 17.12.

You're now looking at the current value of the txt variable. Talk about handy!

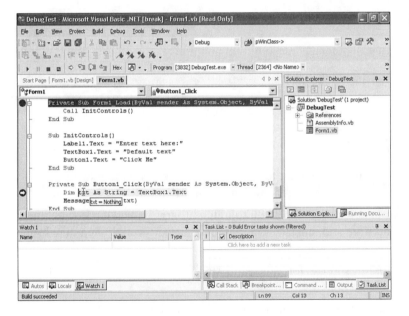

Figure 17.12

Visual Basic .NET displays the values of variables.

9. To prove that Visual Basic .NET is showing the actual value of the variable txt, press F11 to execute the highlighted line, which assigns the text in the text box to the txt variable. Place your mouse cursor over txt again, and this time Visual Basic .NET tells you that txt="Default text", as the Figure 17.13.

10. To turn off the breakpoint, click on the breakpoint line, and press F9 to select the Toggle Breakpoint command.

Now that you can trace through your programs and sneak a peek at the value of your variables as the program executes, you have no excuse for not hunting down those program bugs and squashing them like … well … like *bugs!*

Figure 17.13

Visual Basic .NET displays the correct value even after the value has changed.

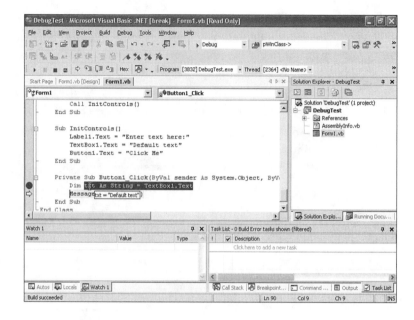

The Least You Need to Know

◆ The Step Into command enables you to watch program execution line by line, jumping into any procedures or functions that the program calls.

◆ The Step Over command also enables you to watch program execution line by line, but it executes procedure and function calls without tracing through them line by line.

◆ By setting a breakpoint, you can force Visual Basic .NET to stop on a specific line and wait for your instructions.

◆ You can turn off all the breakpoints in a program by selecting the Clear All Breakpoints command.

◆ When Visual Basic .NET is running a program in debug mode, you can view the value of a variable by placing the mouse cursor over the variable's name in the code window.

Elements of Visual Basic .NET Windows Programs

Visual Basic makes Windows programming easier and more convenient in a number of ways. Using forms for your application's window is one way. Other ways are the use of controls that you can manipulate through their methods, properties, and events. Guess what you'll learn about here?

A Place to Put Controls

In This Chapter

- ◆ Explore the Form object's properties
- ◆ Learn to call a Form object's methods
- ◆ Discover how Form events enable a program to respond to user and system actions

Now it's time to start digging deeper into Visual Basic .NET. In this chapter, you'll learn about what makes a Visual Basic .NET Windows application tick. The first step towards this goal is to have a close look at Visual Basic .NET Windows Forms, which are nothing more than objects that can hold other objects.

Revisiting the Windows Form

Whether you've given it much thought or not, you already know that a form is a container. How do you know that? Because throughout this book, you've been placing controls on your forms, and only a container object can hold other controls. The Windows Form is, in fact, the most common container object because it represents your Visual Basic .NET application's main window. Figure 18.1 shows an empty Form object in the Visual Basic .NET Project window.

The Project's form

Figure 18.1

A Form object looks like a window because it represents your application's main window.

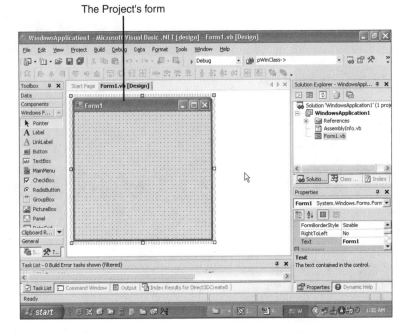

Previously in this book, you've been using a Windows Form for little more than holding the few controls needed to run sample programs. But a form is a powerful object, featuring many properties and methods that your programs can use to control the way the form looks and acts. Moreover, the form responds to a whole host of events. By responding to these events, a program can tap into the interaction going on between the application, the user, and the operating system.

Introducing Form Properties

Okay, I'm going to scare you a little bit now: The Form object features nearly 100 properties! Luckily, until you become a full-fledged Visual Basic .NET geek (you'll know when that happens; you'll have a constant craving for gummy bears, Diet Coke, and Xena dinner plates), you don't need to know all the properties and what they do. The following list describes the seven form properties that are easiest to use and understand, and, for someone just starting out, are also the most useful:

- ◆ BackColor: Determines the form's background color.
- ◆ ForeColor: Determines the color used to draw text and lines in the form.
- ◆ Height: Determines the height of a form.
- ◆ Left: Determines the position of the form's left edge.
- ◆ Text: Determines the text that appears in the form's title bar.

◆ `Top`: Determines the position of the form's top edge.

◆ `Width`: Determines the width of the form.

You can set these properties in the Properties window when you're designing your program. This is the easiest way to handle the properties, because Visual Basic .NET lists a property's possible settings for you. All you have to do is choose one, as shown in Figure 18.2.

The Properties window

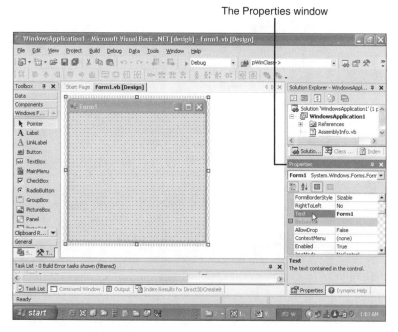

Figure 18.2

The Properties window makes it easy to set a property's value.

Not all properties are available in the Properties window, however. Some are only available when your program is running.

Using Form Properties

There's not enough room in this chapter to cover all the Form properties, even just the easy ones. However, this section will give you some experience with a few of the properties. Once you've familiarized yourself with these, you can experiment with the others on your own.

The ForeColor and BackColor Properties

The `ForeColor` and `BackColor` properties not only affect the form, but also the controls on the form. That is, when you change the form's `ForeColor` property, you also change the ForeColor property of the controls on the form. The exception is when you've explicitly set the control colors separate from the form. To see how this works, follow these steps:

1. Start a new Visual Basic®.NET project named FormTest, and add two buttons to the form, as shown in Figure 18.3.

Figure 18.3

The FormTest program's form.

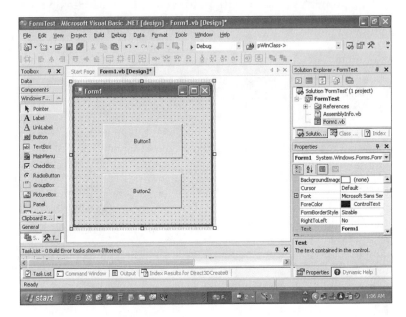

2. Double-click the form and complete the Load procedure with these program lines:

```
Button1.Text = "Form Colors"
Button2.Text = "Button Colors"
```

3. Double-click the Button1 control, and add the following lines to the Click event handler that Visual Studio starts for you:

```
Me.ForeColor = Color.White
Me.BackColor = Color.Blue
```

4. Double-click the Button2 control, and add the following lines to the Click event handler that Visual Studio starts for you:

```
Button1.BackColor = Color.LightGray
Button1.ForeColor = Color.Black
Button2.BackColor = Color.LightGray
Button2.ForeColor = Color.Black
```

5. Save your work, and run the program. If all went well, you should see the program's window, as shown in Figure 18.4.

Figure 18.4

The running FormTest program.

6. Click the Form Colors button. The form changes its BackColor and ForeColor properties, which causes the controls to follow suit, as shown in Figure 18.5.

Figure 18.5

The running FormTest program after changing the form's colors.

7. Click the Button Colors button. The program changes the buttons' BackColor and ForeColor properties, which changes the buttons' colors but has no effect on the form, as you can see in Figure 18.6.

Figure 18.6

The running FormTest program after changing the buttons' colors.

8. Click the Form Colors button again. This time nothing seems to happen. This is because the form is already set to the new colors. Moreover, the controls are no longer affected by the form's colors, because you set the colors of the controls in the program.

By the Way

Notice how, in the program, you refer to a form property with the `Me` keyword followed by a dot and the name of the property. You can't use `Form1` as the form's name, because `Form1` is the name of a class, not the name of an object. The `Me` keyword, on the other hand, refers to the program's object of the `Form1` type.

The Left and Top Properties

The form's `Left` and `Top` properties control where the form appears on the screen. To see how this works, follow these steps:

1. Start a new Visual Basic .NET application named LeftTop, and place one button on the form, as shown in the Figure 18.7.

Figure 18.7

The LeftTop program's form.

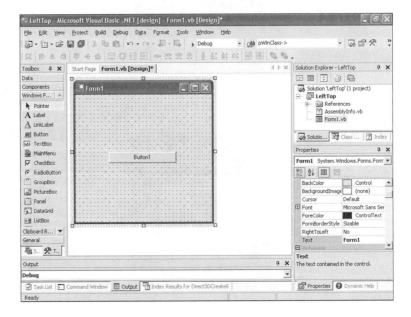

2. Double-click the form and complete the Load procedure with the following program line:

```
Button1.Text = "Move Window"
```

3. Double-click the Button1 control, and add the following lines to the Click event handler that Visual Studio starts for you:

```
If Me.Left = 100 Then
    Me.Left = 400
    Me.Top = 200
Else
    Me.Left = 100
    Me.Top = 75
End If
```

4. Save your work and run the program. When you click the button, the form moves on the screen.

The Width and Height Properties

The form's Width and Height properties control where the form appears on the screen. To see this in action, let's do a little surgery on the LeftTop application you just wrote.

Change the contents of the Load procedure to this:

```
Button1.Text = "Size Window"
```

Next, change the lines in the Click event handler to this:

```
If Me.Width = 300 Then
    Me.Width = 500
    Me.Height = 300
Else
    Me.Width = 300
    Me.Height = 190
End If
```

Save your work and run the program. When you click the button, the form changes size on the screen.

Introducing Form Methods

The Form object also provides a set of methods, which you can call to manipulate the form in various ways. Just as with the properties, though, you don't have to know all the methods to get started with Visual Basic .NET forms. The following list of four will get you going:

- ◆ `Close`: Closes the form.
- ◆ `CreateGraphics`: Creates a Graphics object associated with the form.
- ◆ `Hide`: Hides the form.
- ◆ `Show`: Shows the form.

To see how a few of these methods work, follow these steps:

1. Start a new Visual Basic .NET application named FormMethods, and place one button on the form, as shown in Figure 18.8.

Figure 18.8

The FormMethods program's form.

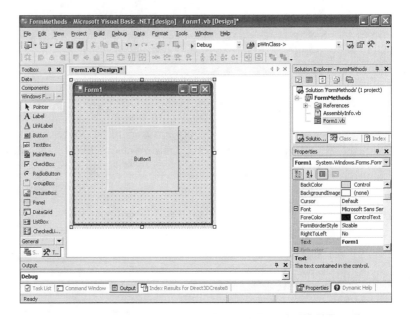

2. Double-click the form and complete the `Load` procedure with this program line:

```
Button1.Text = "Show Form"
```

3. Double-click the `Button1` control, and add the following lines to the `Click` event handler that Visual Studio starts for you:

```
Dim frm As New Form()
Dim g As Graphics = frm.CreateGraphics
frm.Show()
g.DrawRectangle(Pens.Black, 100, 100, 100, 100)
```

4. Save your work and run the program. When you click the button, the program displays a new form with a rectangle drawn on it, as shown in Figure 18.9.

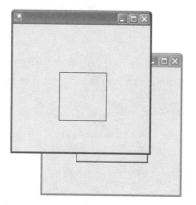

Figure 18.9

The running FormMethods program.

Adding Form Events

The Form object responds to many kinds of events. The more you know about these events, the more control you have over the interactions between your program, the user, and the operating system. Still, some events are more important than others. The following list shows the events most important to a new Visual Basic .NET programmer:

◆ `Click`: This is called when the user clicks the form.

◆ `Closing`: This is called when Visual Basic .NET is about to close the form.

◆ `DblClick`: This is called when the user Double-clicks the form.

◆ `Load`: This is called when Visual Basic .NET first loads the form.

The following program demonstrates how form events cause Visual Basic .NET to call the associated event procedures.

1. Start a new Visual Basic .NET project named FormEvents, and double-click the form to bring up the code window. Type the following source-code lines (Visual Basic .NET will have already started the `Form_Load` procedure for you).

```
Private Sub Form1_Load(ByVal sender As System.Object, _
      ByVal e As System.EventArgs) Handles MyBase.Load
   MessageBox.Show("Load Event")
End Sub


Private Sub Form1_Click(ByVal sender As Object, _
      ByVal e As System.EventArgs) Handles MyBase.Click
   MessageBox.Show("Click Event")
End Sub
```

```
Private Sub Form1_Closing(ByVal sender As Object, _
        ByVal e As System.ComponentModel.CancelEventArgs) Handles
MyBase.Closing
    MessageBox.Show("Closing Event")
End Sub
```

If you want to save on typing, select Base Class Events from the first list box at the top of the code window, and then select the event you want from the second list box, as shown in Figure 18.10.

Set this box for
base class events

Set this box to the
event handler you need

Figure 18.10

Adding event handlers to a form.

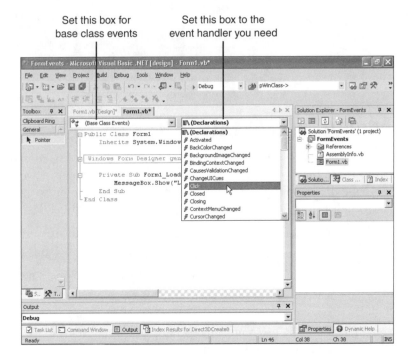

2. Save your work and run the program. When you do, a message box appears that tells you the Load event has occurred. The Load event, which is handled by the Form1_Load event procedure, occurs when Visual Basic .NET first loads the form but has not yet displayed the form.

3. Dismiss the message box, and the application's window appears.

4. Click in the window, and a message box appears that tells you a Click event just occurred, as shown in Figure 18.11.

Figure 18.11

Watching form events as they happen.

5. Dismiss the message box, and terminate the application by clicking its Close button. Right before Visual Basic .NET removes the window from the screen, it calls the Form1_Closing event procedure, as you can tell by the message box that appears.

Feel free to explore Form objects more fully. Look up the different properties, methods, and events in the Visual Studio .NET documentation and experiment with what you've learned. As long as you resist the urge to take an axe to your computer, fiddling with forms won't hurt anything!

The Least You Need to Know

- The Form object is Visual Basic .NET's most important container. A container is an object that can hold other objects.

- The Form object's properties include BackColor, ForeColor, Text, Left, Top, and others.

- The Form object's Show, Hide, Close, and CreateGraphics methods are the most useful to a new Visual Basic .NET programmer.

- The Load and Closing events enable a program to initialize and shut down a program elegantly.

Controls and Objects: There's a Difference?

In This Chapter

♦ Learn the many meanings of "object"

♦ Discover Visual Basic .NET objects

♦ Compare Visual Basic .NET objects with Visual Basic. NET controls

Throughout the previous chapters, you've been reading a lot about controls and objects. You probably have a fuzzy idea of what these things are, but you can't quite bring it into focus. Don't worry; you're not the only one. Unfortunately, although the word "control" has a clear definition in Visual Basic .NET, the word "object" in Visual Basic. NET (and many other languages) tends to mean different things at different times. It's all a matter of context, you know?

Thinking About Objects

So what exactly is a Visual Basic .NET object? Technically, an object is any piece of data in a program. An integer is an object, a string is an object, and a TextBox control is an object. Some objects are much more sophisticated than others. For example, whereas an integer is only a few bytes of memory, a TextBox control is an entire collection of properties, methods, and event handlers and usually (though not always) features some sort of graphical user interface.

In Visual Basic .NET programming, though, an object usually has a more specific definition. Usually, an object is something more abstract than a control. Visual Basic .NET and the .NET Framework provide many types of objects, including `Font`, `File`, `Screen`, `Clipboard`, and `Image` objects. You can tell by the objects' names what type of "real-world" object they represent. For example, the `File` object comprises the properties and methods a program needs to manipulate a disk file, whereas the `Clipboard` object comprises the properties and methods a program needs to manipulate the Windows Clipboard.

> **Techno Talk**
>
> The concept of objects started with something called **object-oriented programming** (OOP), which is a way of representing real-world (and some not-so-real-world) objects in a computer program. In fact, the idea of OOP actually started with the need for simulation programmers to model objects such as a car or a plane.

One thing these objects have in common is that none is interactive. The user can't manipulate them directly; only your program can. You can't see a `Font` object (although you can see the resulting font when text is printed on the screen). It doesn't appear on the screen, and the user can interact with it only indirectly through your program. Yet it represents a set of methods and properties that a program can access to control the object and, indirectly, control the appearance of text.

Something else these kinds of objects have in common is that each is an *instance* of a *class*. You can think of a class as a blueprint and an instance of a class (called an object) as the thing that gets built from the blueprint. You learn more about classes later in this book.

Thinking About Controls

Unlike Visual Basic .NET objects like `Font`, `Clipboard`, and `File`, controls are interactive. Most (though not all) can be manipulated directly by the user, most (though not all) have a graphical user interface, and all respond to events, enabling them to interact not only with the user, but also with the program and the operating system.

Take a TextBox control, for example, which boasts these attributes:

◆ Has a graphical user interface, which is the box into which the user can type text

◆ Is interactive because the user can change its contents

◆ Responds to events that the user generates when he changes the contents of the control

If you still have a hard time telling the difference between a control and an object, just remember that controls appear in your Visual Basic .NET toolbox whereas objects appear only in your program's source code.

Of course, you can refer to a control by its name in your program's source code. In that way, a control also appears in your program's source code. However, a control starts out in the toolbox. An object (using the strict definition) never appears in the toolbox.

Visual Basic .NET comes with many of its own controls, often called *intrinsic controls*. However, many companies and even hobbyist programmers have created many, many other controls that you can add to your Visual Basic .NET toolbox. You may even already have some installed on your system that you don't know about. To see the control packages installed on your machine, right-click Windows Forms in the Toolbox, and then select the Customize Toolbox command in the menu that appears. When you do, the Customize Toolbox dialog box appears, which, on its COM Components and .NET Framework Components pages, lists all the available controls on your machine. Just select a control's check box and click OK. Visual Basic .NET then adds the selected control to your toolbox.

Check This Out

Controls and objects both have properties and methods, but only controls can respond to events. If you can keep that one point in your head, you'll always be able to tell the difference between the two.

The Least You Need to Know

- When used in a general way, the term "object" can refer to just about any piece of data or code in your program, including integers, controls, and more.

- In Visual Basic .NET, an object usually comprises properties and methods that enable the program to access and control a "real-world" object like a disk file.

- Controls differ from Visual Basic .NET objects in that controls respond to events. Moreover, controls usually (but not always) are interactive with a graphical interface.

- Controls appear in your Visual Basic .NET toolbox whereas objects appear only in your program lines.

Chapter

20

The Inner Workings of Controls and Objects

In This Chapter

◆ Learn about properties and how to manage them

◆ Discover how to call methods

◆ Learn how Visual Basic .NET enables your program to respond to events

◆ See how Visual Basic .NET helps you with properties, methods, and event procedures

In Chapter 19, "Controls and Objects: There's a Difference?" you learned to tell the difference between a control and an object. Along the way, you read about properties, methods, and events. In fact, you've seen a little about properties, methods, and events scattered throughout the entire book. Up until now, though, you may have been a little fuzzy on what these important elements of a control or object actually are. In this chapter, you get the inside scoop.

Introducing Properties

Most objects and controls have properties, which you can think of as nothing more complicated than attributes. For example, as you've already learned, a Button control has a property called Text, which determines the text that appears in the button. Lots of other controls, such as the familiar Label control, also have a Text property. Some properties are common in Visual Basic .NET whereas others are associated with only a single control or object.

The Name property is an example of a property that every control has. Without a control's name, your program would have no way to refer to the control. Most visible controls also have Left, Top, Width, and Height properties, which determine the location and size of the control. However, the FormBorderStyle property, which determines the way a window looks and acts, is unique to forms. After all, you wouldn't want a dialog-style border on something like a button.

Setting Properties

Both controls and objects can have properties. However, the way you set a property for a control and an object are different. You can set a control's properties in the Properties window, as shown in Figure 20.1.

Figure 20.1

You can access most properties in a control's Properties window.

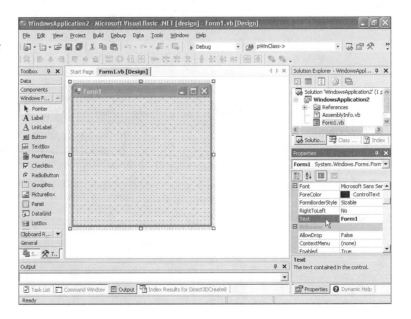

Or you can set a control's properties in your program's source code, as shown in Figure 20.2.

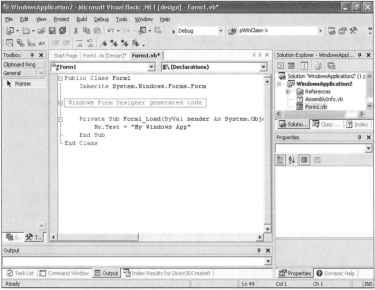

Figure 20.2

Many properties can be set from within the program.

Which way you set a control's properties depends on the property and your preference.

Check This Out _____

When should you set properties using the Properties window, and when should you set properties in a program? Often, that's just a matter of taste. Other times, it's a matter of necessity. For example, you might just prefer to always set a control's properties in your program. However, there are also times when you have no choice. For example, you might want to set a control's properties in response to some input from the user. In this case, of course, you'd have to set the properties in your program. As for this book, I tend to send properties in the programs themselves because it's easier and more concise than telling you to set each property in the Properties window.

On the other hand, you must set an object's properties in your program, because an object doesn't display a Properties window the way a control does. In fact, objects don't even exist until you run your program.

To complicate matters, some properties work differently depending on whether the program is in *design time* (when you're writing the program) or *runtime* (when the program is

Techno Talk

In programming, you run across the terms **read** and **write** a lot. For example, when a program sends data to a disk file, it's writing to the file. Conversely, when a program retrieves data from a file, it's reading the file. The same is true of properties. When a program changes the value of a property, it's writing to the property, and when a program retrieves the value of a property, it's reading the property. In Visual Basic .NET, you usually use `Get` and `Set` procedures for this task.

actually running). For example, you can set almost any form property at design time in its Property window, but only some can be set by a running program. The properties you can set only at design time are *read-only* at runtime.

Some properties are *read* and *write* at both design time and runtime whereas others are read-only at runtime. Some properties don't exist at design time and can be accessed only at runtime. This all goes to show that the ways in which you can access a property depend on the property.

One cool thing about Visual Basic .NET is its ability to help you find the right property as you're writing a program. When you type the name of a control or an object and then type the dot that separates the name from the property or method, Visual Basic .NET displays a list containing all the available properties and methods, as shown in Figure 20.3.

Figure 20.3

Visual Basic .NET displays a form's properties and methods.

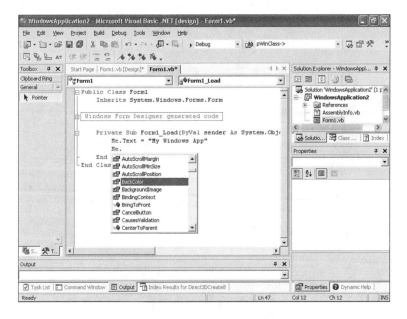

All you have to do is find the name of the property or method you want (if you type a couple of letters, Visual Basic .NET will help you zero in on the property you want) and press the spacebar on your keyboard. No more digging through hundreds of pages of documentation looking for the name of a property or method. More importantly, no more paper cuts from the edges of the pages!

Introducing Methods

If properties represent a control's or object's attributes, methods represent the control's or object's abilities. For example, many controls have a Focus method, which gives the input focus to the control. Similarly, as you learned earlier, the PrintDocument control has a Print method that sends data to the printer.

Although there is a small set of methods that are common to many controls, most controls and objects feature methods that are unique to that particular control or object. No other control or object other than the PrintDocument control has the Print method. Similarly, no other control or object other than the Clipboard object has a SetDataObject method.

Calling Methods

Techno Talk

You learned in a previous chapter's Techno Talk that the idea of objects comes from object-oriented programming (OOP). You also learned that OOP programmers create classes, which are like templates or blueprints for an object. Classes have properties and methods, too, but they are called different things in different languages. If you were programming a class in Visual C++, for example, you'd call properties **data members** or **member variables**, and you'd call methods **member functions**.

Methods are similar to procedures and functions in that your program not only calls them, but also often needs to call them with a set of arguments. To call a control or object's method, you just type the name of the control or object followed by a dot and then the name of the method. Just as with properties, Visual Basic .NET will help you—when it can—to figure out the correct arguments to include in the method call. Figure 20.4, for example, shows a programmer about to enter the arguments for a call to a button's CreateGraphics method.

Figure 20.4

Visual Basic .NET displays the types of arguments needed for a method call.

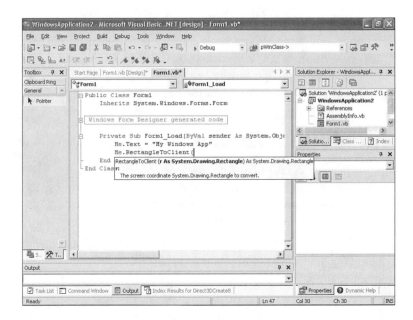

By the Way

There may be times when you have an object or control that contains another object for which you want to access a property or method. In cases like this, you use the object names and the dots to create a kind of map to the property, like this `Object1.Object2.Property`. For example, every Form object has a `MousePosition` property, which holds, among other things, the location of the mouse. In turn, the `MousePosition` property (which is an object itself) holds the values of the mouse's horizontal and vertical position in data members called X and Y. If your program needs the horizontal position of the mouse, you could write something like `mouseX = Form1.MousePosition.X`.

Introducing Events

Event handlers are kind of like methods in that they are called like subroutines and functions. The big difference between methods and event handlers, though, is that, while your program calls a method, Visual Basic .NET calls event handlers on its own in response to events generated by the user or the operating system. In your program, you supply the event handler, which tells Visual Basic .NET what to do when a particular event occurs, and then Visual Basic .NET does the rest.

Take the Button control (please!). As you've noticed in previous chapters, the Button control responds to an event called Click. This means that, when the user clicks the button, Visual Basic .NET calls the button's `Click` event handler and performs whatever the program instructs it to do in the procedure. If the program has no `Click` event handler, and the user clicks the button, nothing happens. (As you'll soon discover, sometimes a button does nothing even when there is a `Click` event handler. This usually means you fell asleep while writing the handler, or when you glanced away, your cat walked across the keyboard, filling the handler with strange feline words Visual Basic .NET can't possibly understand.)

Writing Event Handlers

As was mentioned previously, the program lines that Visual Basic .NET executes when an event occurs make up an event handler. An event handler is not unlike other procedures you might write, except for the fact that Visual Basic .NET itself calls the event handler. (Your program can also call an event handler, but this would be an uncommon thing to do.)

Event handlers are another place where Visual Basic .NET is as smart as Bart Simpson's mouth. First, Visual Basic .NET can list all the events for any control in your program. Just select the control's name in the code window's left-hand list box, and all the available events appear in the second list box, as shown in Figure 20.5.

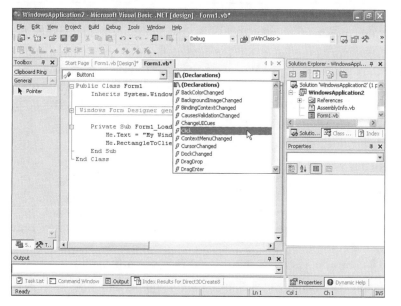

Figure 20.5

Here, Visual Basic .NET lists the events for a Button control called Button1.

Once you find the event you want, just press Enter with the event highlighted. In the code window, Visual Basic .NET automatically starts the event handler for you. All you have to do is complete the handler, adding the program lines you want executed when the event occurs. Figure 20.6 shows the event handler that Visual Basic .NET starts for a button's MouseDown event.

Figure 20.6

Visual Basic .NET starts event procedures for you, so you don't have to remember the syntax and all the arguments.

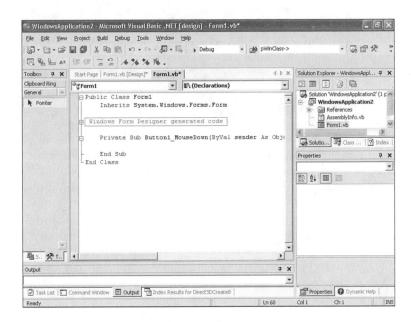

Another way to get Visual Basic .NET to start an event handler for you is to double-click a control or form. When you do, Visual Basic .NET creates the event handler that you'll most likely need (called the default handler). Of course, sometimes Visual Basic .NET guesses wrong and provides an event handler that you don't want. In this case, just ignore the event handler that Visual Basic .NET created (you can even delete it if you want), and choose the event you want from the event list box in the code window.

The Least You Need to Know

◆ Properties represent a control's or object's attributes.

◆ Some properties can be set in the program's source code at runtime while other properties must be set in the Properties window at design time. Some properties can be set either way.

◆ Methods represent a control's or object's abilities, the things that it can do.

◆ Calling a method is much like calling procedures. Often, you need to supply one or more arguments.

◆ An event handler holds the program lines that Visual Basic .NET should execute when a specific event occurs.

Part 4

Modules and Classes

When programs get big, you have do something to get them under control. One of the things you can do is organize the program into modules and classes. Classes, especially, are a great way to separate your program code into logical units. But when you start using classes, you have to know about stuff like encapsulation, inheritance, and polymorphism. Luckily, as you'll see in this part of the book, this stuff isn't as scary as it sounds.

Modules: A Special Place for Handy Stuff

In This Chapter

◆ Adding modules to your program

◆ Organizing code with modules

◆ Reusing code with modules

As your programs get larger, you're going to want to separate your source code into different files. This practice not only enables you to work with smaller files, but also enables you to build libraries of code that you can easily reuse. For example, you may have a number of mathematical functions that you use often in your programs. By placing these functions into a file of their own, you can easily call upon them whenever you need them. In this chapter, you'll see how Visual Basic .NET modules make this kind of code organization easy.

Getting Modular

Simply put, a module is a file of source code. When you first create your Visual Basic .NET project, Visual Studio generates a starting module for you in the guise of the main form's class. (For more details about classes sneak a peek at Chapter 22, "Classes: An Object-Oriented Way of Thinking.") You can, however, have many modules in one program, enabling you to organize your source code into logical components. You might, for example, have a module that contains all your program's file-handling procedures and another one that contains graphics procedures. In this way, when you need to work on a particular procedure, you can find it more quickly.

One New Module Coming Up

Adding a new module to your Visual Basic .NET program is as easy as luring a hungry friend into a steak house. And you don't need anywhere as much A1 sauce.

1. Select the Project menu's Add New Item command. When you do, the Add New Item dialog box appears, as shown in Figure 21.1.

Figure 21.1

The Add New Item dialog box.

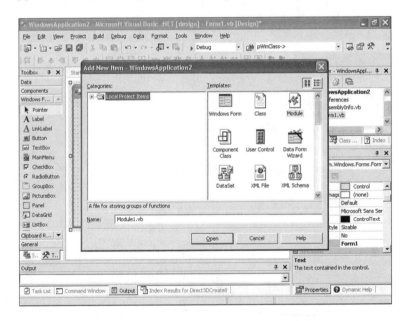

2. In the Templates pane, click Module, and then give the module a name in the Name text box.

3. Click the Open button, and Visual Studio adds the module to your project and places it in the Solution Explorer window, as shown in Figure 21.2.

The new module

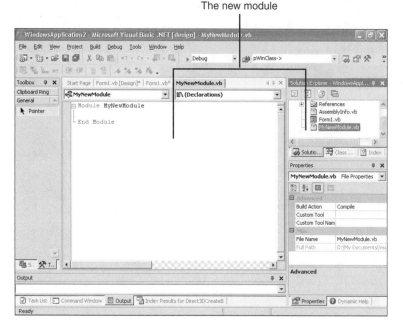

Figure 21.2

The new module added to the project.

Now, when you double-click the module in the Solution Explorer, Visual Basic .NET displays the contents of the module in a code window. If this is the first time you've opened the module, all you'll see in the code window is this snippet:

```
Module Module1

End Module
```

These two lines mark the module's beginning and end. All code you add to the module goes between these lines, except for `Option` statements and directives. In this example, `Module1` is the name of the module. Whatever name you chose for the module when you created it shows up here.

Putting It to Work

To see a module in action, follow these steps:

1. Start a new Visual Basic .NET program (from the Windows Application template) named Modules, and add text boxes and a button to the form, as shown in Figure 21.3.

Figure 21.3

The form for the Modules program.

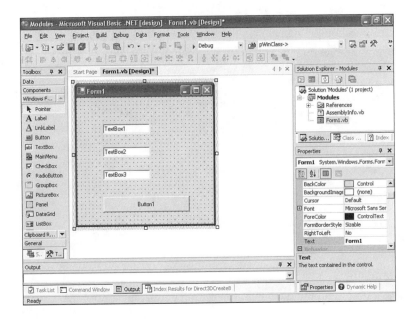

2. Select the Project menu's Add New Item command and then the Module template in the dialog box that appears to add a new module to the program. You don't need to name the module; just accept the default name, Module1.

3. Complete the module so that it looks like this:

```
Module Module1
    Function Avg3(ByVal n1 As Single, ByVal n2 As Single, ByVal n3 As
Single) As Single
        Dim avg = (n1 + n2 + n3) / 3
        Return avg
    End Function
End Module
```

4. In the designer window, double-click the form, and add the following lines to the Load procedure:

```
TextBox1.Text = ""
TextBox2.Text = ""
TextBox3.Text = ""
Button1.Text = "Calculate Average"
```

5. In the designer window (again), double-click the form's button, and complete the Click event handler with these lines:

```
Dim n1 = Single.Parse(TextBox1.Text)
Dim n2 = Single.Parse(TextBox2.Text)
```

```
Dim n3 = Single.Parse(TextBox3.Text)
Dim result As Single
result = Avg3(n1, n2, n3)
MessageBox.Show("Average = " & result)
```

Now, run the program, enter a number into each text box, and click the Calculate Average button. When you do, the program calls the `Avg3` function, which is located in the `Module1` module, and displays the result of the calculation in a message box, as shown in Figure 21.4.

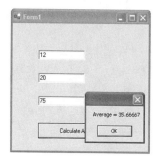

Figure 21.4

Getting the average of three numbers.

The program called the `Avg3` function just as if it were in the same module with the form's class. Now, if you have other mathematical functions you need, you can add them to this module. If you do this, you'll probably also want to rename the module to something more descriptive, such as Math.vb.

Check This Out

Modules are also a great place to put symbols that you need to use in several other modules in your programs. For example, suppose you use a constant named **PI** (which you haven't set to "Blueberry" or "Apple," but rather to 3.14, of course) in three different modules. You could define the constant in every module. But a better way of handling this type of problem is to create a module and put all your constants in it. Then every module automatically gets to use them.

Reuse Is the Key

In these days of huge programs, the word "reuse" gets thrown around a lot. (Computer keyboards get thrown around a lot, too, but for different reasons.) This is because being able to reuse code that's already been written and tested can save a lot of time and money. The Visual Basic .NET modules are a way of implementing code reuse.

To see how code reuse works with modules, follow these steps:

1. Start a new Visual Basic .NET program (from the Windows Application template) named Reuse, and add one button to the form, as shown in Figure 21.5.

Figure 21.5

The form for the Reuse program.

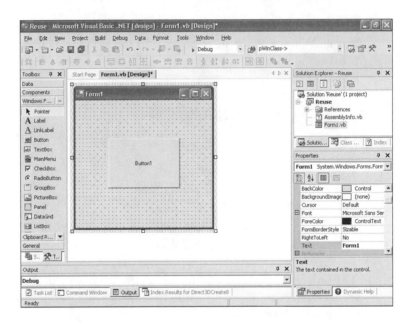

2. Click the Project menu's Add Existing Item command. When you do, the Add Existing Item dialog box appears.

3. Find and select the Module1.vb file that you created in the Modules application (if you're not sure where it is, use the Search command on your Windows Start menu) as shown in Figure 21.6.

4. Click the Open button to add the module to your new project.

5. In the design window, double-click the form's button, and complete the `Click` procedure with these lines:

```
Dim result As Single
result = Avg3(10, 12, 20)
MessageBox.Show(result)
```

6. Run the program, and click the button. Presto! You get the `Avg3` function free this time around.

Imagine how much time you could have saved in this program if the module had dozens of reusable functions in it. Makes you want to get busy writing modules, doesn't it? I'd join you, but I have to finish writing this book.

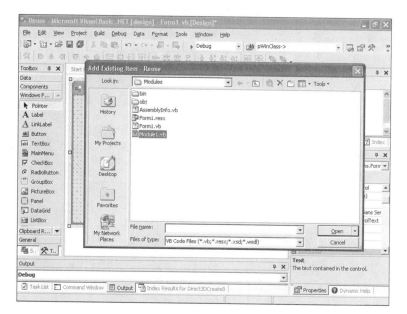

Figure 21.6

Adding a module to the Reuse program.

Check This Out

You may run into problems when you need to access your program's objects in other modules. For example, what if you need to change the text of your form's title bar in another module? You can't just access the form in another module. You have to pass to the function a reference to the form. For example, in your form's class, you might call a procedure in another module like this: `SetTitleBar(Me, "New Title")`. Here, `Me` is the reference to the form. Inside the module, the procedure's signature looks something like this: `Sub SetTitleBar(ByVal f as Form, ByVal t as String)`. In `SetTitleBar`, you would change the form's text like this: `f.Text = t`.

The Least You Need to Know

◆ You can have many modules in one program, enabling you to organize your source code into logical components.

◆ You can add a new module to your program with the Project menu's Add New Item command.

◆ The modules in Visual Basic .NET are a way of implementing code reuse.

Classes: An Object-Oriented Way of Thinking

In This Chapter

◆ Learn to think in terms of objects

◆ Discover how to write classes

◆ Explore encapsulation, inheritance, and polymorphism

◆ See how classes represent objects

Throughout this book, you've used the many classes that Microsoft created for Visual Basic .NET and the .NET Framework. Creating classes, however, is not a magical trick that only master programmers who work for Microsoft can accomplish. Any Visual Basic .NET programmer (including you) can create classes and incorporate them into his or her programs. If you've never created your own classes, however, you may find the process to be a bit mysterious. In this chapter, you start to dispel that mystery, as you learn how to supplement programs with your own custom-written classes.

Looking at Object-Oriented Programming Techniques

Before you can start writing your own classes, you have to be comfortable with object-oriented programming techniques. Not comfortable like with a sweater, all fuzzy and warm, but rather comfortable like having a general idea of what all this object-oriented stuff is about.

Object-oriented programming (OOP) enables you to think of program elements as objects. For example, think of an application's window. You don't need to know the details of how it works nor do you need to know about the window's private data. As a programmer, you need to know only how to call the various functions that make the window operate.

Now, think about a car. If you're thinking of an Oldsmobile rather than a Corvette, you need to get a better imagination. But more important to the topic at hand, to drive a car, you don't have to know the details of how a car works. You need to know only how to drive it. What's going on under the hood is none of your business. If you try to make it your business, plan to face an amused mechanic who will have to straighten out your mess!

If this were all there were to OOP, you wouldn't have gained much over standard programming techniques. After all, anybody can create "black box" routines, which a programmer could then use without knowing how they work. Obviously, there must be much more to OOP than just hiding the details of a process and that great party OOP programmers always have on Friday night. There's also more to it than dreaming of cruising down the highway in a Corvette. In this section, you'll discover cool techie stuff like encapsulation, inheritance, and polymorphism—the features that give OOP its true power.

Encapsulation

One major difference between conventional procedural programming and OOP is a handy thing called *encapsulation*. Encapsulation enables you to package both the data and the functions that act on that data inside the object. Once you do this, you can control access to the data, forcing programs to retrieve or modify data only through the object's interface, which provides access to the object's methods. In strict object-oriented design, an object's data is always private to the object. No messing with those private parts! Other parts of a program should never have direct access to that data.

How is this data hiding different from a conventional programming approach? After all, you could always hide data inside of functions, just by making that data local to the function. A problem arises, however, when you want to make the data of one function available to other functions. The way to do this in a structured program is to make the data global to the program, which gives any function access to it. It seems that you could use another level of scope—one that would make your data global to the functions that need it—but still prevent other functions from gaining access. Encapsulation does just that.

Inheritance

Inheritance enables you to create a class that is similar to a previously defined class but that still has some of its own properties. Consider a car again. Suppose you want to create a car that has a high-speed passing gear. In a traditional program, that would require a lot of code modification. As you modified the code, you would probably introduce bugs into a tested program.

To avoid these hassles, use the object-oriented approach: Create a new class by inheritance. This new class inherits all the data and function members from the base class (the class from which the new class is derived). Of course, the new class also inherits the original class's problems, but if there's a problem with a base class, fixing it in the base class fixes it for all the classes that inherit from the base class.

Polymorphism

The last major feature of OOP is *polymorphism*. By using polymorphism, you can create new objects that perform the same functions found in the base object but that perform one or more of these functions in a different way.

For example, think of a car. (Here we go again.) All cars are the same type of object. They all start, steer, brake, and so on. However, each car may handle these tasks in a different way. The first car (okay, an Oldsmobile) may have an automatic transmission while the next (the Corvette!) may have a standard transmission. Both cars shift gears, but they do it in different ways.

In OOP, you would implement these kinds of differences using polymorphism. Yeah, it's a kind of intimidating word, but you'll feel better about it after you write a program or two that uses this technique. For now, you should be proud if you can even spell polymorf … uh … pollymore … er … pollywanna … never mind.

Writing a Class

Creating your own classes is actually pretty easy from a syntax point of view. To write the code for a simple class, you need to know only one new keyword, `Class`. For example, here's the simplest Visual Basic .NET class you can write:

```
Public Class MyClass

End Class
```

It'd be very tough to make this process any easier! This is almost exactly the same way you'd write a subroutine, except that you substitute the word Class wherever you'd use Sub. Also, the class name isn't followed by arguments in parentheses.

Believe it or not, though, Visual Basic .NET actually *does* make the process easier, because it can create the new class for you. All you have to do is select the Project menu's Add Class command, as shown in Figure 22.1.

Figure 22.1

Adding a class to a project.

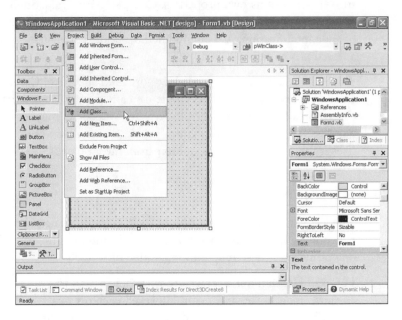

When the Add New Item dialog box appears, click the Class template and then type a new name for the class in the Name text box, as shown in Figure 22.2.

In the next chapter, you'll learn what to put between those lines that mark the beginning and end of a class. I promise you all sorts of wonderful experiences. And ice cream. Until then, let's continue in a more philosophical direction.

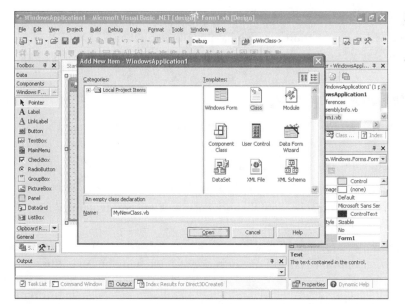

Figure 22.2

The Add New Item dialog box.

Classes Versus Objects

You can think of a class as a template for an object. You can also think of a class as a room full of students, but that won't help you here. In order to take advantage of your new class, you must first create an object of the class, as shown in this example:

```
Dim myObject As MyClass = New MyClass()
```

Here, `myObject` is the name of the object you're creating from the class, and `MyClass` is the name of the class from which you're creating the object. Whew. Does this make sense? Think of a car. No, just kidding. Think of a blueprint for a dog house. The blueprint tells you everything you know about how to build the dog house—except how to use a hammer and how many six-packs you'll need to make it through to the end of the project. You take that blueprint, and using it as a guide, you build a dog house.

Classes and objects work the same way, except that you won't bash your thumb with a hammer when you're building an object from a class. The class you write is the blueprint the computer uses to build objects. When you ask the computer to create an object, the computer goes down to the hardware store ... whoops, I'm still thinking about dog houses. When you ask the computer to make an object from a class, the computer takes the instructions you provided (the class) and creates the object. Did I mention that you can create as many objects as you like from a single class? This is just like how you can make a whole pile of dog houses from a single blueprint. Then, not only will you have a lot of great experience bashing your thumb with a hammer, but you'll also have places for you and your friends to stay when you annoy the people who live in your real house.

The Least You Need to Know

- OOP uses classes with properties and methods instead of using functions and sub-routines.
- OOP enables you to think of program elements as objects.
- Encapsulation enables you to package both data and functions inside an object.
- Inheritance enables you to create a class that is similar to a previously defined class but that still has some of its own properties.
- Using polymorphism, you can create new objects that perform the same functions found in a base object but that perform one or more of these functions in a different way.
- To write the code for the simplest class, you need to know only one new keyword, `Class`.
- A class is a template for an object.

Chapter

23

Properties, Methods, and Events: A Class's Innards

In This Chapter

- ◆ Write a class
- ◆ Add properties to a class
- ◆ Add methods to a class
- ◆ Use classes in your programs

In the previous chapter, you got a quick overview of what classes are and why you might want to use them. Now you're ready to really dig in and see how to use object-oriented programming to improve your programs. Get your shovels!

Introducing Properties and Methods

Although the simple class you learned to add to your project in the previous chapter works (in that the program will run okay), the class doesn't do anything. To make a class useful, you need to add properties and methods. You can think of properties as being attributes of an object. For example, in the real world a car has attributes such as color and body style.

Methods, on the other hand, represent actions that can be performed with an object. Sticking with the car example, such actions might be starting the car and putting on the brakes. In this chapter, you'll learn why you need properties and methods, and you'll discover how to add them to your classes.

Properties

Conceptually, a property is nothing fancier than a variable that's contained in the class. This variable represents an attribute of the class. For example, if you created a class named Book, you might have Title and Author properties. To create the Book class and add the Title and Author properties, you might start with something like this:

```
Public Class Book
    Private Title As String
    Private Author As String
End Class
```

Because of the rules of encapsulation, properties are always private to the class. This means that code from outside the class cannot access the properties directly. This may seem like a clumsy limitation at first, until you realize that limiting direct access to properties enables the class to retain complete control over them. But, how then, I hear you asking, can a program get or set the values of the properties? I mean, they're private, dude!

The words "get" and "set" are a huge clue here. The truth is that when you declared the Title and Author strings in the previous code, you only created storage for the properties' values. To make these variables into full-fledged properties, you have to add *property procedures*, which are special kinds of methods that enable the properties to be initialized and returned from objects of the class. The following example demonstrates a property procedure for Title:

```
Public Property BookTitle() As String
    Get
        Return Title
    End Get
    Set(ByVal Value As String)
        Title = Value
    End Set
End Property
```

Here's some stuff you need to notice about this property procedure:

◆ The property procedure is declared as Public because code outside of the class must be able to call the procedure.

◆ The Property keyword identifies this method as a property procedure.

◆ As far as code outside of the class goes, the name of the property is the same as the name of the property procedure: `BookTitle`. The variable `Title` cannot be seen from outside the class and simply acts as storage for the property.

◆ Between the `Get` and `End Get` lines, the property procedure returns the property's value, which, in this case, is the value stored in the `Title` variable.

◆ The `Set` keyword is followed by a name and data type for the value that will be used to set the property's value.

◆ Between the `Set` and `End Set` lines, the procedure assigns the value received by the `Set` statement to the property's storage area, which in this case is the variable `Title`.

◆ This sure is a lot of stuff to notice!

Each property procedure is a method of the class, so it must be written as part of the class. So far, then, your `Book` class looks like this example:

```
Public Class Book
    Private Title As String
    Private Author As String

    Public Property BookTitle() As String
        Get
            Return Title
        End Get
        Set(ByVal Value As String)
            Title = Value
        End Set
    End Property

    Public Property BookAuthor() As String
        Get
            Return Author
        End Get
        Set(ByVal Value As String)
            Author = Value
        End Set
    End Property
End Class
```

If all this is making you as nervous as a cat in a swimming pool, don't sweat it. You'll get plenty of practice with this class stuff in the course of the following chapters. So, clear your head, take a deep breath, and let's move on.

Construction and Destruction Underway

The property procedures you just added to your Book class enable your programs to get or set the value of a property at any time. However, a program can set the starting values for properties when creating an object of the class. To do this, you need to write a special method called a *constructor*. A constructor is a method that gets called when your program creates an object of a class. You may remember creating an object like this:

```
Dim myObject As MyClass = New MyClass()
```

You probably don't remember writing a constructor for the MyClass class. That's because you partied too hard last night. Actually, you don't remember writing the constructor because you *didn't* write one. In this case, the class's constructor is the default constructor provided by Visual Basic .NET for all classes. (It's called the default because if it doesn't work it's "default" of Visual Basic .NET. Get it? Huh? Huh?) You can create your own constructor for a class and enable the constructor to initialize the class's properties. The following example shows what a constructor for your Book class might look like:

```
Public Sub New(ByVal Title As String, ByVal Author As String)
    Me.Title = Title
    Me.Author = Author
End Sub
```

And here's a list of stuff you should notice about the Book class's constructor:

♦ The constructor is declared as a Public subroutine. It has to be Public so that code outside of the class can call it.

♦ The constructor's name is New. This is the name you use for any class's constructor.

♦ The constructor accepts as arguments whatever values a program needs to pass into the class. In this case, the constructor accepts the title and author of the book.

♦ The constructor assigns the values it receives as arguments to the appropriate property storage areas.

♦ There isn't as much stuff in this list as there was in the last one.

The opposite of a constructor is a *destructor*. Honest. I'm not making this up. A class's destructor gets called right before your program removes an object of a class from your computer's memory. You can use a class's destructor to do any kind of clean up you need to do for the class. You know, like wiping the chocolate off little Jimmie's face and cutting the gum out of Sarah's hair. Probably, though, chocolate and gum won't have anything to do with it. (By the way, I should note here that Visual Basic .NET classes don't have destructors in the sense that other OOP languages do. However, the term destructor is often used in OOP discussions, so I'll stick with that term here.) The following example shows what your Book class's destructor might look like:

```
Public Sub dispose()
    ' Do cleanup here.
End Sub
```

And here's a list of stuff you should notice about the `Book` class's destructor:

◆ The destructor is declared as a `Public` subroutine. It has to be `Public` so that code outside of the class can call it.

◆ The destructor's name is `Dispose`. This is the name you use for any class's destructor.

◆ The destructor accepts no arguments.

◆ These lists are getting shorter all the time.

The `Book` class's destructor contains nothing but a comment because the `Book` class doesn't need to do any cleanup chores. In this case, you probably wouldn't bother writing the destructor at all, but I included it here because I wanted you to waste your time typing. No, wait! I meant to say that I included it for demonstration purposes. The following code sample shows what the `Book` class looks like now:

```
Public Class Book
    Private Title As String
    Private Author As String

    Public Sub New(ByVal Title As String, ByVal Author As String)
        Me.Title = Title
        Me.Author = Author
    End Sub

    Public Sub dispose()
        ' Do cleanup here.
    End Sub

    Public Property BookTitle() As String
        Get
            Return Title
        End Get
        Set(ByVal Value As String)
            Title = Value
        End Set
    End Property

    Public Property BookAuthor() As String
        Get
            Return Author
        End Get
```

```
        Set(ByVal Value As String)
            Author = Value
        End Set
    End Property
End Class
```

A Method to the Madness

Suppose that the Book class is going to be used for managing computer-based electronic books. Along with the class's properties then, you're also going to need methods that perform actions on the book. For example, you may want the reader to be able to turn a page in the book in order to view the next chunk of the book's text. You perform actions in classes by writing *methods*.

A method is very similar to the other types of procedures you've written in Visual Basic .NET. The main difference is that a method is encapsulated (remember that cool word?) in a class and so has access to the class's properties. The following snippet presents a method you might write to turn a page of the book:

```
Public Sub TurnPage()
    Page = Page + 1
    If Page = 501 Then Page = 1
End Sub
```

Of course, all this method really does is update a variable called Page. There's no program code here to actually display text on the screen. We'll leave that to your imagination. The important thing here is that the method is declared as Public so code outside of the class can call it. Also, notice that the Book class doesn't have a variable named Page, so what's it doing in the TurnPage method?

Obviously (well, obviously if you're as brilliant as you and I are), you need to add the Page variable to the class, and the best way to do this is to create a new property. However, this time you'll create a *read-only property*, which is a property that the program can look at but not change. The following snippet shows the new property's storage variable and property procedure:

```
Private Page As Integer
Public ReadOnly Property BookPage() As Integer
    Get
        Return Page
    End Get
End Property
```

This property procedure is different from the others you've written in this chapter in two significant ways:

♦ The addition of the ReadOnly keyword.

♦ No Set program code, only Get.

Besides adding the Page variable to the class, you'll also need to set it to a starting value. You can do that in the class's constructor. However, you don't need to add it to the constructor's arguments, because the program won't be able to set the page number when creating a book object. Why? Because you're not going to let it! So, here's the final Book class:

```
Public Class Book
    Private Title As String
    Private Author As String
    Private Page As Integer

    Public Sub New(ByVal Title As String, ByVal Author As String)
        Me.Title = Title
        Me.Author = Author
        Page = 1
    End Sub

    Public Sub dispose()
        ' Do cleanup here.
    End Sub

    Public Sub TurnPage()
        Page = Page + 1
        If Page = 101 Then Page = 1
    End Sub

    Public Property BookTitle() As String
        Get
            Return Title
        End Get
        Set(ByVal Value As String)
            Title = Value
        End Set
    End Property

    Public Property BookAuthor() As String
        Get
            Return Author
        End Get
```

By the Way

Classes can have three types of properties: read/write, read-only, and write-only. The most common properties are read/write, which enable a program to read the property's value as well as set the value. Read-only properties, on the other hand, can only be read from outside the class and can be set only by the class itself. Write-only properties are just the opposite. They can be set from outside the class, but can be read only from within the class. Frankly, I've never run into a case when I wanted a write-only property in a class.

```
        Set(ByVal Value As String)
            Author = Value
        End Set
    End Property

    Public ReadOnly Property BookPage() As Integer
        Get
            Return Page
        End Get
    End Property
End Class
```

Reading Your Books

Now, you've created Visual Basic .NET source code that tells Visual Basic what a book object is like. Next, you can create book objects from the class and "read" them on screen. To do this, follow these steps:

1. Start a new Visual Basic .NET project using the Windows Application template, and name the application Classes. Add the controls shown in Figure 23.1 to the application's form. (Make sure that you add GroupBox1 to the form before you add the controls that the group box holds. This ensures that the group box "owns" the controls.)

Figure 23.1

The Classes application's form.

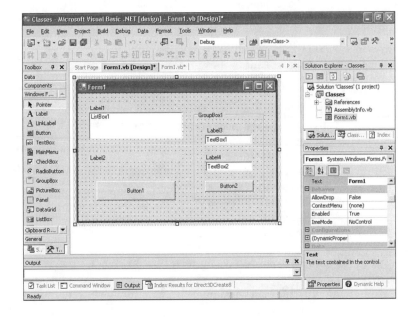

2. Double-click the form, and add the following lines to the `Form1_Load` procedure that Visual Studio starts for you:

```
Label1.Text = "Current Book"
Label2.Text = "You are reading page #0"
Label3.Text = "Title"
Label4.Text = "Author"
ListBox1.Text = ""
TextBox1.Text = ""
TextBox2.Text = ""
GroupBox1.Text = "Add New Book"
Button1.Text = "Turn Page"
Button2.Text = "Add Book"
bookCount = 0
currentBookNum = -1
currentBook = Nothing
```

3. Add the following lines near the top of the program, right before the `Form1_Load` procedure:

```
Const MAXBOOKS = 5
Dim books(MAXBOOKS-1) As Book
Dim bookCount As Integer
Dim currentBookNum As Integer
Dim currentBook As Book
```

4. Double-click the `Button1` control and add the following lines to the `Button1_Click` procedure that Visual Studio starts for you:

```
If currentBook Is Nothing Then
    MessageBox.Show("Please select a book first.")
Else
    currentBook.TurnPage()
    Label2.Text = "You are reading page #" & currentBook.BookPage
End If
```

5. Double-click the `Button2` control and add the following lines to the `Button2_Click` procedure that Visual Studio starts for you:

```
If bookCount < MAXBOOKS And TextBox1.Text <> "" Then
    Dim title As String = TextBox1.Text
    Dim author As String = TextBox2.Text
    books(bookCount) = New Book(title, author)
    bookCount = bookCount + 1
    ListBox1.Items.Add(title)
```

```
    Else
        MessageBox.Show("Can't add book.")
    End If
    TextBox1.Text = ""
    TextBox2.Text = ""
```

6. Double-click the `ListBox1` control, and add the following lines to the `ListBox1_SelectedIndexChanged` procedure that Visual Studio starts for you:

```
currentBookNum = ListBox1.SelectedIndex()
currentBook = books(currentBookNum)
Label2.Text = "You are reading page #" & currentBook.BookPage
```

7. Add a class module to the project, as you learned to do earlier in this chapter. Name the class `Book`, and complete it with the code from the `Book` class, as shown in Figure 23.2.

Figure 23.2

Adding the Book class to the project.

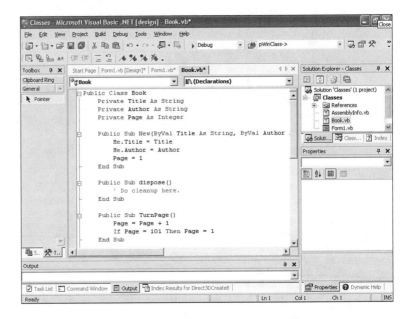

8. When the project is complete, save your work, and run the program. When you do, you see the window shown in Figure 23.3.

9. Type the title and author of a book into the text boxes on the right, and click the Add Book button. The book then appears in the list box. You can add up to five books to the list.

10. After adding at least two books to the list, select a book by clicking it. When you do, the program informs you that you are reading page 1.

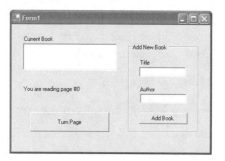

Figure 23.3

The running Classes application.

11. Click the Turn Page button to "read" the book. Each click of the button advances the book's current page.

12. Select another book in the list and do the same thing. Switch between books and notice how every book remembers the last page read. Digital bookmarks are way better than the paper kind, huh? You could try to save your place by folding over the corner of your monitor, but I wouldn't suggest it.

Figure 23.4 shows what the application looks like with a few books added to the list and the current book having been read to page 15.

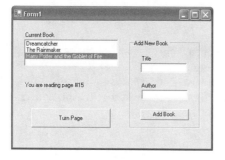

Figure 23.4

Reading books with the Classes application.

The Stuff You Need to Know

A lot of the Classes program is straight-forward Visual Basic .NET programming, but there are a few points worth going over. First, notice how the program stores its Book objects in an array:

```
Dim books(MAXBOOKS-1) As Book
```

Because the program sets the constant MAXBOOKS to 5, the books array can hold five Book objects, numbered 0 through 4. The program also declares a Book object for the book the user is currently reading:

```
Dim currentBook As Book
```

When the user selects a book, the list box control's `SelectedIndexChanged` event handler gets called. (You'll learn more about list boxes in Chapter 28, "List Controls: It's the User's Choice.") There, the program gets the selected book's number from the list box:

```
currentBookNum = ListBox1.SelectedIndex()
```

The program uses the book number to get the current book from the array:

```
currentBook = books(currentBookNum)
```

Finally, the program displays the current `Book` object's last-read page, which it gets from the, `BookPage` property:

```
Label4.Text = "You are reading page #" & currentBook.BookPage
```

Clicking the Turn Page button causes Visual Basic .NET to call the button's `Click` event handler, which first makes sure that the user has chosen a book to read:

```
If currentBook Is Nothing Then
    MessageBox.Show("Please select a book first.")
```

The `Nothing` keyword represents the value an object has when it hasn't yet been set.

If the user has selected a book, the program calls the `Book` object's `TurnPage` method to advance the page count and displays the new current page in the window:

```
currentBook.TurnPage()
Label4.Text = "You are reading page #" & currentBook.BookPage
```

Adding, a `Book` object to the list occurs when the user clicks the Add Book button. In that button's `Click` procedure, the program first makes sure that the book array has room and that the user has typed a book title into the text box:

```
If bookCount < MAXBOOKS And TextBox1.Text <> "" Then
```

If everything checks out, the program creates a new `Book` object with the title and author supplied by the user, adding the book to the `Book` array:

```
Dim title As String = TextBox1.Text
Dim author As String = TextBox2.Text
books(bookCount) = New Book(title, author)
```

After updating the book count, the program adds the new book's title to the list box (again, you'll learn more about list boxes in Chapter 28):

```
bookCount = bookCount + 1
ListBox1.Items.Add(title)
```

The rest of the program you should be able to understand on your own. If you have trouble, take two button controls and call me in the, morning.

The Least You Need to Know

- ◆ You can think of properties as being attributes of an object.
- ◆ Methods represent actions that can be performed with an object.
- ◆ Because of the rules of encapsulation, properties are always private to the class.
- ◆ Classes implement property procedures for getting and setting the value of the properties.
- ◆ Property procedures are declared as `Public` because code outside of the class must be able to call the procedure.
- ◆ The name of a property is the same as the name of its property procedure.
- ◆ A constructor is a method that gets called when your program creates an object of a class.
- ◆ A constructor is declared as a `Public` subroutine. It has to be `Public` so that code outside of the class can call it.
- ◆ The constructor's name is always `New`.
- ◆ The constructor accepts as arguments whatever values a program needs to pass into the class.
- ◆ A class's destructor gets called right before your program removes an object of a class from your computer's memory.
- ◆ You can use a class's destructor to do any kind of cleanup you need to do for the class.
- ◆ The destructor is declared as a `Public` subroutine. It has to be `Public` so that code outside of the class can call it.
- ◆ The destructor's name is `Dispose`.
- ◆ The destructor accepts no arguments.

Chapter 24

Inheritance: Reproduction the Visual Basic .NET Way

In This Chapter

- ◆ Write a base class
- ◆ Write derived classes using inheritance
- ◆ Design class hierarchies

You now have a good idea of what classes are and how they work. However, you can't believe how much more there is to learn about classes. In fact, I could write an entire book on classes alone. You'll be glad to hear, however, that you don't have to know *that* much about classes. You do need to know about a little thing called inheritance, though—and, no, I'm not referring to that house you think Grandma Sarah is going to leave you.

The Basics of Inheritance

One of the great things about classes is the way they can help you reuse code. That is, once you have created and perfected a class, you can use it again and again, knowing that it'll work fine every time. However, there's even more to the code-reuse abilities of classes than that. You can use an existing class as the starting point for a new class that's similar to the starting class, but that has new abilities. To see how this works, look at the following simple Visual Basic .NET class:

```
Public Class Class1
    Private num As Integer
    Public Property Number() As Integer
        Get
            Return num
        End Get
        Set(ByVal Value As Integer)
            num = Value
        End Set
    End Property
End Class
```

This class has a single property named `Number` that the class stores in the private class variable `num`. The `Get` and `Set` parts of the property procedure enable a program to get and set the property's value. If you want to test this class, you could pay a big company tons of money to perform months of research; or you could just write these program lines:

```
Dim Class1Obj As New Class1()
Class1Obj.Number = 10
Dim n = Class1Obj.Number
MessageBox.Show(n)
```

Here's what these lines do:

1   Creates an object of the `Class1` class.

2   Sets the object's `Number` property to 10.

3   Gets the value of the `Number` property.

4   Displays the value of the `Number` property in a message box.

Now, write a new class that looks like this:

```
Public Class Class2
    Inherits Class1
End Class
```

See that line `Inherits Class1`? That line tells VB that you want `Class2` to start off exactly like `Class1`. What does this mean to you? It means that, even though you haven't written the program lines needed to create a property named `Number`, `Class2` has that property, anyway. `Class2` inherits the `Number` property from `Class1`. Don't believe me? I'll prove it, as soon as you stop standing on your head and start paying attention! The following program lines put `Class2` to the test:

```
Dim Class2Obj As New Class2()
Class2Obj.Number = 15
Dim n = Class2Obj.Number
MessageBox.Show(n)
```

Here's what these lines do:

1   Creates an object of the Class2 class.

2   Sets the object's Number property to 15.

3   Gets the value of the Number property.

4   Displays the value of the Number property in a message box.

Now both Class1 and Class2 are identical. The more astute among you will be asking, "What good are two classes that are exactly alike?"

The whole point of this inheritance stuff is not to make classes that are exactly alike, but rather to start with a tested class and build new features into it. Suppose, for example, you want a class just like Class1, except you also need a property named Number2. Here's what you could write:

```
Public Class Class2
    Inherits Class1
    Private num2 As Integer
    Public Property Number2() As Integer
        Get
            Return num2
        End Get
        Set(ByVal Value As Integer)
            num2 = Value
        End Set
    End Property
End Class
```

Now, Class2 has two properties, Number and Number2. Class2 inherits Number from Class1 and then defines the new property Number2 within the class. Here's the proof:

```
Dim Class2Obj As New Class2()
Class2Obj.Number = 15
Class2Obj.Number2 = 25
Dim n = Class2Obj.Number
Dim n2 = Class2Obj.Number2
MessageBox.Show(n)
MessageBox.Show(n2)
```

Techno Talk

When using inheritance with classes, the starting class is called the **base class**, and the class that inherits from the base class is called the **derived class**.

Here's what these lines do:

1 Creates an object of the Class2 class.

2 Sets the object's Number property to 15.

3 Sets the object's Number2 property to 25.

4 Gets the value of the Number property.

5 Gets the value of the Number2 property.

6 Displays the value of the Number property in a message box.

7 Displays the value of the Number2 property in a message box.

Inheritance for Real

Okay, enough of the theoretical stuff. I don't know about you, but I'm getting a headache. Let's put object-oriented programming with inheritance to work in an actual program.

Start a new Visual Basic .NET project (using the Windows Application template) named Inheritance, and add a single button to the form, as shown in Figure 24.1.

Figure 24.1

The form with its button.

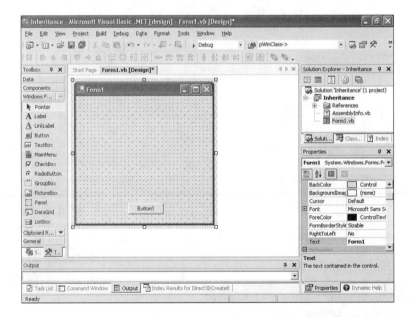

Now, you need to decide what kind of class you want to write. A class hierarchy, which is what programmers call a tree of classes that inherit from each other, can be a little tricky. The base class of the hierarchy should comprise all the features that all the derived classes will have in common. After all, it doesn't make sense for a class to inherit things it doesn't need (you know, like that extra eyeball in the back of your head). It also doesn't make sense to duplicate something in all the classes when all you have to do is put it in the base class where all the other classes will automatically get it. You'll probably have to read this paragraph again. It really does make sense. I promise.

Let's start with a class called Shape from which you can create more specific classes like Rectangle and Circle. Let's say that all shapes in your class hierarchy will have the following properties:

◆ PositionX: The shape's horizontal position.

◆ PositionY: The shape's vertical position.

To create this base class, first start a new class module named Shape, as shown in Figure 24.2.

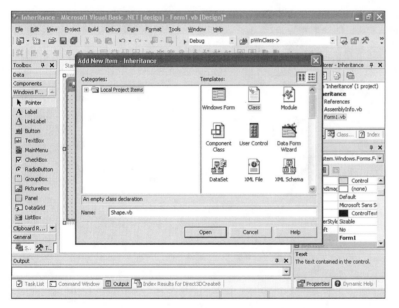

Figure 24.2

Add the Shape *class to the project.*

Now, type these program lines into the new Shape class (between the Public Class Shape and End Class lines, of course):

```
Private posx As Integer
Private posy As Integer
Public Property PositionX() As Integer
    Get
        Return posx
    End Get
    Set(ByVal Value As Integer)
        posx = Value
    End Set
```

```
End Property
Public Property PositionY() As Integer
    Get
        Return posy
    End Get
    Set(ByVal Value As Integer)
        posy = Value
    End Set
End Property
```

Now that you've got your base class, you can create a `Rectangle` class by inheriting from `Shape`. To do this, first start a new class module named Rectangle, and then type these program lines into it:

```
Inherits Shape
Private w As Integer
Private h As Integer
Public Property Width() As Integer
    Get
        Return w
    End Get
    Set(ByVal Value As Integer)
        w = Value
    End Set
End Property
Public Property Height() As Integer
    Get
        Return h
    End Get
    Set(ByVal Value As Integer)
        h = Value
    End Set
End Property
```

As you can see from this class, a `Rectangle` object has—besides the `PositionX` and `PositionY` properties it inherited from `Shape`—the new properties `Width` and `Height`, which are necessary in order to draw a rectangle.

Now, how about a `Circle` class? To draw a circle, you don't need width and height. In a circle, width and height are the same value, a value called diameter. So, create a new class module named `Circle` that looks like this:

```
Inherits Shape
Private d As Integer
Public Property Diameter() As Integer
```

```
    Get
        Return d
    End Get
    Set(ByVal Value As Integer)
        d = Value
    End Set
End Property
```

Now, it's time to test your new classes. Double-click the form's button control, and add the following program lines to the Click event handler:

```
Dim s As New Shape()
Dim r As New Rectangle()
Dim c As New Circle()
s.PositionX = 10
s.PositionY = 15
r.PositionX = 20
r.PositionY = 25
r.Width = 20
r.Height = 25
c.PositionX = 50
c.PositionY = 75
c.Diameter = 30
MessageBox.Show(s.ToString() & " : " & _
    s.PositionX & " : " & s.PositionY)
MessageBox.Show(r.ToString() & " : " & _
    r.PositionX & " : " & r.PositionY & " : " & _
    r.Width & " : " & r.Height)
MessageBox.Show(c.ToString() & " : " & _
    c.PositionX & " : " & c.PositionY & " : " & _
    c.Diameter)
```

Check This Out

If you had a special type of circle you wanted to draw, you could inherit a new class from the general Circle class. For example, you might create a class called SolidCircle. In this way, you can build a circle class hierarchy with as many classes as you need, all those classes tracing their chain of inheritance all the way back to Shape.

Finally, run the program and click the form's button. When you do, the program creates objects of each of the classes and displays the object values in message boxes, as shown in Figure 24.3.

Figure 24.3

The running Inheritance program.

You haven't seen the end of these shape classes. In the next chapter, you'll use them to learn even more about object-oriented programming.

The Least You Need to Know

♦ One of the great things about classes is the way they can help you reuse code.

♦ With inheritance, you can use an existing class as the starting point for a new class that's similar to the starting class, but that has new abilities.

♦ You use the `Inherits` keyword to tell Visual Basic .NET that you want a class to inherit the properties and methods of another class.

♦ When a class inherits from another class, the new class automatically gets the properties and methods of the original class.

♦ In object-oriented programming, the starting class in a hierarchy is called the base class, and the classes that inherit from the base class are called derived classes.

♦ The base class of a class hierarchy should comprise all the features that the derived classes will have in common.

Chapter 25

Polymorphism: Teaching Objects Special Tricks

In This Chapter

- ◆ Understand polymorphism
- ◆ Write polymorphic classes
- ◆ Program a class hierarchy

Okay, folks, get your thinking caps polished and perched on top of your pointy little heads, because this will probably be the toughest chapter in the book. So far, you've learned quite a bit about classes and object-oriented programming. If you're confused about any of that stuff, you should probably reread the previous two chapters before you start on this one. In this chapter, you're not only going to learn about something called polymorphism (there's a scary word for you), but you're also going to put all your knowledge of classes to the test as you build on the shape classes you started with in Chapter 23, "Properties, Methods, and Events: A Class's Innards."

Getting Polymorphic

Let's get right to the scary stuff first—you know, that word polymorphism that just gave you goose bumps and a headache. The idea of polymorphism really isn't all that hard to understand. Polymorphism is just the ability to create objects that perform the same functions in different ways. For example, think about the Shape, Rectangle, and Circle classes you wrote in the previous chapter. Suppose now that you not only want to store data such as position and size in these classes, but that you also want to draw the shapes on the screen. To do this, you plan to add a method called Draw to each class. However, you draw a circle differently than you draw a rectangle, right? This is an example of performing the same function—in this case, drawing a shape—in different ways.

Polymorphism on the Loose

The best way to explore polymorphism is to see it in action, so let's start off this chapter by creating a new Visual Basic .NET project named Shapes, then add a single button to the top of the form.

Now, you're ready to start writing the program. Because all the shapes you'll use in the program derive from the Shape base class, you'll start there. First, add a new class module to the program named Shape. When the class's code window appears, complete the class so that it looks like this:

```
Public MustInherit Class Shape
    Private posx As Integer
    Private posy As Integer

    Sub New(ByVal x As Integer, ByVal y As Integer)
        posx = x
        posy = y
    End Sub

    Public Property PositionX() As Integer
        Get
            Return posx
        End Get
        Set(ByVal Value As Integer)
            posx = Value
        End Set
    End Property

    Public Property PositionY() As Integer
        Get
            Return posy
        End Get
        Set(ByVal Value As Integer)
            posy = Value
        End Set
    End Property
```

```
    MustOverride Sub Draw(ByVal g As Graphics)
End Class
```

If you're paying attention, you will have noticed a few new things about this class as compared to the version you wrote in Chapter 24, "Inheritance: Reproduction the Visual Basic .NET Way." For example, the first line of the class definition includes the MustInherit keyword:

```
Public MustInherit Class Shape
```

This keyword tells Visual Basic .NET that no program will be allowed to create a Shape object. Instead, programs must inherit classes from Shape and then create objects from those classes. Why? Because the Shape class is so general that it doesn't even represent a real object. I mean, how would you draw it? What does it look like? The only reason we have the Shape class is to provide a storage place for the properties and methods that are common to all shapes, like circles and rectangles. The MustInherit keyword ensures that the Shape class is used only in this way.

The next thing to notice is that the Shape class now has a constructor:

```
Sub New(ByVal x As Integer, ByVal y As Integer)
    posx = x
    posy = y
End Sub
```

You learned about constructors in Chapter 23. In case you've forgotten, a constructor provides a place for the Shape class to initialize itself. By providing the constructor with the x and y parameters, a program can create a Shape object like this:

```
Dim s = New Shape(15, 25)
```

Of course, thanks to the MustInherit keyword, no program can create a Shape object directly, so this program line would not compile. But you get the point. You'll soon see the right way to call the Shape class's constructor.

The last new thing in the Shape class is this line:

```
    MustOverride Sub Draw(ByVal g As Graphics)
```

See the MustOverride keyword? This keyword tells Visual Basic .NET that every class that uses Shape as a base class must define a Draw method that matches the declaration in the Shape class. That is, the method must be called Draw and must accept a Graphics object as its single parameter. You're confused, right? Don't worry about it. You'll see what I mean when you write the Draw method in other classes. In fact, let's write one of those classes right now.

A Shape That Actually Does Something

Add a new class module named Rectangle to your project, and then complete the class so that it looks like this:

```
Public Class Rectangle
    Inherits Shape
    Private w As Integer
    Private h As Integer

    Sub New(ByVal x As Integer, ByVal y As Integer, _
            ByVal w As Integer, ByVal h As Integer)
        MyBase.New(x, y)
        Me.w = w
        Me.h = h
    End Sub

    Public Property Width() As Integer
        Get
            Return w
        End Get
        Set(ByVal Value As Integer)
            w = Value
        End Set
    End Property
    Public Property Height() As Integer
        Get
            Return h
        End Get
        Set(ByVal Value As Integer)
            h = Value
        End Set
    End Property

    Overrides Sub Draw(ByVal g As Graphics)
        g.DrawRectangle(Pens.Black, PositionX, PositionY, w, h)
    End Sub
End Class
```

This Rectangle class is the same as the one you wrote in Chapter 24, except it now has a constructor, and it also has the Draw method.

Look at the constructor. In order to create a Rectangle object, the program needs to provide the rectangle's horizontal (PositionX) and vertical (PositionY) positions as well as its width and height. The Rectangle class inherits its PositionX and PositionY properties from the Shape class. The Width and Height properties, on the other hand, are defined right in the Rectangle class itself.

The Base Class Again

Splitting the properties between two classes this way leads to a problem. How can you initialize the rectangle's `PositionX` and `PositionY` properties when they are located somewhere else? Easy! The first line in the constructor of a derived class always calls the base class's constructor with the values required to initialize the base class's properties:

```
MyBase.New(x, y)
```

As you can see, you don't need to use the base class's actual name, but should type `MyBase.New` instead. Visual Basic .NET already knows the base class's name. Just be sure to include the right arguments, which, in this case, are the values for the `PositionX` and `PositionY` properties. After the call to the base class's constructor executes, the base class's inheritable properties are initialized and ready to go.

As for the properties that are unique to the `Rectangle` class, you initialize them in the constructor exactly as you learned in Chapter 23:

```
Me.w = w
Me.h = h
```

The Key to Polymorphism

Now the `Rectangle` class's properties are ready, but the class is required to define the `Draw` method, remember? Here's what that method looks like:

```
Overrides Sub Draw(ByVal g As Graphics)
    g.DrawRectangle(Pens.Black, PositionX, PositionY, w, h)
End Sub
```

The `Overrides` keyword tells Visual Basic .NET that this function is a replacement for a function of the same name in the base class. Because this version of `Draw` is in the `Rectangle` class, it must draw a rectangle using the `Rectangle` class's properties. That, of course, is what the call to `Draw` does. The `Draw` method will get its `Graphics` object when the main program calls the method.

Another Shape That Does Something

Now, add a `Circle` class to the program. Create a new class module named Circle, and complete the module so that it looks like this:

```
Public Class Circle
    Inherits Shape
    Private d As Integer
```

```
    Public Sub New(ByVal x As Integer, ByVal y As Integer, _
            ByVal d As Integer)
        MyBase.New(x, y)
        Me.d = d
    End Sub

    Public Property Diameter() As Integer
        Get
            Return d
        End Get
        Set(ByVal Value As Integer)
            d = Value
        End Set
    End Property

    Overrides Sub Draw(ByVal g As Graphics)
        g.DrawEllipse(Pens.Black, PositionX, PositionY, d, d)
    End Sub
End Class
```

This `Circle` class is just like the `Circle` class from Chapter 24 except, like the `Rectangle` class, it now has a constructor and a `Draw` method. If you're slow on the draw today, please notice that the `Circle` class's `Draw` method draws a circle rather than a rectangle.

Another Branch on the Family Tree

Now, let's go one step further with the shape classes. Let's add a specialized circle shape called `FilledCircle`. A filled circle shape will be exactly like a regular circle shape, except that the circle will be drawn in a solid color, rather than just as an outline. Because a `FilledCircle` object is so much like a `Circle` object, you'll derive `FilledCircle` from `Circle`.

Add a new class module named `FilledCircle` to your program, and complete the class so that it looks like this:

```
Public Class FilledCircle
    Inherits Circle
    Private b As Brush

    Public Sub New(ByVal x As Integer, ByVal y As Integer, _
            ByVal d As Integer, ByVal b As Brush)
        MyBase.New(x, y, d)
        Me.b = b
    End Sub
```

```
    Public Property FillColor() As Brush
        Get
            Return b
        End Get
        Set(ByVal Value As Brush)
            b = Value
        End Set
    End Property

    Overrides Sub Draw(ByVal g As Graphics)
        g.FillEllipse(b, PositionX, PositionY, _
            Diameter, Diameter)
    End Sub
End Class
```

Here are a few things to notice about the new `FilledCircle` class:

◆ It inherits from the `Circle` class.

◆ The constructor calls `MyBase.New`. In this case, `MyBase.New` refers to `Circle.New`. Inside `Circle.New`, the first line is also `MyBase.New`, but this time `MyBase.New` refers to `Shape.New`. This is how the values for `PositionX` and `PositionY` make it all the way back to `Shape`.

◆ The required `Draw` method draws a filled circle rather than an outlined circle.

So now you have a class inheritance tree that looks like the one shown in Figure 25.1.

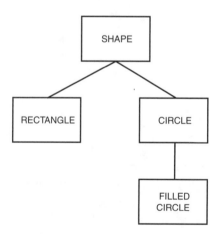

Figure 25.1

The Shape inheritance tree.

Putting It All to Work

With all your classes in place, it's time to put them to work. Double-click the form's button and add the following program lines to the `Click` event procedure:

```
Dim myRectangle As New Rectangle(20, 25, 20, 25)
Dim myCircle As New Circle(50, 75, 50)
Dim myFilledCircle As New FilledCircle(70, 195, 40, Brushes.Red)
Dim g As Graphics = CreateGraphics()
myRectangle.Draw(g)
myCircle.Draw(g)
myFilledCircle.Draw(g)
myRectangle.PositionX = 200
myRectangle.PositionY = 100
myRectangle.Width = 75
myRectangle.Height = 50
myRectangle.Draw(g)
myCircle.PositionX = 150
myCircle.PositionY = 125
myCircle.Diameter = 100
myCircle.Draw(g)
myFilledCircle.PositionX = 150
myFilledCircle.PositionY = 30
myFilledCircle.Diameter = 60
myFilledCircle.FillColor = Brushes.Blue
myFilledCircle.Draw(g)
```

Now you can run the program. When you do, click the button, and you'll see the window shown in Figure 25.2.

Figure 25.2

The running Shapes program.

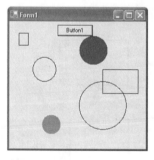

There's nothing too tricky going on in the main program. First, it creates `Rectangle`, `Circle`, and `FilledCircle` objects after which the program gets a `Graphics` object to use for drawing. By calling each object's `Draw` method, the associated shape appears on the screen. The program then changes the shapes' properties and calls their `Draw` methods once again, displaying a new set of shapes.

To make sure you have this class stuff down, see if you can add a `FillRectangle` class to the hierarchy. Hint: to draw a filled rectangle, call the Graphics object's `FillRectangle` method. Look `FillRectangle` up in your online documentation to get the details.

The Least You Need to Know

- Polymorphism is the ability to create objects that perform the same functions in different ways.

- The `MustInherit` keyword tells Visual Basic .NET that no program will be allowed to create a `Shape` object directly. Instead, programs must inherit classes from `Shape` and then create objects from those classes.

- Declaring a method as `MustOverride` tells Visual Basic .NET that every derived class must define the method.

- In a derived class, the class's constructor should call the base class's constructor using the `MyBase.New()` call.

- The `Overrides` keyword tells Visual Basic .NET that the function being defined is a replacement for a function of the same name in the base class.

Part 5

Writing Windows Applications

Knowing the Visual Basic programming language is only half the battle (okay, maybe three-quarters of the battle). You also need to know how to build a user interface for your programs using the controls provided by Visual Basic .NET programming environment. Here, you'll learn about all sorts of cool stuff like forms, buttons, list boxes, scroll bars, timers, and menus. All right!

Chapter **26**

Button Controls: Clicking Your Way to Success

In This Chapter

- ◆ Learn more about Button controls
- ◆ See how to use CheckBox controls to represent application options
- ◆ Discover RadioButton controls

Button controls are nothing new to you. You've used one or more of them in almost every Visual Basic .NET program so far. What you don't know is that there is a lot more to Button controls than just a Click event procedure. In fact, there are more kinds of buttons than just Button controls; there are also RadioButton and CheckBox controls, which are also considered to be buttons. In this chapter, you get a chance to go button crazy, so put on your party hat.

Digging Into Button Controls

Button controls are the kind of button that you think of when you think of the word "button." That is, just like buttons in the real world, you press these on-screen buttons to issue commands to the device. However, because it's very difficult to get flesh and bone into a computer's memory, you have to use a magical device called a mouse to click an on-screen button. Of course, you already know all this—unless you're one of those folks who always has sore fingers from poking at on-screen buttons.

In your previous Visual Basic .NET programs, you've learned to respond to button clicks in the Button control's `Click` event procedure. This is the most common way to handle buttons. There's a lot more you can do with a button, however, considering that it has dozens of properties, methods, and events—all this power in that little rectangle. What a bargain!

I won't force you to use all those properties, methods, and events—you'll only examine some of the more useful ones. Along the way, you'll see how versatile a button can really be.

Button Properties

You'll probably use button properties more than its methods and events. In fact, that's likely to be the case with most controls. Table 26.1 lists some of the Button control's more useful properties.

Table 26.1 Button Control Properties

Property	Description
BackColor	Represents the button's background color. For this property to have an effect, the button's `Style` property must be set to graphical.
Enabled	Represents whether the user can interact with the button.
FlatStyle	Represents whether the button is standard or flat.
ForeColor	Represents the color of the button's text.
Height	Represents the button's height.
Image	Represents the image that's displayed in the button.
Left	Represents the position of the button's left edge.
Text	Represents the button's text.
Top	Represents the position of the button's top edge.
Visible	Represents whether the button is visible.
Width	Represents the button's width.

The following program demonstrates a few of the Button control's properties.

1. Start a new Visual Basic .NET project named Buttons, and then place four Button controls on the form, as shown in Figure 26.1.

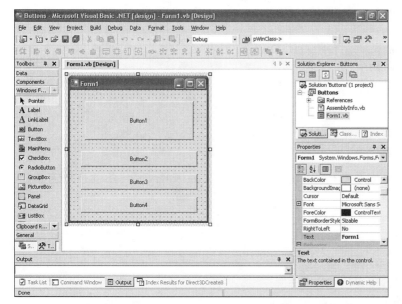

Figure 26.1

Position the buttons as shown in this figure.

2. Double-click the form to bring up the Visual Basic .NET code window, and type the following program lines into the Load procedure (Visual Basic .NET will have already started the Form1_Load procedure for you):

```
Button1.Text = "TEST BUTTON"
Button2.Text = "Disable Button"
Button3.Text = "Change Button Color"
Button4.Text = "Change Button Size"
```

3. Double-click the Button1 Button control, and type the following program line into the Click procedure (Visual Basic .NET will have already started the Button1_Click procedure for you):

```
MessageBox.Show("Yep, the button works.")
```

4. Double-click the Button2 Button control, and type the following program lines into its Click procedure:

```
If Button1.Enabled = True Then
    Button1.Enabled = False
    Button2.Text = "Enable Button"
Else
    Button1.Enabled = True
    Button2.Text = "Disable Button"
End If
```

5. Double-click the Button3 Button control, and type the following program lines into its Click procedure:

```
Static isButtonBlue As Boolean = False
If isButtonBlue Then
    Button1.BackColor = Color.Red
Else
    Button1.BackColor = Color.Blue
End If
isButtonBlue = Not isButtonBlue
```

6. Double-click the Button4 Button control, and type the following program lines into its Click procedure:

```
If Button1.Height = 80 Then
    Button1.Height = 40
    Button1.Width = 100
    Button1.Top = 40
    Button1.Left = 80
Else
    Button1.Height = 80
    Button1.Width = 250
    Button1.Top = 20
    Button1.Left = 30
End If
```

7. Save your work, and run the program. When you do, the main window appears. To prove that the Button1 button is working normally, give it a click. A message box appears.

8. Dismiss the message box, and click the Disable Button button. Visual Basic .NET disables the Button1 button; if you try to click it, nothing will happen.

9. Click the Enable button (it used to be the Disable button; fancy trickery, eh?) to reenable the Button1 button. Now the button will work normally.

10. Click the Change Color button to toggle the button's background color between red and blue.

11. Click the Change Button Size button to toggle between two button sizes. Figure 26.2 shows the application when the Button1 button is set to its small size with a red background.

Figure 26.2

Here's the button sample program in action.

If you look at the `Button3_Click` procedure, you'll see this line:

```
Static isButtonBlue As Boolean = False
```

What the heck is that `Static` keyword? The `Static` keyword takes the place of `Dim`, but it has a special effect on the variable. When you use `Dim` to declare a variable inside a procedure, the program forgets all about the variable when the procedure ends. When you declare the variable as `Static`, the program remembers the variable's value, even when the procedure ends.

In the case of `isButtonBlue`, you have a variable that appears only in Button3's `Click` procedure. Because the variable is needed nowhere else in the program, it's kind of silly to declare it as a global variable, yet the program needs to remember the variable's value. The solution is to make the variable `Static`, which enables the variable to be declared where it's used, but also to remember its value from one procedure call to the next.

Button Methods

The Button control features seven methods, but only two are of interest to a Visual Basic .NET novice. Those methods are `Hide` and `Show`, which make the button invisible or visible, respectively.

To see `Hide` and `Show` in action, replace the contents of your program's `Button4_Click` event procedure with the following:

```
If Button1.Visible Then
    Button1.Hide()
Else
    Button1.Show()
End If
```

You'll also need to go to the program's `Form1_Load` procedure, and change the following line:

```
Button4.Text = "Change Button Size"
```

to this line:

```
Button4.Text = "Change Button Visibility"
```

Now, when you run the program, you can use the lower button to make the upper button appear and disappear. Calling the `Hide` method changes the value of the button's `Visible` property to false whereas calling the `Show` method changes the `Visible` property to true.

Button Events

The Button control responds to lots of different events. However, none except `Click` is likely to be useful to you for a while. Once you become a Visual Basic .NET guru, you might want to check into some of the other events. Even then, however, `Click` will be the one you use 99 percent of the time.

Checking Out CheckBox Controls

If you've been using Windows for any time at all, you've seen almost as many CheckBox controls as Button controls in windows, dialog boxes, and property sheets. CheckBox controls are usually used to represent program options. When you click the control, a checkmark appears in its box, indicating that the associated option is active. A second click removes the checkmark and turns off the option. Figure 26.3 shows several CheckBox controls in a window.

Figure 26.3

CheckBox controls enable a user to select options.

Like Button controls, CheckBox controls have dozens of properties, methods, and events. As with Button controls, however, you'll only need to master a few of these controls.

CheckBox Properties

The CheckBox control has even more properties than the Button control. Table 26.2 lists some of the more useful CheckBox control properties.

Table 26.2   CheckBox Control Properties

Property	Description
Appearance	Represents whether the check box looks like a traditional check box or like a button.
BackColor	Represents the check box's background color.
Checked	Represents whether or not the box is checked.
Enabled	Represents whether the user can interact with the check box.
ForeColor	Represents the color of the check box's text.
Height	Represents the check box's height.
Image	Represents the image that's displayed in the button.
Left	Represents the position of the check box's left edge.
Text	Represents the check box's text.
Top	Represents the position of the check box's top edge.
Visible	Represents whether the check box is visible.
Width	Represents the check box's width.

The CheckBox properties that have the same name as the Button properties work about the same way, so there's no point in demonstrating them here. One point of interest, however, is the difference between a standard check box and a button-style check box. Specifically, when you set a CheckBox control's Appearance property to the button style, it no longer looks like a check box, but more like a regular button. What's special about this button is that when it's clicked, the button stays pressed to indicate the checked state, rather than showing a check mark. Figure 26.4 shows the CheckBox control's four different looks.

In this figure, the first control is a standard check box in its unchecked state, the second control is a standard check box in its checked state, the third control is a button-like check box in its unchecked state, and the fourth control is a button-like check box in its checked state.

The following program demonstrates a few of the CheckBox control's properties. To build this program, follow these steps:

1. Start a new Visual Basic .NET project named CheckBoxes, and then place one Button and three CheckBox controls on the form, as shown in Figure 26.5.

Figure 26.4

The CheckBox control doesn't always look like a check box.

Figure 26.5

Position the buttons as shown in this figure.

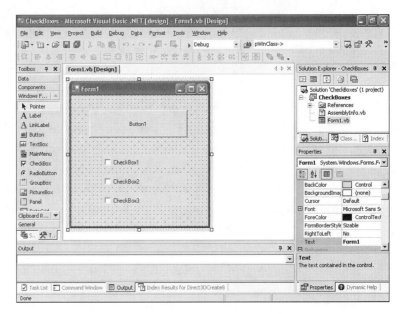

2. Double-click the form to bring up the Visual Basic .NET code window, and type the following program lines into the Load procedure (Visual Basic .NET will have already started the Form1_Load procedure for you):

```
Button1.Text = "TEST BUTTON"
CheckBox1.Text = "Disable Button"
CheckBox2.Text = "Change Button Color"
CheckBox3.Text = "Change Button Size"
```

3. Double-click the Button1 Button control, and type the following program line into the Click procedure (Visual Basic .NET will have already started the Button1_Click procedure for you):

```
MessageBox.Show("Yep, the button works.")
```

4. Double-click the `CheckBox1` control, and type the following program lines into its `Click` procedure:

```
If CheckBox1.Checked Then
    Button1.Enabled = False
Else
    Button1.Enabled = True
End If
```

5. Double-click the `CheckBox2` control, and type the following program lines into its `Click` procedure:

```
If Not CheckBox2.Checked Then
    Button1.BackColor = Color.LightGray
Else
    Button1.BackColor = Color.Red
End If
```

6. Double-click the `CheckBox3` control, and type the following program lines into its `Click` procedure:

```
If Not CheckBox3.Checked Then
    Button1.Height = 40
    Button1.Width = 100
    Button1.Top = 40
    Button1.Left = 80
Else
    Button1.Height = 80
    Button1.Width = 250
    Button1.Top = 20
    Button1.Left = 30
End If
```

> **By the Way**
>
> Notice in the source code how the program uses the value of a CheckBox control's `Checked` property as a Boolean expression in the `If` statements. This works because the value of the `Checked` property is either true or false, which not so coincidentally is exactly the values to which a Boolean expression must evaluate.

7. Save your work, and run the program. When you do, the main window appears. To prove that the `Button1` button is working normally, give it a click. A message box appears.

8. Dismiss the message box, and click the Disable Button check box. Visual Basic .NET checks the box and disables the `Button1` button; if you try to click the `Button1` button, nothing will happen.

9. Click the Disable Button check box a second time to remove the check mark and to reenable the `Button1` button.

10. Click the Change Color check box to toggle the `Button1` button's background color between red and gray.

11. Click the Change Button Size check box to toggle between two button sizes. Figure 26.6 shows the application when the Button1 button is disabled and set to its large size.

Figure 26.6

The check boxes take over the task formally handled by regular Button controls.

CheckBox Methods and Events

In the previous program, you can see that the Click event is every bit as important to a CheckBox control as it is to a Button control. The added bonus is that Visual Basic .NET automatically shows or hides the control's checkmark for you. Send all thank-you's to the Microsoft Visual Basic .NET programming team. Send all money to your humble author (that's me).

> **By the Way**
>
> The name "radio button" comes from the car radio buttons that enable you to select a station. Even though you have two ears, you can listen to only one station at a time, right? If you have more than two ears, you better be carrying your intergalactic green card.

Outside of the Hide and Show methods, which you already learned about in the section on Button controls, and the Click event procedure, you can pretty much ignore the rest of the CheckBox stuff. Someday, when you're really bored, you might want to look over the other methods and events, just to see what's there. On the other hand, if you ever get that bored, I'd seriously consider taking up a hobby.

Tuning Into the RadioButton Controls

Like CheckBoxes, you've undoubtedly seen plenty of RadioButton controls before. RadioButton controls, like CheckBox controls, are commonly used to represent program options. However, RadioButton controls represent a set of options in which only one can be selected simultaneously. When you click the control, a dark circle appears in its box, indicating that the associated option is active. However, if you want to change the option, you cannot simply click the selection again (as is the case with check boxes)—you must click another RadioButton control in the group.

RadioButton Properties

The RadioButton control has about the same number of properties as a Button control, though for most you'll have little need. Table 26.3 lists some of the more useful RadioButton control properties.

Table 26.3   RadioButton Control Properties

Property	Description
Appearance	Represents whether the radio button looks like a traditional radio button or like a button.
BackColor	Represents the radio button's background color.
Checked	Represents whether the button is checked.
Enabled	Represents whether the user can interact with the radio button.
ForeColor	Represents the color of the radio button's text.
Height	Represents the radio button's height.
Image	Represents the image that's displayed in the button.
Left	Represents the position of the radio button's left edge.
Text	Represents the radio button's text.
Top	Represents the position of the radio button's top edge.
Visible	Represents whether the radio button is visible.
Width	Represents the radio button's width.

As you can see, the RadioButton control's properties are much like the CheckBox control's properties. The two controls are closely related. Like a check box, when you set a RadioButton control's Appearance property to Button, it no longer looks like a radio button, but more like a regular button. This button stays pressed to indicate the selected state. Figure 26.7 shows the RadioButton control's four different looks.

In this figure, the first control is a standard radio button in its unselected state, the second control is a standard radio button in its selected state, the third control is a button-like radio button in its unselected state, and the fourth control is a button-like radio button in its checked state. Notice how the GroupBox controls separate the two sets of buttons. Without the group boxes, Visual Basic .NET would treat all four radio buttons as a single set, and you'd be able to select only one rather than the two selected in the figure.

Figure 26.7

The RadioButton control has four different looks, not counting its disabled look.

The following program demonstrates how to use RadioButton controls.

1. Start a new Visual Basic .NET project named RadioButtons, and then place one Button, one GroupBox, and three RadioButton controls on the form, as shown in Figure 26.8. When placing the RadioButtons, make sure you create the GroupBox first, and then place the RadioButtons into the GroupBox.

Figure 26.8

Position the controls as shown in this figure.

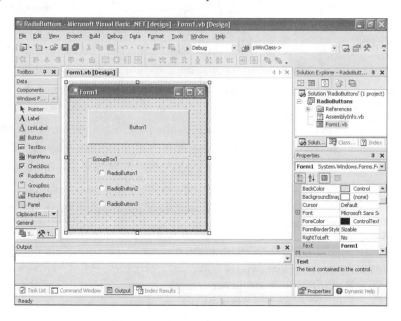

2. Double-click the form to bring up the Visual Basic .NET code window, and type the following program lines into the Load procedure (Visual Basic .NET will have already started the Form1_Load procedure for you):

```
Button1.Text = "TEST BUTTON"
GroupBox1.Text = "Button Color"
```

```
RadioButton1.Text = "Gray Button"
RadioButton2.Text = "Red Button"
RadioButton3.Text = "Green Button"
RadioButton1.Checked = True
```

3. Double-click the Button1 Button control, and type the following program line into the Click procedure (Visual Basic .NET will have already started the Button1_Click procedure for you):

```
MessageBox.Show("Yep, the button works.")
```

4. Double-click the RadioButton1 control. Visual Basic .NET starts the control's CheckedChanged procedure into which you should type this program line:

```
Button1.BackColor = Color.LightGray
```

5. Double-click the RadioButton2 control, and type the following program line into its CheckedChanged procedure:

```
Button1.BackColor = Color.Red
```

6. Double-click the RadioButton3 control, and type the following program line into its CheckedChanged procedure:

```
Button1.BackColor = Color.Green
```

7. Save your work, and run the program. When you do, the main window appears. To prove that the Button1 button is working normally, give it a click. A message box appears.

8. Dismiss the message box, and click the Red Button radio button. Visual Basic .NET selects the button, deselects the previously selected button, and changes the Button1 button's background color to red.

9. Click the Green Button radio button to change the Button1 control to green. As you can see, you can select only one color at a time. Figure 26.9 shows the application when the Button1 button is set to green.

By the Way

As you've noticed in the sample program, GroupBox controls are great for grouping together controls that have similar functions. In Chapter 27, "Text Controls: Computers and the English Language," you'll use GroupBox controls again.

Figure 26.9

The radio buttons enable the user to choose a color for the Button1 *button.*

RadioButton Methods and Events

In the previous program, you can see that the CheckedChanged event is as important to a RadioButton control, as the Clicked procedure is to a CheckBox or Button control. (Actually, both the CheckBox and RadioButton controls have the Click and CheckedChanged events.) Outside of the Hide and Show methods, and the Click and CheckedChanged event procedures, there's only one other event that you might find interesting—the DoubleClick event, whose event procedure looks almost exactly like the Click event procedure. The only difference between the two is that Visual Basic .NET jumps to the DoubleClick event procedure when the user double-clicks the button rather than just single-clicking it.

The Least You Need to Know

◆ Button controls look and act like regular buttons.

◆ Button controls support many properties, methods, and events, but the Text property and the Click event are the most important.

◆ CheckBox controls usually represent application options. When the user selects a check box, he also selects the option.

◆ Like a Button control, the most important CheckBox event is Click, and the most important property is Text.

◆ RadioButton controls enable the user to select only one option from a group of options.

◆ The Text property and the CheckedChanged event procedure are most important for the RadioButton control.

27

Text Controls: Computers and the English Language

In This Chapter

- ◆ Learn about the Label control's many properties, methods, and events
- ◆ Set the appearance of Label controls
- ◆ Learn new TextBox programming techniques
- ◆ Discover the most useful TextBox properties, methods, and events

Just like Button controls, you've been using a lot of Label and TextBox controls in the programs you've explored so far in this book. Although you're pretty familiar by now with their basic use, these handy controls have a few tricks up their sleeves that you may not know about. This chapter will fix that.

Introducing Label Controls

Label controls are sometimes called *static text* controls, because they hold text that the user cannot edit. As such, Label controls are great for, as their name hints, creating labels. Labels are important on your application's user interface, so that the user knows what different controls do and what's expected of him. If you present the user of your application with a screen full of unlabeled controls, he'll make a voodoo doll in your image and poke at it with floppy disks. Ouch!

Although the text in a Label control cannot be edited by the user, it can be changed easily by your program. For this reason, Label controls are also a great way to put a line of text in a window, a line of text that your program can change as needed. For example, you could use a Label control to hold the name of the currently loaded file or the name of the directory to which the file will be saved.

Label Properties

The Label control features more than 70 (!) properties that enable a program to do everything from align the text in the label to change the colors used to display the control. Table 27.1 presents the most useful label properties.

Table 27.1   Label Control Properties

Property	Description
AutoSize	Represents whether the label will automatically size itself to fit its contents.
BackColor	Represents the label's background color. This property has an effect only if the label's BackStyle property is set to opaque.
BorderStyle	Represents the type of border used to display the label.
Enabled	Represents whether the label is displayed grayed out.
ForeColor	Represents the color of the label's text.
Height	Represents the label's height.
Left	Represents the position of the label's left edge.
Text	Represents the label's text.
TextAlign	Represents the position of the label's text.
Top	Represents the position of the label's top edge.
Visible	Determines whether the control is visible.
Width	Represents the label's width.

Although reading a list of properties can be informative (do I hear snoring?), nothing beats seeing the properties in action—except maybe a huge bowl of mint chocolate chip ice cream. The following program gives you a chance to experiment with many of a Label control's properties.

Check This Out ⎯⎯⎯⎯⎯⎯⎯⎯⎯⎯⎯

One of the best ways to learn about a control's properties, methods, and events is to start up Visual Basic .NET and experiment with the control, changing things to see what happens. In fact, you can use the sample programs provided in this book as your starting point. When you get a program working properly, save your work, and then see what else you can do with the controls in the program. Nothing you can do with Visual Basic .NET will hurt your computer as long as you don't do something like delete files or change your registry. (Although, you could end up having to reboot the computer.) Dig in and have fun!

---

1. Start a new Visual Basic .NET project named Labels, and then position 1 Label control, 4 GroupBox controls, and 14 RadioButton controls, as shown in Figure 27.1.

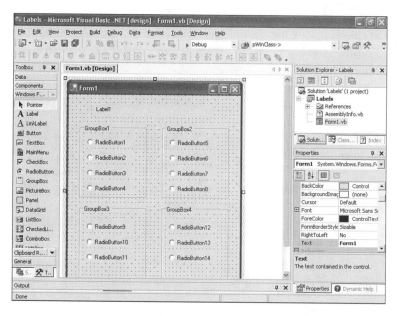

Figure 27.1

Position the buttons as shown in this figure.

Sure, that's a lot of controls, but you need some experience building larger programs. And I'm just the guy to give it to you (evil chuckle).

2. Double-click the form to bring up the Visual Basic .NET code window, and type the following program lines into the Load procedure (Visual Basic .NET will have already started the Form1_Load procedure for you):

```
Label1.Text = "THIS IS A TEST LABEL"
GroupBox1.Text = "BackColor"
```

```
GroupBox2.Text = "ForeColor"
GroupBox3.Text = "Alignment"
GroupBox4.Text = "Border"
RadioButton1.Text = "Red"
RadioButton2.Text = "Green"
RadioButton3.Text = "Blue"
RadioButton4.Text = "Transparent"
RadioButton5.Text = "Red"
RadioButton6.Text = "Green"
RadioButton7.Text = "Blue"
RadioButton8.Text = "Black"
RadioButton9.Text = "Left"
RadioButton10.Text = "Right"
RadioButton11.Text = "Center"
RadioButton12.Text = "None"
RadioButton13.Text = "Fixed Single"
RadioButton14.Text = "Fixed 3D"
RadioButton4.Checked = True
RadioButton8.Checked = True
RadioButton11.Checked = True
RadioButton12.Checked = True
```

3. Double-click the RadioButton1 control, and type the following program lines into the CheckedChanged procedure:

```
Label1.BorderStyle = 1
Label1.BackColor = Color.Red
```

Do the same thing for the remaining RadioButtons as you did for the first one, but complete each CheckedChanged procedure with the following lines. The comments (that's the text after the apostrophe) tell you what goes where.

```
' Place these lines in RadioButton1_CheckedChanged.
Label1.BackColor = Color.Red

' Place these lines in RadioButton2_CheckedChanged.
Label1.BackColor = Color.Green

' Place these lines in RadioButton3_CheckedChanged.
Label1.BackColor = Color.Blue

' Place these lines in RadioButton4_CheckedChanged.
Label1.BackColor = Color.Transparent
```

```
' Place these lines in RadioButton5_CheckedChanged.
Label1.ForeColor = Color.Red

' Place these lines in RadioButton6_CheckedChanged.
Label1.ForeColor = Color.Green

' Place these lines in RadioButton7_CheckedChanged.
Label1.ForeColor = Color.Blue

' Place these lines in RadioButton8_CheckedChanged.
Label1.ForeColor = Color.Black

' Place these lines in RadioButton9_CheckedChanged.
Label1.TextAlign = ContentAlignment.MiddleLeft

' Place these lines in RadioButton10_CheckedChanged.
Label1.TextAlign = ContentAlignment.MiddleRight

' Place these lines in RadioButton11_CheckedChanged.
Label1.TextAlign = ContentAlignment.MiddleCenter

' Place these lines in RadioButton12_CheckedChanged.
Label1.BorderStyle = BorderStyle.None

' Place these lines in RadioButton13_CheckedChanged.
Label1.BorderStyle = BorderStyle.FixedSingle

' Place these lines in RadioButton14_CheckedChanged.
Label1.BorderStyle = BorderStyle.Fixed3D
```

4. Save your work, and run the program. When you do, the main window appears. Click the appropriate radio buttons to set the Label control's BackColor, ForeColor, TextAlign, and BorderStyle properties. Have you ever had so much fun?

Figure 27.2 shows the application with the Label control's BackColor property set to green, the ForeColor property set to red, the TextAlign property set to center, and the BorderStyle property set to Fixed Single.

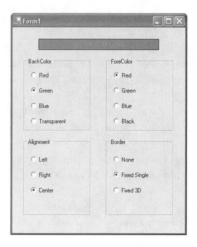

Label Methods and Events

The only Label methods you need to know at this point are `Hide` and `Show`, which do the same thing for a Label control as they do for any other control. (In case you've forgotten, the `Hide` method makes the control invisible and the `Show` method makes it visible.)

Because the Label control isn't commonly used in an interactive way, your programs probably won't need to handle Label events. However, even though the Label control represents static text, it does respond to over 50 events. Of these events, only `Click` and `DoubleClick` are likely to be useful to you until you learn more about Visual Basic .NET. As you've already learned, the `Click` event occurs when the user clicks a control, and the `DoubleClick` event occurs when the user double-clicks a control.

Using TextBox Controls

The TextBox is the last of the controls with which you've had previous experience. For example, you know that you can use a TextBox control to retrieve input from the user. You can also give information back to the user by setting the TextBox control's text, but that would be an unusual way of providing output. In the following sections, you'll stumble upon some other cool ways to use a TextBox control.

TextBox Properties

The TextBox control features more properties than any other control you've looked at so far. Table 27.2 presents the most useful TextBox properties.

Table 27.2   TextBox Control Properties

Property	Description
AutoSize	Represents whether the text box will automatically size itself to fit its contents.
BackColor	Represents the text box's background color.
BorderStyle	Represents the type of border used to display the text box.
Enabled	Represents whether the text box can accept input from the user.
ForeColor	Represents the color of the text box's text.
Height	Represents the text box's height.
Left	Represents the position of the text box's left edge.
MaxLength	Represents the number of characters that the text box can hold.
Multiline	Represents whether the text box can display multiple lines of text.
ReadOnly	Represents whether the control's text can be edited by the user.
Top	Represents the position of the text box's top edge.
Text	Represents the text box's contents.
TextAlign	Represents whether the text box's text is left justified, right justified, or centered.
Visible	Determines whether the control is visible.
Width	Represents the text box's width.

In the next section, you'll experiment with a program that puts TextBox properties to the test. First, however, read on to learn a little about this control's methods and events.

TextBox Methods and Events

The TextBox control features several methods and events that you might find useful. There's the usual Hide and Show, of course, not to mention the Click and DoubleClick events. They work the same for the TextBox control as for any other control. However, the Focus method and the TextChanged event, which are new to you, are handy to know when you're working with TextBox controls.

The Focus method gives the *input focus* to the TextBox control. A control that has input focus can accept input from the user. Visual Basic .NET sends the TextChanged event every time a TextBox control's contents changes. In the following

Check This Out

Clicking a control with your mouse is only one way to give the control the focus. You can also move the focus around from one control to the next by pressing your keyboard's Tab key.

program, you'll see how to use the Focus method and the TextChanged event as well as experiment with a few TextBox properties.

1. Start a new Visual Basic .NET project named TextBoxes, and then position two TextBox controls and one CheckBox control, as shown in Figure 27.3.

Figure 27.3

Position the controls as shown in this figure.

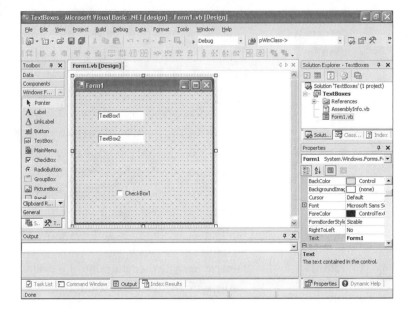

2. Select the first TextBox control on the form (click it with your mouse), and change its Multiline property in the Properties window to True, as shown in Figure 27.4.

3. Set the Multiline property for the second TextBox control in the same way. You have to set the Multiline property in the Properties window because, until you do, you won't be able to size the control in any way except its length.

4. After setting the Multiline property for each control, resize the controls so that they look as shown in Figure 27.5.

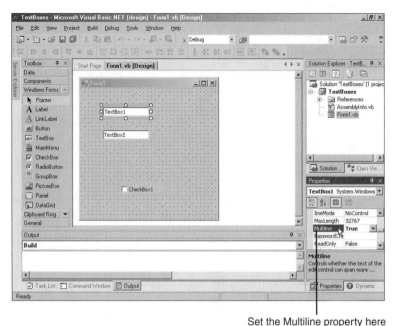

Figure 27.4

The Multiline *property enables a TextBox to display more than one line of text.*

Set the Multiline property here

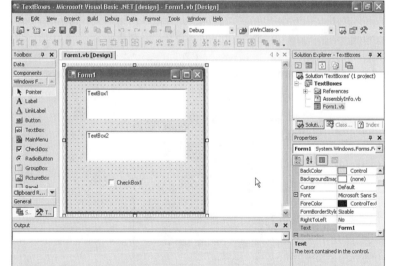

Figure 27.5

Size the controls as shown in this figure.

5. Double-click the form to bring up the Visual Basic .NET code window, and type the following program lines into the Load procedure (Visual Basic .NET will have already started the Form1_Load procedure for you):

```
Dim str As String
str = "This is a test of a TextBox " & _
    "control's Locked, Enabled, " & _
    " and Multiline properties. " & _
    "As long as the check box " & _
    "below is not checked " & _
    "you can edit this text."
TextBox1.Text = str
TextBox2.Text = str
TextBox2.Enabled = False
CheckBox1.Text = "Lock Text"
```

6. Double-click the TextBox1 control, and type the following program line into the
TextChanged procedure:

```
TextBox2.Text = TextBox1.Text
```

7. Double-click the CheckBox control, and type the following lines into its
CheckedChanged procedure:

```
If CheckBox1.Checked Then
    TextBox1.ReadOnly = True
Else
    TextBox1.ReadOnly = False
End If
TextBox1.Focus()
```

8. Save your work, and run the program. When you do, the main window appears, as
shown in Figure 27.6.

Figure 27.6

*This application demon-
strates handy things you can
do with a text box.*

9. Try deleting or adding text to the first TextBox control. The second TextBox control
mirrors all your changes, thanks to the TextChanged event. If you look at the
TextChanged event procedure in the source code, you'll see that the procedure

assigns the first TextBox control's text to the second TextBox control. This happens every time you change even a single character in the first text box.

10. Click the Lock Text check box to turn on its check mark. You've now locked the text in the first TextBox control so that it cannot be edited. Go ahead and try. Can't change the text, can you? If you do manage to change the text, you've either mistyped the program, or you've been transported to a parallel universe where Visual Basic .NET works differently.

The text gets locked in the `Check1_CheckedChanged` event procedure, to which Visual Basic .NET jumps when you click the check box. In that procedure, the program sets the TextBox control's `ReadOnly` property to true or false, depending on the state (checked or un-checked) of the check box control.

The `Check1_CheckedChanged` event procedure also calls the TextBox control's `Focus` method. Here's why: The input focus automatically goes to the last control you selected. So, when you click the check box, it gets the input focus. Worse, it *keeps* the input focus, which means that, before you can type more text in the text box, you first have to click the text box with your mouse. By calling `Focus` on behalf of the text box, you can keep typing right after clicking the check box.

> ### By the Way
>
> As you now know, the `Focus` method gives the input focus to a control. Most Visual Basic .NET controls feature two event procedures that are related to the input focus. When the control receives the input focus, the control generates a `GotFocus` event, to which your program can respond in the `GotFocus` event procedure. When a control loses the focus, it generates a `LostFocus` event.

The Least You Need to Know

- Programmers usually use Label controls to label controls on the application's user interface and to display lines of text in a window.
- The user cannot edit the text in a Label control, which is often called a static-text control. (The term "static" means unchanging.)
- Of all the Label control's properties, `TextAlign`, `BorderStyle`, and `Text` are probably the most important.
- TextBox controls enable a user to input text to an application. A program can also use a text box to present text to the user.
- The most important TextBox properties are probably `Enabled`, `ReadOnly`, `Multiline`, and `Text`.
- When the user changes the text in a text box, the control generates a `TextChanged` event, which the program can handle in the `TextChanged` event procedure.
- The `Focus` method enables a program to return the input focus to a text box after the user has made a selection from another control.

Chapter 28

List Controls: It's the User's Choice

In This Chapter

- ◆ Discover the ListBox control and its properties, methods, and events
- ◆ Respond to a user's selections in a ListBox control
- ◆ Explore the differences between a ListBox control and a ComboBox control
- ◆ Learn to program a ComboBox

Often in your Visual Basic .NET programs, you need to enable the user to select an item from a list of possibilities. Although you can use check boxes and option buttons for presenting limited choices, ListBox and ComboBox control can hold a list of many more choices that takes up little screen real estate. In this chapter, you'll see how these handy controls work.

Introducing ListBox Controls

A ListBox control is little more than a box that contains a list of selections. The user can use his mouse to select a choice from the list, and the program can respond to the choice through the control's event procedures. You might use a list box control to present a list of choices that are too long to accommodate with check boxes or option buttons, but still short enough not to take up too much screen space.

ListBox Properties

The ListBox control features over 80 properties. Table 28.1 presents the most useful ones.

Table 28.1 ListBox Control Properties

Property	Description
BackColor	Represents the list box's background color.
Enabled	Represents whether the user can interact with the list box.
ForeColor	Represents the color of the list box's text.
Height	Represents the list box's height.
Items	Represents the items contained in the list box.
Left	Represents the position of the list box's left edge.
SelectedIndex	Represents the index of the currently selected item in the control.
SelectedItem	Represents the selected item in the control.
Sorted	Represents whether the items in the control's list are sorted.
Text	Represents the text of the currently selected item in the list.
Top	Represents the position of the control's top edge.
Width	Represents the control's width.

The Items property is actually an object that features its own properties and methods. You use the Items object's properties and methods to manipulate the items in your list. In the next section, you'll build a program that shows how the properties of the ListBox and Items controls work.

ListBox Methods and Events

The ListBox control features about 70 methods, most of which you'll rarely need to bother with. As with all controls, the ListBox control supports the Hide and Show methods. These are the only two methods you need to worry about at this point.

Besides its properties and methods, the ListBox control responds to over 60 events, two of which are particularly useful to you at this time. Those events are Click and DoubleClick, both of which you've encounter previously in this book. In case you've forgotten, the Click event occurs when the user clicks the control, and the DoubleClick event occurs when the user double-clicks the control. (The triple-click event occurs when the user accidentally sits on the mouse.)

Because you've probably sensed a pattern to these chapters, you know that a sample program is next.

1. Start a new Visual Basic .NET project named ListBoxes, and then position one ListBox control, one Label control, one TextBox control, and three Button controls, as shown in Figure 28.1.

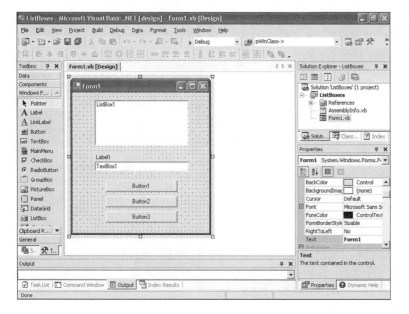

Figure 28.1

Position the controls as shown in this figure.

2. Double-click the form to bring up the Visual Basic .NET code window, and type the following program lines into the Load procedure (Visual Basic .NET will have already started the Form1_Load procedure for you):

```
ListBox1.Items.Add("Elephant")
ListBox1.Items.Add("Cheetah")
ListBox1.Items.Add("Lion")
ListBox1.Items.Add("Giraffe")
ListBox1.Items.Add("Monkey")
ListBox1.Items.Add("Boa Constrictor")
ListBox1.Items.Add("Antelope")
ListBox1.Items.Add("Water Buffalo")
ListBox1.BackColor = Color.Yellow
ListBox1.ForeColor = Color.Blue
Label1.Text = "Enter a new item:"
```

```
Button1.Text = "Add New Item"
Button2.Text = "Remove All Items"
Button3.Text = "Remove Selected Item"
TextBox1.Text = "Default Item"
```

3. Double-click the Button1 control, and type the following program lines into the Click procedure that Visual Basic .NET starts for you:

```
Dim newItem As String = TextBox1.Text
If newItem <> "" Then ListBox1.Items.Add(newItem)
```

4. Double-click the Button2 control, and type the following program lines into the Click procedure that Visual Basic .NET starts for you:

```
ListBox1.Items.Clear()
```

5. Double-click the Button3 control, and type the following program lines into the Click procedure that Visual Basic .NET starts for you:

```
Dim selItemIndex As Integer = ListBox1.SelectedIndex
If selItemIndex = -1 Then
    MessageBox.Show("No item selected.")
Else
    ListBox1.Items.RemoveAt(selItemIndex)
End If
```

6. Finally, you need to add a DoubleClick procedure for the ListBox control. However, if you double-click the control, Visual Basic .NET starts the SelectedIndexChanged procedure for you, which isn't what you want. So, here's what to do:

   a. Go to the code window.

   b. In the list box near the top left corner of your source code, select ListBox1 (see Figure 28.2).

   c. In the list box near the top right corner of your source code, select DoubleClick. Visual Basic .NET then starts the procedure for you.

7. Now, type the following program lines into the DoubleClick procedure that Visual Basic .NET started for you:

```
Dim selItem As String = ListBox1.Text
MessageBox.Show("You selected: " & selItem)
```

8. Select the list box in the form. In the Properties window, set the list box's Sorted property to True, as shown in Figure 28.3.

9. Save your work, and run the program. When you do, the main window appears, as shown in Figure 28.4.

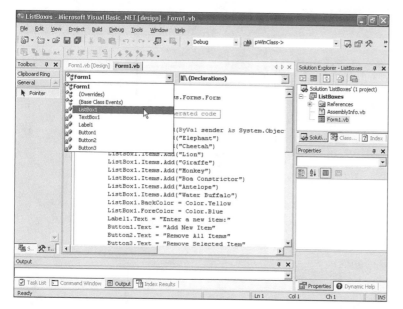

Figure 28.2

Adding an event handler.

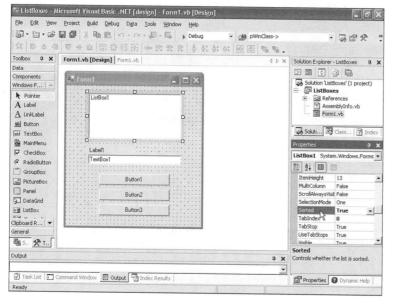

Figure 28.3

The Properties window provides a way to set properties when you're designing the application's interface.

10. Double-click an item in the list box, and a message box appears showing the item you picked. You can add your own items to the list box by typing the item into the text box and clicking the Add New Item button. You can clear all items from the list box by clicking the Remove All Items button. Finally, you can remove any single item from the list box, by selecting the item in the list and clicking the Remove Selected Item button.

Figure 28.4

This program puts a ListBox control through its paces.

This program demonstrates how to use many ListBox properties, methods, and events. Let's take a look. First, the Form1_Load procedure calls the Items.Add method to load items into the list box:

```
ListBox1.Items.Add("Elephant")
ListBox1.Items.Add("Cheetah")
ListBox1.Items.Add("Lion")
ListBox1.Items.Add("Giraffe")
ListBox1.Items.Add("Monkey")
ListBox1.Items.Add("Boa Constrictor")
ListBox1.Items.Add("Antelope")
ListBox1.Items.Add("Water Buffalo")
```

As you can see, the Items.Add method's single argument is the text of the item to add to the list. Couldn't get much easier than that, eh?

Next, Form1_Load sets the list box's BackColor and ForeColor properties to yellow and blue, respectively:

```
ListBox1.BackColor = Color.Yellow
ListBox1.ForeColor = Color.Blue
```

It's the DoubleClick event procedure that displays the user's selection:

```
Private Sub ListBox1_DoubleClick(ByVal sender As System.Object, _
        ByVal e As System.EventArgs) Handles ListBox1.DoubleClick
    Dim selItem As String = ListBox1.Text
    MessageBox.Show("You selected: " & selItem)
End Sub
```

In this procedure, the program gets the selected item from the list box's `Text` property, which holds the text of the selected item. The program then displays the text in a message box. Nothing tricky going on here.

The `Button1_Click` procedure adds new items to the list:

```
Private Sub Button1_Click(ByVal sender As System.Object, _
        ByVal e As System.EventArgs) Handles Button1.Click
    Dim newItem As String = TextBox1.Text
    If newItem <> "" Then ListBox1.Items.Add(newItem)
End Sub
```

First, this procedure gets the text from the text box. The `If` statement ensures that the text box actually contains text before it adds the item to the list box. If the text box contains no text, the `Text` property returns an empty string, which you represent in a program by two double quotes ("") with nothing between them, which is kind of like what my wife says is between my ears.

The `Button2_Click` event procedure gets the job of removing all items from the list box, which it does by calling the `Items.Clear` method, as shown here:

```
Private Sub Button2_Click(ByVal sender As System.Object, _
        ByVal e As System.EventArgs) Handles Button2.Click
    ListBox1.Items.Clear()
End Sub
```

Finally, the `Button3_Click` event procedure removes the selected item from the list box:

```
Private Sub Button3_Click(ByVal sender As System.Object, _
        ByVal e As System.EventArgs) Handles Button3.Click
    Dim selItemIndex As Integer = ListBox1.SelectedIndex
    If selItemIndex = -1 Then
        MessageBox.Show("No item selected.")
    Else
        ListBox1.Items.RemoveAt(selItemIndex)
    End If
End Sub
```

This procedure gets the index of the selected item from the list box's `SelectedIndex` property. If this index is –1, the list box has no selected item, and the procedure shows a message box that presents the user with an error message. Otherwise, the procedure calls the `Items.RemoveAt` method to remove the selected item from the list. This method's single argument is the index of the item to remove.

Introducing ComboBox Controls

A ComboBox control is like a ListBox control combined with a TextBox control. I've long suspected that that's where the name "ComboBox" came from. (Duh!) The user can select items from the combo box's list or can type a selection into the control's text box. If the user selects an item from the list, the selected item automatically appears in the text box. Because the ComboBox control's items appear in a drop-down list (that doesn't appear until the user clicks an on-screen arrow), a ComboBox control is great for long lists.

ComboBox Properties

Like the ListBox control, the ComboBox control features over 80 properties. Table 28.2 presents the most useful ComboBox properties, which are pretty much the same as the ListBox control's handiest properties.

Table 28.2   ComboBox Properties

Property	Description
BackColor	Represents the combo box's background color.
DropDownStyle	Determines how the ComboBox control looks and how items can be selected from the control's list.
Enabled	Represents whether the user can interact with the combo box.
ForeColor	Represents the color of the combo box's text.
Height	Represents the combo box's height.
Items	Represents the items contained in the combo box.
Left	Represents the position of the combo box's left edge.
SelectedIndex	Represents the index of the currently selected item in the control.
SelectedItem	Represents the selected item in the control.
Sorted	Represents whether the items in the control's list are sorted.
Text	Represents the currently selected item in the list.
Top	Represents the position of the control's top edge.
Width	Represents the control's width.

As you now know, you use the Items object's properties and methods to manipulate the items in your list. Later in this chapter, you'll build a program that demonstrates how many of the properties of the ComboBox control and Items object work. In the next section, though, you'll look over the ComboBox control's most important methods and events.

Check This Out _____

By setting a ComboBox control's `DropDownStyle` property, you can create several different kinds of combo boxes. For example, set the `DropDownStyle` property to `DropDownStyle.DropDown` (which is the default), and you get the standard ComboBox with a drop-down list and a text box. However, set the `DropDownStyle` property to `DropDownStyle.Simple`, and you get a combo box whose list is always visible (doesn't drop down). Finally, the `DropDownStyle.DropDownList` style yields a combo box in which the user must select items only from the list and can't type selections into the control's text box.

ComboBox Methods and Events

Like the ListBox control, the ComboBox control features about 70 methods, most of which you'll rarely need to bother with. As with all controls, the ComboBox control supports the `Hide` and `Show` methods, which are the only two methods you need to worry about at this point.

Besides its properties and methods, the ComboBox control responds to plenty of events, three of which are particularly useful to a Visual Basic .NET novice. Those events are `TextChanged`, `Click`, and `DoubleClick`. You reviewed the `Click` and `DoubleClick` events in the section on the ListBox control. You should recognize the `TextChanged` event from your work with the TextBox control. The `TextChanged` event occurs when the user changes the text in the control's text box. (I know, tell you something you don't already know.)

Time for the inevitable sample program. Please face the front of the class, throw away your gum, and stop passing notes. To build the program, follow these steps:

1. Start a new Visual Basic .NET project named ComboBoxes, and then position one ComboBox control, one Label control, one TextBox control, and three Button controls, as shown in Figure 28.5.

2. Double-click the form to display the code window, and type the following lines (Visual Basic .NET will have already started the `Form1_Load` event procedure for you):

```
ComboBox1.Items.Add("Elephant")
ComboBox1.Items.Add("Cheetah")
ComboBox1.Items.Add("Lion")
ComboBox1.Items.Add("Giraffe")
ComboBox1.Items.Add("Monkey")
ComboBox1.Items.Add("Boa Constrictor")
ComboBox1.Items.Add("Antelope")
ComboBox1.Items.Add("Water Buffalo")
ComboBox1.BackColor = Color.Yellow
ComboBox1.ForeColor = Color.Blue
```

```
ComboBox1.Text = ""
ComboBox1.Sorted = True
Label1.Text = "Enter a new item:"
Button1.Text = "Add New Item"
Button2.Text = "Remove All Items"
Button3.Text = "Remove Selected Item"
TextBox1.Text = "Default Item"
```

Figure 28.5

Position the controls as shown in this figure.

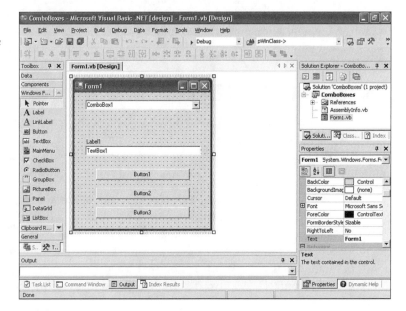

3. Double-click the Button1 control, and type the following program lines into the Click procedure that Visual Basic .NET starts for you:

```
Dim newItem As String = TextBox1.Text
If newItem <> "" Then ComboBox1.Items.Add(newItem)
```

4. Double-click the Button2 control, and type the following program line into the Click procedure that Visual Basic .NET starts for you:

```
ComboBox1.Items.Clear()
```

5. Double-click the Button3 control, and type the following program lines into the Click procedure that Visual Basic .NET starts for you:

```
Dim selItemIndex As Integer = ComboBox1.SelectedIndex
If selItemIndex = -1 Then
    MessageBox.Show("No item selected.")
Else
    ComboBox1.Items.RemoveAt(selItemIndex)
End If
```

6. Double-click the `CommboBox1` control, and type the following program lines into the `SelectedIndexChanged` procedure that Visual Basic .NET starts for you:

```
Dim selItem As String = ComboBox1.Text
MessageBox.Show("You selected: " & selItem)
```

Figure 28.6

The running ComboBoxes program.

7. Save your work, and run the program. When you do, the main window appears, as shown in Figure 28.6.

   Because a ComboBox control works much like a ListBox control, this program is very similar to the ListBox demo program.

8. Click the combo box's arrow to display its drop-down list, as shown in Figure 28.7.

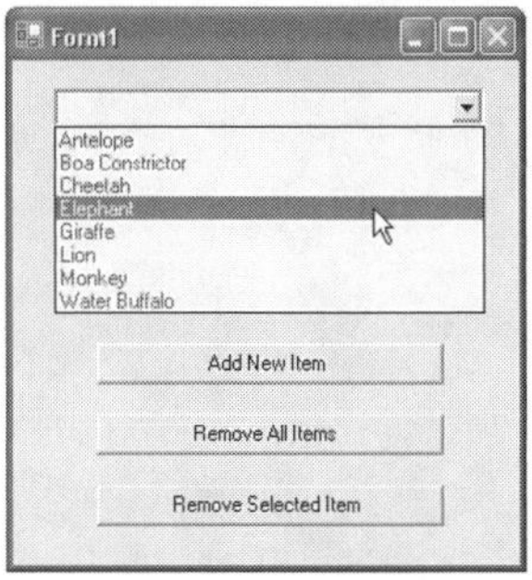

Figure 28.7

Unlike a ListBox control, a ComboBox control has a drop-down list.

9. Click an item in the list, and a message box appears showing the item you picked. Add your own items to the list box by typing the item into the text box and clicking the Add New Item button. Remove any single item from the list box by selecting the item in the list and clicking the Remove Selected Item button. Finally, clear all items from the list box by clicking the Remove All Items button.

The Least You Need to Know

♦ A ListBox control is a small box that contains a list of selectable items.

♦ The most useful ListBox properties are Items, SelectedIndex, Sorted, and Text.

♦ The ListBox control's Items object gives you access to the important Add, Clear, and RemoveAt methods.

♦ The Click and DoubleClick events enable a program to respond to a user's selection in a ListBox control.

♦ A ComboBox control is like a ListBox control combined with a TextBox control.

♦ The most useful ComboBox properties are Items, SelectedIndex, Locked, Sorted, and Text.

♦ The ComboBox control's Items object gives you access to the important Add, Clear, and RemoveAt methods.

♦ The TextChanged, Click, and DoubleClick events enable a program to respond to a user's interactions with a ComboBox control.

29

Scrolling Controls: Getting from Here to There

In This Chapter

- ◆ Learn to use scroll bars in a program
- ◆ Get the scroll bar's current setting
- ◆ Discover how to set a scroll bar's properties
- ◆ Explore a scroll bar control's methods and events

A program can get a value from the user in several ways. The most obvious way is to have the user enter the value into a text box. However, your programs can have greater control over the values entered by the user by incorporating a scroll bar control into the application's user interface. In this chapter, you'll see how.

Using Scroll Bar Controls

Scroll bars are everywhere in Windows. Usually, applications have scroll bars that enable the user to view data that doesn't currently appear on the screen, as shown in Figure 29.1.

Figure 29.1

In many applications, scroll bars enable the user to manipulate the application's view of the data.

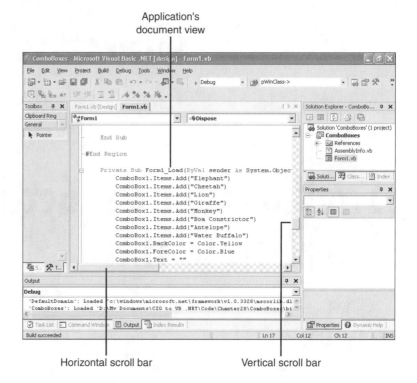

Application's document view

Horizontal scroll bar   Vertical scroll bar

However, scroll bars have many other uses. In a Visual Basic .NET application, for example, you might use a scroll bar to get a value from the user. Because a scroll bar forces the user to select the value from a predetermined, limited range, the program is guaranteed to get a valid value. On the other hand, if you tried to use a text box to get a value from the user, you could get anything from –9,847 to an order for a pizza without anchovies.

The Visual Basic .NET toolbox offers two types of scroll bars. The first is the HScrollBar control, which represents a horizontal scroll bar. The second type is the VScrollBar control, which is a vertical scroll bar. Because both of these controls work virtually identically, the following sections show you how to use both.

By the Way

In Windows applications, a horizontal scroll bar usually scrolls that application's display from left to right, whereas a vertical scroll bar scrolls the display up and down. However, because both controls work almost identically, which one you choose to use in your program's interface depends on your taste and a little bit of common sense.

For example, if a program needed a scroll bar to move an object on the screen left and right, the horizontal scroll bar would be the logical choice. If the program only needs to get a value from 1 to 100, though, either the horizontal or vertical scroll bar will work just fine. In short, the type of scroll bar you use depends mostly on the layout of your user interface.

Scroll Bar Properties

As with most controls, a scroll bar's properties determine, for the most part, the way the control looks and acts. Some of the scroll bar controls' properties are for advanced users. (You know, the folks who wear Spock ears and say "May the force be with you" whenever they leave a room.) In fact, the scroll bar controls feature over 60 properties, all told, only 10 of which will interest you at this time. Table 29.1 introduces those interesting properties.

Table 29.1   Scroll Bar Control Properties

Property	Description
Enabled	Represents whether the user can interact with the scroll bar.
Height	Represents the scroll bar's height.
LargeChange	Represents how much the scroll bar's value changes when the user clicks inside the scroll bar.
Left	Represents the position of the scroll bar's left edge.
Maximum	Represents the scroll bar's maximum value.
Minimum	Represents the scroll bar's minimum value.
SmallChange	Represents how much the scroll bar's value changes when the user clicks the scroll bar's arrow buttons.
Top	Represents the position of the control's top edge.
Value	Represents the scroll bar's current value.
Width	Represents the control's width.

Later in this chapter, you'll build a program that shows how many of these properties work. First, however, you'll have to look over the scroll bar's most important methods and events.

Scroll Bar Methods and Events

The scroll bar controls feature six methods, only two of which—Show and Hide—you might find especially useful at this point in your Visual Basic .NET programming career. As luck would have it, you already know about these methods from previous controls in this book, so you might as well dive right into the control's events.

Besides its properties and methods, the scroll bar controls respond to around 60 events, one of which is particularly useful to you at this time. This event is Scroll, which occurs whenever the user changes the value of the scroll bar.

Creating a Sample Program

As you can guess by now, a program responds to the Scroll event in the Scroll event procedure, which you'll see in the following sample program—provided you follow these steps:

1. Start a new Visual Basic .NET project named Scrollers, and then position one HScrollBar control, one VScrollBar control, and two Label controls, as shown in Figure 29.2.

Figure 29.2

Position the controls as shown in this figure.

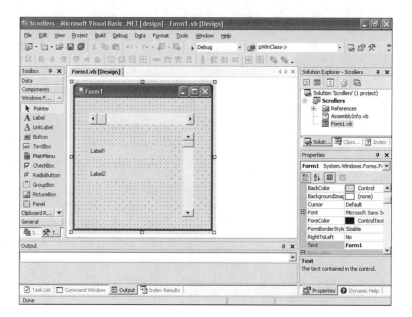

2. Double-click the form to display the code window, and type the following lines into the Load procedure (Visual Basic .NET will have already started the Form1_Load event procedure for you):

```
HScrollBar1.Minimum = 0
HScrollBar1.Maximum = 100
HScrollBar1.LargeChange = 10
HScrollBar1.SmallChange = 1
VScrollBar1.Minimum = 0
VScrollBar1.Maximum = 32767
VScrollBar1.LargeChange = 1000
VScrollBar1.SmallChange = 100
Label1.Text = "Horizontal Scroll bar: 0"
Label2.Text = "Vertical Scroll bar: 0"
```

3. Double-click the HscrollBar1 control, and type the following lines into the Scroll procedure that Visual Basic .NET starts for you:

```
Dim scrollValue As Integer = HScrollBar1.Value
Label1.Text = "Horizontal Scroll bar: " & scrollValue
```

4. Double-click the VscrollBar1 control, and type the following lines into the Scroll procedure that Visual Basic .NET starts for you:

```
Dim scrollValue As Integer = VScrollBar1.Value
Label2.Text = "Vertical Scroll bar: " & scrollValue
```

5. Save your work, and run the program. When you do, the main window appears.

6. Manipulate either of the scroll bar controls, by clicking inside the scroll bar, by dragging the small box (called the *scroll thumb*) in the scroll bar, or by clicking a scroll bar's arrow buttons. The application's Label controls keep you up to date with the scroll bars' current settings. For example, Figure 29.3 shows the application after the user has set the scroll bars to the values 23 and 10,100.

Figure 29.3

This program demonstrates scroll bar controls.

This program demonstrates how to use many scroll bar properties and events. For example, turn your attention from that bag of potato chips you snuck from the kitchen (caught you!) to the Form1_Load event procedure. First, the Form1_Load procedure sets the horizontal scroll bar's minimum and maximum values:

```
HScrollBar1.Minimum = 0
HScrollBar1.Maximum = 100
```

A horizontal scroll bar's minimum value is the value when the scroll bar's thumb is set fully to the left. Conversely, a horizontal scroll bar's maximum value is the value when the scroll bar's thumb is fully to the right. In the case of a vertical scroll bar, the minimum value is at the top of the scroll bar, and the maximum value is at the bottom.

There is one thing to keep in mind, however: The value returned from the control is based on the left or top edge of the scroll thumb, which means that the scroll bar can't actually return its highest value. To accommodate this problem, you can make the scroll bar's Maximum property higher than the maximum value you want returned in order to accommodate for the width of the scroll thumb.

After setting the scroll bar's Minimum and Maximum properties, the Form1_Load procedure sets the LargeChange and SmallChange properties:

```
HScrollBar1.LargeChange = 10
HScrollBar1.SmallChange = 1
```

The first of the previous lines sets the scroll bar so that when the user clicks inside the scroll bar, the control's value goes up or down by 10. Which way the value goes depends on whether the user clicks to the left of the scroll bar's thumb (the value goes down) or to the right (the value goes up). The second line sets the scroll bar so that when the user clicks one of the scroll bar's arrow buttons, the value changes by only 1. Whether the value goes up by 1 or down by 1 depends on whether the user clicks the left arrow button or the right arrow button.

After setting the horizontal scroll bar's properties, the procedure sets the vertical scroll bar's properties:

```
VScrollBar1.Minimum = 0
VScrollBar1.Maximum = 32767
VScrollBar1.LargeChange = 1000
VScrollBar1.SmallChange = 100
```

These property settings have a similar effect on the vertical scroll bar that they have on the horizontal scroll bar. The difference (besides the different values being used for the properties) is that the VScrollBar1 control is oriented up and down rather than left to right.

Finally, Form1_Load sets the Label controls to their starting text:

```
Label1.Text = "Horizontal Scroll bar: 0"
Label2.Text = "Vertical Scroll bar: 0"
```

Whenever the user changes the value of a scroll bar, Visual Basic .NET jumps to the scroll bar's Scroll event procedure. For example, in the case of this program's horizontal scroll bar, the Scroll event procedure looks like this:

```
Private Sub HScrollBar1_Scroll(ByVal sender As System.Object, _
        ByVal e As System.Windows.Forms.ScrollEventArgs) Handles
HScrollBar1.Scroll
    Dim scrollValue As Integer = HScrollBar1.Value
    Label1.Text = "Horizontal Scroll bar: " & scrollValue
End Sub
```

Here, the program gets the value of the scroll bar's `Value` property, which is the scroll bar's current setting. The program does nothing more than display this value in the first Label control.

The vertical scroll bar's `Scroll` event procedure is very similar to the horizontal scroll bar's:

```
Private Sub VScrollBar1_Scroll(ByVal sender As System.Object, _
        ByVal e As System.Windows.Forms.ScrollEventArgs) Handles
VScrollBar1.Scroll
    Dim scrollValue As Integer = VScrollBar1.Value
    Label2.Text = "Vertical Scroll bar: " & scrollValue
End Sub
```

Amazingly, you've already reached the point in this chapter when you get to prove how smart you are. Put on your thinking cap and follow me.

The Least You Need to Know

- ◆ A scroll bar control enables a user to select a value from a range of acceptable values.
- ◆ There are two types of scroll bars: horizontal (represented by the HScrollBar control) and vertical (represented by the VScrollBar control).
- ◆ Horizontal and vertical scroll bars work almost identically. Their only real difference is their on-screen orientation.
- ◆ A scroll bar's most useful properties are `Minimum`, `Maximum`, `LargeChange`, `SmallChange`, and `Value`.
- ◆ To respond to changes in a scroll bar's value, a program needs to supply a `Scroll` event procedure for the scroll bar.

30

The Timer Control: Tick, Tick, Tick ...

In This Chapter

◆ Use a timer to wait a specified period of time

◆ Perform repeating actions with continuous Timer events

◆ Write your first Windows game program

Some programs require that an action occur at a regular interval. For example, a program that displays an animation needs to time when to replace one image with another. A program may need to track elapsing time for many other reasons, as well. Luckily, Visual Basic .NET features a special control that enables programs to keep track of time intervals—the Timer control.

Using the Timer Control

Managing a timer in your program may at first sound like a complicated task, but the truth is that the Visual Basic .NET Timer control is easier to use than a squirt gun in a swimming pool. The timer control does nothing more than send a Timer event to your program at whatever interval you set. Every time the Timer control sends a timer event, Visual Basic .NET jumps to the Timer control's `Tick` event procedure, where you place the program lines required to handle the event.

Your program may need to receive only a single timer event. For example, you might want to give the user a limited time period in which to respond to some aspect of your program. On the other hand, you may need to have a steady stream of Timer events arriving at your program at an interval you specify. The Timer control can handle either of these eventualities, as you'll see in the following sections.

Timer Properties, Methods, and Events

From a programmer's point of view, the Timer control is one of the least complicated controls you'll ever use. If you find this hard to believe, consider that the Timer control has only 4 properties and 11 methods and responds to only 2 events.

Of the control's properties, only `Enabled` and `Interval` are useful to you at this time. The `Enabled` property determines whether the control is on or off. That is, when `Enabled` is set to `True`, the control is on and sends Timer events to the program at the interval specified by the `Interval` property. Conversely, when `Enabled` is set to `False`, the Timer control is turned off and does not generate Timer messages. When the `Enabled` property is set to `Maybe`, it's time to get a new copy of Visual Basic .NET.

As was hinted in the previous paragraph, the `Interval` property determines how often the Timer control sends Timer events to your program. This property is measured in milliseconds. (A millisecond is $1/1000$ of a second.) So, if you want Timer messages to arrive at your program every second, you set the `Interval` property to 1,000. If you want Timer messages every half second, you set the `Interval` property to 500. Finally, setting the Timer control to a negative number (such as –100) causes time to run backwards, which is a great way to regain your lost youth. (Just kidding. You can't set the timer to a negative number.)

The only event the Timer control responds to that you'd be interested in is the `Tick` event. (Aptly named, don't you think?) Visual Basic .NET jumps to the Timer control's `Tick` event procedure each time a Timer event arrives. So, if you were to set a Timer control's `Interval` property to 1,000, Visual Basic .NET would jump to the `Tick` event procedure once a second.

A Single Timer Event

One way to use a Timer control is to determine when a specified period of time has elapsed. For example, you may want your program to display a prompt if the user doesn't react to some sort of request within a given period of time. The following sample program demonstrates how to use a Timer control in this way.

1. Start a new Visual Basic .NET project named TimerTest, and place one Label control, one TextBox control, two Button controls, and one Timer control (the Timer control will appear at the bottom of the design window), as shown in Figure 30.1.

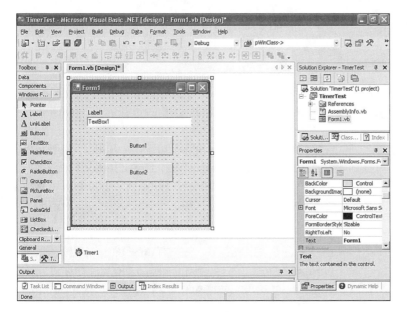

Figure 30.1

Position the controls as shown in this figure.

2. Double-click the form to bring up the code window, and type the following program lines into the Load procedure (Visual Basic .NET will have already started the Form1_Load procedure for you):

```
Label1.Text = "Enter Timer Interval:"
TextBox1.Text = "5"
Button1.Text = "Set Timer Interval"
Button2.Text = "Start Timer"
Timer1.Enabled = False
```

3. Double-click the Button1 control, and type the following lines into its Click procedure:

```
Dim timeInterval As Integer
Dim msg As String
timeInterval = Int32.Parse(TextBox1.Text)
Timer1.Interval = timeInterval * 1000
msg = "Timer interval set to " & timeInterval & " second"
If timeInterval > 1 Then msg = msg & "s"
MessageBox.Show(msg)
```

Whoops!

Don't try to set the Timer to 0 by typing 0 into the program's text box. If you do, your program will come to a screeching halt because the Timer control's Interval property must be greater than 0. You learned to stop errors of this kind from happening in Chapter 16, "Catching Runtime Errors."

4. Double-click the Button2 control, and type the following line into its Click procedure:

```
Timer1.Enabled = True
```

5. Double-click the Timer1 control, and type the following lines into its Tick procedure:

```
Timer1.Enabled = False
MessageBox.Show("Time is up.")
```

6. Save your work and run the program. When you do, you see the main window.

7. Type the number of seconds you want to set the timer to, and click the Set Timer Interval button. A message box appears telling you that the interval has been set, as shown in Figure 30.2.

Now that you've set the timer's interval, you can start the timer by clicking the Start Timer button. After the number of seconds you requested, a message box appears, informing you that the time is up, as shown in Figure 30.3.

Figure 30.2

The message box verifies the timer interval setting.

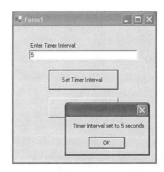

Figure 30.3

The message box notifies you that the requested time has elapsed.

Digging Into the TimerTest Program

There's a lot of stuff going on in this program. First, in the Form1_Load event procedure, the program sets the Label, Text, and Button controls' Text properties:

```
Label1.Text = "Enter Timer Interval:"
TextBox1.Text = "5"
Button1.Text = "Set Timer Interval"
Button2.Text = "Start Timer"
```

Also in the Form1_Load procedure, the program turns off the Timer control:

```
Timer1.Enabled = False
```

Turning off the Timer control ensures that the timer won't start running until the user clicks the Start Timer button.

To set the Timer's interval, the user must type a value into the text box and click the Set Timer Interval button. When the user clicks the button, Visual Basic .NET jumps to the Button1_Click procedure, which first declares integer and string variables:

```
Dim timeInterval As Integer
Dim msg As String
```

Then the procedure gets the user's entry from the text box and multiplies the requested value by 1000 in order to set the Timer control's Interval property correctly:

```
timeInterval = Int32.Parse(TextBox1.Text)
Timer1.Interval = timeInterval * 1000
```

Why multiply the value from the text box by 1000? Remember that the Timer control expects the time interval to be measured in $\frac{1}{1000}$ths of a second. Multiplying the user's entry by 1,000 converts seconds to milliseconds.

Next, the program builds a message string to display in the message box:

```
msg = "Timer interval set to " & timeInterval & " second"
If timeInterval > 1 Then msg = msg & "s"
```

Notice that if the timer interval is larger than one second, the program tacks an "s" onto the end of the message, which makes the word "second" plural.

Finally, the Button1_Click procedure displays the message it just constructed:

```
MessageBox.Show(msg)
```

To start the timer, the user must click the Start Timer button, which causes Visual Basic .NET to jump to the Button2_Click event procedure. This procedure does nothing more than turn on the timer by setting the Timer control's `Enabled` property to `True`, as shown in the following snippet:

```
Private Sub Button2_Click(ByVal sender As System.Object, _
        ByVal e As System.EventArgs) Handles Button2.Click
    Timer1.Enabled = True
End Sub
```

Now, the timer starts keeping track of time. When the number of milliseconds specified in the `Interval` property has elapsed, the Timer goes off like an alarm clock and sends a Timer message to the program, which causes Visual Basic .NET to jump to the `Timer1_Tick` event procedure. This procedure shuts off the timer and displays a message box:

```
Private Sub Timer1_Tick(ByVal sender As System.Object, _
        ByVal e As System.EventArgs) Handles Timer1.Tick
    Timer1.Enabled = False
    MessageBox.Show("Time is up.")
End Sub
```

Working with Multiple Timer Events

Another way to use the Timer control is to send a constant stream of Timer messages to the program. You would do this when you want your program to repeatedly perform some action at a regular interval. The following sample program demonstrates how this programming technique works. It's also a complete, albeit simple, game that you just might find amusing.

For this program, you'll try something a little different. You'll set most control properties in the Properties window at design time rather than setting them in the program source code. This is a more typical way to build a Visual Basic .NET program than you've gotten used to in this book. As I mentioned earlier in this book, it's more concise for me as an author to give you code to set properties, but you may prefer to use the Properties window with your own programs.

To get going, follow these steps:

1. Start a new Visual Basic .NET project named TimerTest2, and place two Button controls, one Timer control, and one Label control on your form, as shown in Figure 30.4.

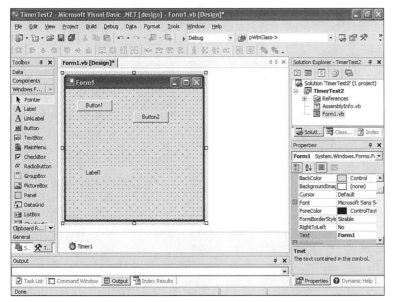

Figure 30.4

Place the controls as shown in this figure.

2. Click the Button1 button on the form. The control's properties appear in the Properties window.

3. Set the following Button properties in the Properties window (note that for text shown below, you don't type the quotes just the text between the quotes):

   ◆ Name: btnTarget

   ◆ Size: 100,100

   ◆ Text: "Target"

4. Set the Label1 control's properties:

   ◆ Name: lblScore

   ◆ Font: 18 points

   ◆ Location: 20,226

   ◆ Size: 200,30

   ◆ Text: "SCORE:"

5. Set the Button2 button's properties:

   ◆ Name: btnStart

   ◆ Location: 232,208

   ◆ Size: 50,50

   ◆ Text: "Start Game"

Figure 30.5 illustrates what your form should look like after you've set the controls' properties.

Figure 30.5

The final user interface.

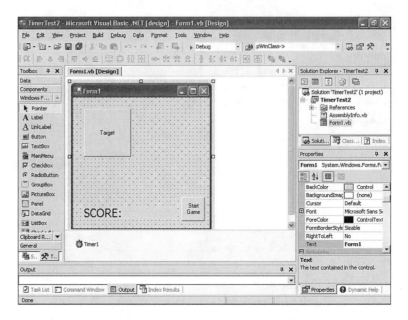

6. Bring up the code window, and type the following program lines right before the `End Class` statement. Remember that you don't need to type all the lines in the program listing. That is, you can have Visual Basic .NET start event procedures for you, either by double-clicking a control (which starts the control's default procedure) or by selecting an event from the list boxes at the top of the code window:

```
Dim score As Integer
Dim jumpCount As Integer

Private Sub btnStart_Click(ByVal sender As System.Object, _
        ByVal e As System.EventArgs) Handles btnStart.Click
    score = 0
    jumpCount = 0
    lblScore.Text = "SCORE:"
    btnTarget.Text = "Target"
    Timer1.Interval = 750
    Timer1.Enabled = True
    btnStart.Enabled = False
    Randomize()
End Sub
```

```
Private Sub Timer1_Tick(ByVal sender As System.Object, _
        ByVal e As System.EventArgs) Handles Timer1.Tick
    Call MoveButton()
    jumpCount = jumpCount + 1
    If jumpCount = 25 Then Call EndGame()
End Sub

Private Sub MoveButton()
    Dim rndNumber As Single = Rnd()
    Dim xPos As Integer = Int((200) * rndNumber)
    rndNumber = Rnd()
    Dim yPos As Integer = Int((100) * rndNumber)
    btnTarget.Left = xPos
    btnTarget.Top = yPos
End Sub

Private Sub EndGame()
    Timer1.Enabled = False
    btnStart.Enabled = True
    btnTarget.Text = "Game Over"
End Sub

Private Sub btnTarget_Click(ByVal sender As System.Object, _
        ByVal e As System.EventArgs) Handles btnTarget.Click
    If Not Timer1.Enabled Then Exit Sub
    score = score + 1
    lblScore.Text = "SCORE: " & Int32.Parse(score)
    Beep()
End Sub
```

7. Save your work, and run the program.

8. When the main window appears, click the Start Game button. When you do the Target button starts jumping around the window. Try to click the button before it moves. Each time you manage to click the button, your score goes up one. The button will jump 25 times, at which point its caption changes to "Game Over" and the game ends. To start a new game, click the Start Game button again. Figure 30.6 shows the Button Chase game after the user has played.

> **By the Way**
>
> When you get the mouse pointer over the button, click as many times as you can. You can often get three, or even four, points before the button moves to its next location. With a little practice you should be able to get scores of 30 or more.

Figure 30.6

You need fast reflexes to get high scores in this game.

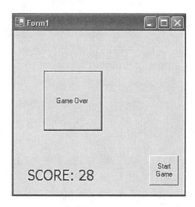

Digging Into the TimerTest2 Program

If you've been putting your nose to the grindstone throughout this book, you should be able to figure out most of what this game program's source code does. You'll also probably have a flat nose. For those of you who still have their nicely rounded nose ends, here's a program explanation.

First, the program declares two global variables:

```
Dim score As Integer
Dim jumpCount As Integer
```

Because the program declares these variables outside of any procedure, the variables can be used anywhere in the program. This is important, because if the variables were declared inside a procedure, they would lose their values every time the procedure ended, which would not be good because several procedures in the program rely on the values of these variables.

> **By the Way**
>
> You may have noticed that this program doesn't have a `Form1_Load` procedure. That's because you already set most control properties in the Properties window. Moreover, no variables need to have their values set at the very start of the program.

When the user clicks the Start Game button, Visual Basic .NET jumps to the `btnStart_Click` procedure, which is the event procedure that responds to the Start Game button. That procedure first sets the `score` and `jumpCount` variables to their game-start values:

```
score = 0
jumpCount = 0
```

The `score` variable holds the player's score, of course, and the `jumpCount` variable counts how many times the button has jumped since the start of the game. You can see why it's important that these variables are set to 0 at the start of a game.

Next, after setting button text, the program sets the Timer control's interval to 750 milliseconds and enables the timer:

```
Timer1.Interval = 750
Timer1.Enabled = True
```

After setting the timer's interval, the btnStart_Click procedure turns off the Start Game button, so that the user can't click it while the game is in progress:

```
btnStart.Enabled = False
```

The program then calls the Randomize statement, which ensures that random numbers retrieved by the program in the MoveButton procedure are different for every game. This may not make a lot of sense to you at the moment. Just take it on faith that whenever you use random numbers in a program, you need to call the Randomize statement.

Check This Out

Changing the game's difficulty is easier than licking a stamp with a hose. If you want to make the game harder, set the Timer control's **Interval** property to a lower value. Similarly, if you want to make the game easier, set the **Interval** property to a higher value.

When the game begins, the Timer control starts sending Timer messages to the program every 750 milliseconds. Those Timer messages find their way to the Timer1_Tick event procedure:

```
Private Sub Timer1_Tick(ByVal sender As System.Object, _
     ByVal e As System.EventArgs) Handles Timer1.Tick
    Call MoveButton()
    jumpCount = jumpCount + 1
    If jumpCount = 25 Then Call EndGame()
End Sub
```

This procedure first calls the MoveButton procedure, which makes the button jump to its new location. The procedure then adds 1 to the jump count. If the jumpCount variable is 25, the procedure calls the EndGame procedure, which, as the name suggests, ends the game.

The MoveButton procedure is a little tricky. First, the procedure calls Visual Basic .NET's Rnd function, which returns a random number between 0 and 1:

```
Dim rndNumber As Single = Rnd()
```

If you think a number between 0 and 1 isn't all that useful, join the club. To fix this problem, the program performs a little math trickery to convert the random number to a number between 0 and 200:

```
Dim xPos As Integer = Int((200) * rndNumber)
```

The number 200 is the farthest to the right the Target button can move. (Any further and it would be off the window.) So the previous statement takes the random number and converts it to a value between 0 and 200. You don't need to know exactly how this works. Just know that the number in parentheses is the largest random number you need. For example, to get a random number between 0 and 10, you'd write the following code:

```
rndNumber = Rnd
xPos = Int((10) * rndNumber)
```

You can also combine these two statements into the following statement:

```
xPos = Int((10) * Rnd)
```

After getting a random horizontal position for the button, the procedure gets a random vertical position the same way:

```
rndNumber = Rnd()
Dim yPos As Integer = Int((100) * rndNumber)
```

Having fun yet? Now that the procedure has a random X and Y position for the button, moving the button is as simple as setting the button's Left and Top properties:

```
btnTarget.Left = xPos
btnTarget.Top = yPos
```

Now you see how the program gets the button to jump around and make the player crazy. But what happens when the player manages to tag the button? You might think that the button's Click event procedure might fit the bill. And you'd be right! Here's what the Click procedure looks like:

```
Private Sub btnTarget_Click(ByVal sender As System.Object, _
        ByVal e As System.EventArgs) Handles btnTarget.Click
    If Not Timer1.Enabled Then Exit Sub
    score = score + 1
    lblScore.Text = "SCORE: " & Int32.Parse(score)
    Beep()
End Sub
```

Notice that the first line inside the procedure checks to see whether the Timer control's Enabled property is True. If Enabled is False, the game has already ended, and the program shouldn't increase the player's score, even if she's clicking the button. No cheating allowed! In the case of the timer being disabled, the program immediately leaves the procedure thanks to the Exit Sub statement.

If the game isn't over yet, the procedure increases the player's score, displays the new score in the Label control, and beeps the computer's beeper.

After the Target button has bounced around the window 25 times, which should be frustrating enough to make the player punch out the screen, the program calls the EndGame procedure:

```
Private Sub EndGame()
    Timer1.Enabled = False
    btnStart.Enabled = True
    btnTarget.Text = "Game Over"
End Sub
```

This procedure turns off the Timer control by setting its Enabled property to False, turns on the Start Game button, and changes the Target button's text to "Game Over."

That was easy! (I know. Easy for me to say.)

Whoops!

Notice how the Exit Sub statement in the program avoids the need for an If statement. Don't smirk yet, though! A lot of programmers consider this to be a bad programming practice, because a procedure shouldn't exit anywhere except at the end. Personally, I think this sort of thing is okay in a simple case like this. Don't overuse it, though.

The Least You Need to Know

♦ A Timer control enables a program to determine when a specified period of time has passed.

♦ The Timer control's Interval property determines how often Timer events arrive at the program.

♦ To turn the Timer control on and off, you set the control's Enabled property to True or False, respectively.

♦ By turning off the Timer control when the first Timer event arrives, you can use the timer to wait a specified period of time.

♦ Unless it's turned off, the Timer control sends a steady stream of Timer messages to the program.

Message Boxes: Your Program Speaks Out

In This Chapter

♦ Display system icons in your message boxes

♦ Choose between various combinations of message box buttons

♦ Add a title to your message box

♦ Respond to the user's message box button selection

In a Windows program, communicating with the user can be trickier than it was in the old days (you know, 10 years ago). In most cases, when your program has something to tell the user, it will display a message box. Message boxes, however, can be much more useful than you might imagine at this point in your Visual Basic .NET programming career. In this chapter, you'll learn to use message boxes to their best advantage.

Introducing the Message Box

At this point in the book, message boxes are nothing new to you. You've already displayed message boxes in many of the sample programs you've explored. However, there's still a lot you don't know about message boxes. For example, a message box can display one of four system icons, depending upon the type of message being displayed. Moreover, a message box can contain not only the familiar OK button, but also Yes, No, Cancel, Ignore, and Retry buttons. You can even change the message box's title.

Message Box Titles

A message box, just like any other kind of window, can have a title in its title bar. You can put whatever title you like in a message box, even "Everything You Wanted to Know About Q-Tips but Were Afraid to Ask." All you have to do is add the title after the argument that gives the message box's text, like this:

```
MessageBox.Show("Is anyone out there?", "Test Message")
```

This program line produces the message box shown in Figure 31.1.

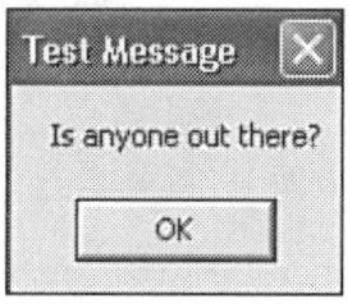

Figure 31.1

A message box with a title.

Message Box Buttons

In the examples used in the previous chapters, you probably noticed that the message boxes always had just an OK button. Isn't it weird to ask a question in a message box and then have only an OK button? If you can answer a question with a single button, you're a cleverer person than I am. For a question message box to make sense, you need at least two buttons, probably of the Yes or No variety. (If you're working with that new technology called fuzzy logic, you could try a Maybe button, but I suspect you won't have much luck.)

Displaying different types of buttons in a message box is easy. You need only add one of the following predefined values to your `MessageBox.Show` line:

◆ `MessageBoxButtons.AbortRetryIgnore`: Displays Abort, Retry, and Ignore buttons in the message box, as shown in Figure 31.2.

Figure 31.2

A message box with Abort, Retry, and Ignore buttons.

◆ `MessageBoxButtons.OKCancel`: Displays OK and Cancel buttons in the message box, as shown in Figure 31.3.

Figure 31.3

A message box with OK and Cancel buttons.

◆ `MessageBoxButtons.OK`: Displays only an OK button in the message box, as shown in Figure 31.4.

Figure 31.4

A message box with an OK button.

◆ `MessageBoxButtons.RetryCancel`: Displays Retry and Cancel buttons in the message box, as shown in Figure 31.5.

Figure 31.5

A message box with Retry and Cancel buttons.

◆ `MessageBoxButtons.YesNo`: Displays Yes and No buttons in the message box, as shown in Figure 31.6.

Figure 31.6

A message box with Yes and No buttons.

◆ `MessageBoxButtons.YesNoCancel`: Displays Yes, No, and Cancel buttons in the message box, as shown in Figure 31.7.

Figure 31.7

A message box with Yes, No, and Cancel buttons.

So, now how about fixing up that question message box from the previous example? To do so, you might write something like this:

```
MessageBox.Show("Is anyone out there?", "Test Message", _
    MessageBoxButtons.YesNo)
```

Think you got it made now, eh? OK, smart guy, how do you know whether the user clicked the Yes or No button? Lucky for you the answer to that question is "Easy!" First, the MessageBox.Show call is actually a function call, which means that it returns a value. Guess what value MessageBox.Show returns? Yep. It returns the value of the button the user clicked to dismiss the message box. To get the user's response, you might write program lines that are similar to this snippet:

```
Dim response As Integer
response = MessageBox.Show("Is anyone out there?", _
    "Test Message", MessageBoxButtons.YesNo)
If response = DialogResult.Yes Then
    MessageBox.Show("You chose Yes.")
ElseIf response = DialogResult.No Then
    MessageBox.Show("You chose No.")
End If
```

Notice that the program compares the value returned from MessageBox.Show to the predefined values DialogResult.Yes and DialogResult.No. The other types of buttons have similar predefined values, which are DialogResult.Abort, DialogResult.vbOK, DialogResult.vbCancel, DialogResult.Ignore, and DialogResult.Retry.

Message Box Icons

As you learned earlier in this chapter, a message box can display one of four system icons, depending on the type of message the message box will display and the message's urgency. (Actually, Visual Basic .NET defines eight different types of icons, but several of them use the same image.) The four types of message icons are:

 ◆ **Error:** Indicates that the message box displays information critical to the application's performance. This type of message and icon often appears to report fatal program errors. Figure 31.8 shows a message box with a critical icon.

Figure 31.8

This message box displays a critical message.

 ◆ **Exclamation:** Indicates that the message box displays important information that requires the user's attention. For example, a program might display this type of message box when a requested file could not be loaded. Figure 31.9 shows a message box with the exclamation icon.

Figure 31.9

This message box displays an exclamatory message.

◆ **Information:** Indicates that the message box displays information that the user may find useful. For example, a program might display this type of message box to inform the user that a file has loaded successfully. Figure 31.10 shows a message box with the informational icon.

Figure 31.10

This message box displays an informational message.

◆ **Question:** Indicates that the message box displays a question that requires an answer from the user. For example, a program might display this type of message box to ask the user if he'd like to save his work before exiting the program. Figure 31.11 shows a message box with the question-type icon.

Figure 31.11

This message box asks a question.

By the Way

How come, you ask, you never had to bother with all this icon and button stuff with your message boxes before? All you did was supply a message and call it a day. When you leave the specifications for an icon and buttons out of the `MessageBox.Show` statement, Visual Basic .NET uses the defaults, which are an OK button and no icon. Having defaults makes the `MessageBox.Show` statement easier to use when you don't care about all the extra stuff. Just another way Visual Basic .NET helps keep you from muttering under your breath and using the latest issue of *Visual Basic .NET Guru World* as a dartboard.

To add one of these informative icons to your message box, you need only write a letter to Bill Gates begging his permission. When Mr. Gates receives your letter—and assuming he likes your penmanship and that your letter arrived on a Wednesday between 1:00 P.M. and 3:00 P.M.—he will chant a prayer to the Universal Binary Silicon Gods, who will enable your machine to use message-box icons. *Ahem.* The truth is that adding an icon to a message box is as easy as tacking on a comma and the predefined value `MessageBoxIcon.Error`, `MessageBoxIcon.Exclamation`, `MessageBoxIcon.Information`, or `MessageBoxIcon.vbQuestion` onto your `MessageBox.Show` line, as shown in the following snippet:

```
MessageBox.Show("Is anyone out there?", _
    "Test Message", MessageBoxButtons.YesNo, MessageBoxIcon.Question)
```

This line results in the message box shown in Figure 31.12.

Figure 31.12

This message box displays a question icon.

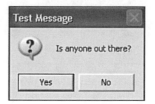

Putting It All Together

Got all this message box stuff down? In this section, you'll build a program that enables you to experiment with message-box options.

1. Create a new Visual Basic .NET project named Messages, and place two GroupBox controls, nine RadioButton controls, two Label controls, two TextBox controls, and one Button control, as shown in Figure 31.13.

Figure 31.13

Position the controls as shown in this figure.

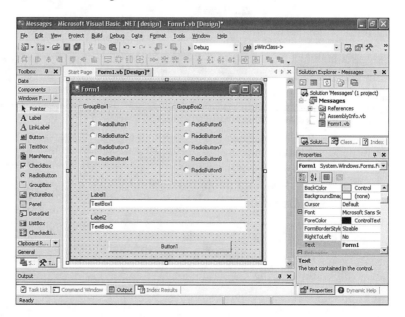

2. Bring up the code window and add the following program lines to the project, right before the `End Class` line:

```
Dim MsgBoxIcon As Integer
Dim MsgBoxButtons As Integer

Private Sub Form1_Load(ByVal sender As System.Object, _
        ByVal e As System.EventArgs) Handles MyBase.Load
    GroupBox1.Text = "Icons"
    GroupBox2.Text = "Buttons"
    RadioButton1.Text = "Critical"
    RadioButton2.Text = "Exclamation"
    RadioButton3.Text = "Information"
    RadioButton4.Text = "Question"
    RadioButton5.Text = "OK"
    RadioButton6.Text = "OK/Cancel"
    RadioButton7.Text = "Yes/No"
    RadioButton8.Text = "Retry/Cancel"
    RadioButton9.Text = "Yes/No/Cancel"
    Label1.Text = "Enter Title:"
    Label2.Text = "Enter Message:"
    Button1.Text = "Show Message Box"
    TextBox1.Text = "Default Title"
    TextBox2.Text = "Default Message"
    RadioButton1.Checked = True
    RadioButton5.Checked = True
    MsgBoxIcon = vbCritical
    MsgBoxButtons = vbOKOnly
End Sub

Private Sub Button1_Click(ByVal sender As System.Object, _
        ByVal e As System.EventArgs) Handles Button1.Click
    Dim response As Integer
    Dim MsgBoxTitle As String
    Dim MsgBoxMessage As String
    MsgBoxTitle = TextBox1.Text
    MsgBoxMessage = TextBox2.Text
    response = MessageBox.Show(MsgBoxMessage, MsgBoxTitle, _
        MsgBoxButtons, MsgBoxIcon)
    If response = DialogResult.OK Then
        MessageBox.Show("You chose OK.")
    ElseIf response = DialogResult.Cancel Then
        MessageBox.Show("You chose cancel.")
    ElseIf response = DialogResult.Retry Then
        MessageBox.Show("You chose Retry.")
```

```
        ElseIf response = DialogResult.Yes Then
            MessageBox.Show("You chose Yes.")
        ElseIf response = DialogResult.No Then
            MessageBox.Show("You chose No.")
        End If


End Sub


Private Sub RadioButton1_CheckedChanged(ByVal sender As System.Object, _
        ByVal e As System.EventArgs) Handles RadioButton1.CheckedChanged
    MsgBoxIcon = MessageBoxIcon.Error
End Sub


Private Sub RadioButton2_CheckedChanged(ByVal sender As System.Object, _
        ByVal e As System.EventArgs) Handles RadioButton2.CheckedChanged
    MsgBoxIcon = MessageBoxIcon.Exclamation
End Sub


Private Sub RadioButton3_CheckedChanged(ByVal sender As System.Object, _
        ByVal e As System.EventArgs) Handles RadioButton3.CheckedChanged
    MsgBoxIcon = MessageBoxIcon.Information
End Sub


Private Sub RadioButton4_CheckedChanged(ByVal sender As System.Object, _
        ByVal e As System.EventArgs) Handles RadioButton4.CheckedChanged
    MsgBoxIcon = MessageBoxIcon.Question
End Sub


Private Sub RadioButton5_CheckedChanged(ByVal sender As System.Object, _
        ByVal e As System.EventArgs) Handles RadioButton5.CheckedChanged
    MsgBoxButtons = MessageBoxButtons.OK
End Sub


Private Sub RadioButton6_CheckedChanged(ByVal sender As System.Object, _
        ByVal e As System.EventArgs) Handles RadioButton6.CheckedChanged
    MsgBoxButtons = MessageBoxButtons.OKCancel
End Sub


Private Sub RadioButton7_CheckedChanged(ByVal sender As System.Object, _
        ByVal e As System.EventArgs) Handles RadioButton7.CheckedChanged
    MsgBoxButtons = MessageBoxButtons.YesNo
End Sub
```

```
Private Sub RadioButton8_CheckedChanged(ByVal sender As System.Object, _
        ByVal e As System.EventArgs) Handles RadioButton8.CheckedChanged
    MsgBoxButtons = MessageBoxButtons.RetryCancel
End Sub


Private Sub RadioButton9_CheckedChanged(ByVal sender As System.Object, _
        ByVal e As System.EventArgs) Handles RadioButton9.CheckedChanged
    MsgBoxButtons = MessageBoxButtons.YesNoCancel
End Sub
```

3. Save your work, and run the program. When you do, you see the window shown in Figure 31.14.

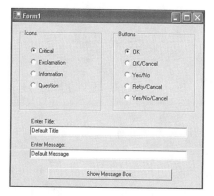

Figure 31.14

This program can display many types of message boxes.

How you use the program should be fairly obvious. Just set the options that you want to appear in your message box, and then click the Show Message Box button to reveal your specified message box. Click a button to dismiss the message box, and another message box pops up (startles you, doesn't it?) showing the button you clicked.

This program contains no tricky programming. There's nothing here that you haven't seen before. So take a few moments to look over the program and figure it all out. Bet it won't take you more than 10 minutes.

The Least You Need to Know

◆ A message box can display one of four different icons: error, exclamation, information, and question.

◆ A program can display in a message box various combinations of OK, Cancel, Abort, Yes, No, and Retry buttons.

◆ The `MessageBox.Show` function returns a value that represents the button the user selected to dismiss the dialog box.

◆ When you call the `MessageBox.Show` function you can supply not only the message text, but also a title for the message box.

Menus: Great Selections at a Great Price

In This Chapter

◆ Learn about standard types of menus

◆ Add a menu bar to your application's form

◆ Write event procedures for your menu commands

Most Windows applications worth their weight in bits contain a menu bar that houses the commands needed to operate the program. The menu bar contains menu titles that, when clicked, drop down to display all the commands associated with the menu name. For example, in the Visual Basic .NET File menu, you can find most of the commands you need to manipulate your program files. In this chapter, you'll discover how to add menus to your own Visual Basic .NET programs.

Introducing Menu Bars

If you didn't skip the introduction to this chapter, you know that a menu bar is an area near the top of a window that contains menu titles. Figure 32.1 shows the menu bar on Windows' NotePad application.

Figure 32.1

The NotePad application has four menus on its menu bar.

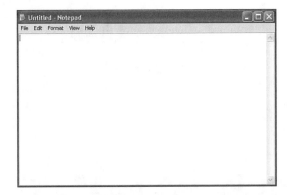

Each of the menu titles represents a group of related commands. For example, the File menu contains commands related to files (duh!), including saving files, loading files, and printing files. The Edit menu, by contrast, contains commands related to editing the contents of the currently loaded file. As shown in Figure 32.2, these commands include Undo, Copy, Cut, Paste, Delete, among others.

Figure 32.2

Each menu title represents a group of related commands.

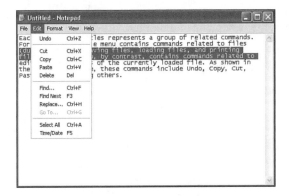

The point is that when you create your menus, you try to keep related commands grouped together. Moreover, menu bars usually have standard menus, such as File, Edit, and Help that contain a particular set of commands. Your applications should always follow the standards set up by Microsoft for an application's menus. The most important menus are the aforementioned File, Edit, and Help menus, which should contain the following commands:

- ◆ **File menu**: Contains the New, Open, Close, Save, Save As, Print, and Exit commands.

- ◆ **Edit menu**: Contains the Cut, Copy, Delete, and Paste commands.

◆ **Help menu**: Contains the About command, which displays a dialog box containing information about the application. Also contains commands for accessing the application's help system.

Of course, nothing about menus is cast in stone. If, for example, your application doesn't enable the user to edit a document, you don't need an Edit menu. Moreover, if your application supports only a Delete command, you don't need to have Cut, Copy, and Paste commands in your Edit menu. However, your Delete command should appear in the Edit menu—nowhere else—because that's where the user expects to find it.

> **By the Way**
>
> You can create menus that are nonstandard and specific to your application. For example, an application that displays colored objects might have a Color menu. Just be sure that the standard commands, like Save or Paste, appear in the appropriate standard menus.

Using the Visual Basic .NET MainMenu Control

You'll be pleased to know that creating a menu for your Visual Basic .NET programs requires no programming at all. All you have to do is add a MainMenu control to your program, and then create your menus visually in much the same way you create the rest of your program's user interface.

To add a MainMenu control, just double-click it in the Toolbox. When you do, the menu control appears below your application's form. Click the control, and a starting menu appears in the form itself, as shown in Figure 32.3.

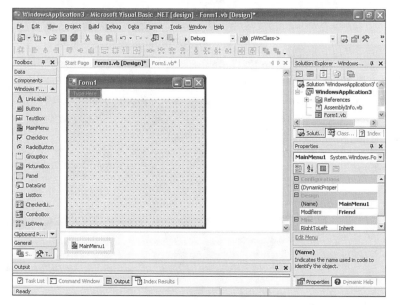

Figure 32.3

The MainMenu control enables you to add menus to your programs.

To create your own menus, follow these steps:

1. Start by typing **File** in the box that displays the text "Type Here."

    The instant you do, Visual Basic .NET creates not only the File menu, but also a new starting menu and a new menu item, as shown in Figure 32.4.

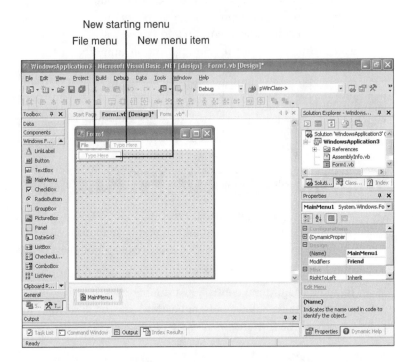

Figure 32.4

This figure shows the MainMenu control after adding a File menu.

2. To continue with the File menu, click the "Type Here" box under the File menu, and type the next command, which is usually **New.**

    Now, you get not only the New menu item, but also starting entries for the next File menu item and a possible submenu for the New command, as shown in Figure 32.5.

3. To finish the File menu, add whatever commands you need, as shown in Figure 32.6.

Menu item for the New command

New submenu

New starting menu item

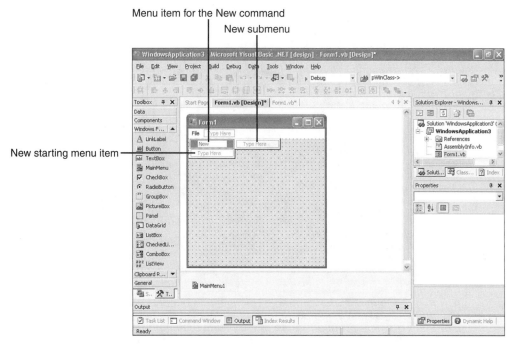

Figure 32.5

This is the MainMenu control after adding a New command to the File menu.

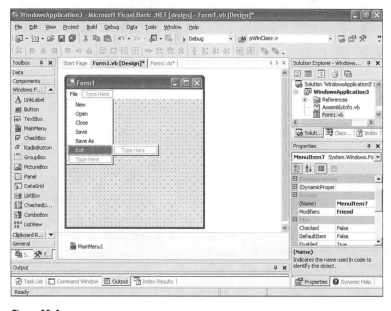

Figure 32.6

Here is the MainMenu control with a complete File menu.

4. To add other menus, go back to the uppermost "Type Here" box and repeat the procedure you used with the File menu. Figure 32.7 shows what you might see on the screen after finishing an Edit menu.

Figure 32.7

This is the MainMenu control with a complete File menu and a new Edit menu.

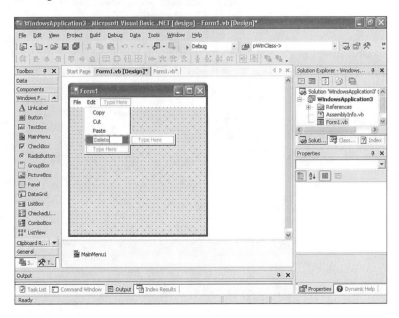

Now that you have a couple of menus, you can give your menu commands better names than the ones assigned by Visual Basic .NET. You might be tempted to use names like Ted, Bob, Heather, and Gertrude, but you don't need to be on first-name basis with elements of your program. Rather, I suggest names like mnuFileNew, mnuFileOpen, or mnuEditDelete. Are you beginning to see a pattern here? Yes? Then follow these steps:

1. Click the New command in your File menu. When you do, the command's properties appear in the Properties window.

2. Click the property you want to change (in this case, click Name), and then type the property's new setting. For example, Figure 32.8 shows the properties for the New command after the command's name has been changed to mnuFileNew.

You may be interested to read that there is a special type of menu item called a separator. A separator is a line that separates one group of menu items from other. For example, if you look at the Visual Basic .NET File menu, you'll see more than a half dozen lines that separate the menu commands from each other. To add a menu separator to your own menus, just type a hyphen in the menu item's "Type Here" box.

The New command

The New command's properties

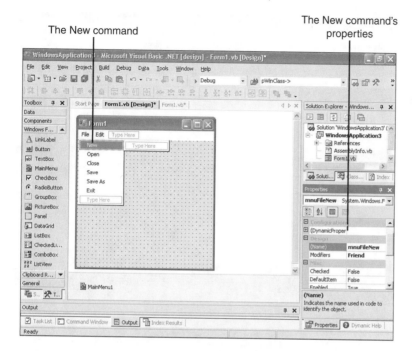

Figure 32.8

Changing the properties of a menu item.

Responding to Menu Commands

Just as promised, you've created a menu bar without typing even a single line of source code. For your program to respond to its menu commands, however, requires a little bit of programming—but nothing trickier than responding to a button click. To respond to a menu command, you must write an event procedure for the command by following these steps:

1. Put your mouse pointer over the New menu command in your form and double-click. Visual Basic .NET creates a `Click` procedure for the command, as shown in Figure 32.9.

2. Complete the `Click` procedure so that it looks as follows:

```
Private Sub mnuFileNew_Click(ByVal sender As System.Object, _
        ByVal e As System.EventArgs) Handles mnuFileNew.Click
    MessageBox.Show("Cool! My menu works!")
End Sub
```

Now, you're ready to test your menu. Save your work, and run the program. Click the New command on the File menu, and the message box shown in Figure 32.10 appears.

Figure 32.9

You can start menu event procedures by double-clicking a menu item.

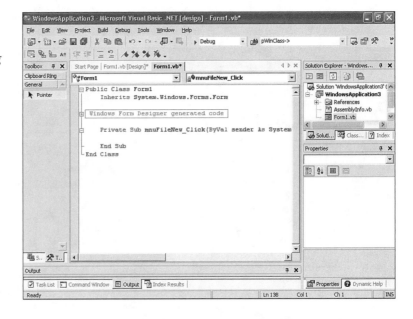

Figure 32.10

The "New" message box.

The Least You Need to Know

♦ A menu bar displays the titles for the menus that contain the commands needed to use an application.

♦ There are several standard menus provided by most Windows applications. The most important of these are File, Edit, and Help.

♦ You create your menu bar using the Visual Basic .NET MainMenu control.

♦ After creating a menu bar, you write Click event procedures for the commands in the menus.

Installing Visual Studio .NET

Visual Studio .NET, of which Visual Basic .NET is a component, comes in a variety of versions. Each of the languages—Visual Basic .NET, Visual C# .NET, and Visual C++ .NET—are available individually in standard editions. Moreover, those with deep pockets can get the entire Visual Studio .NET, with all the full .NET languages, in various editions, including Professional, Enterprise Developer, Enterprise Architect, and Academic.

As you can guess, exactly how you install Visual Studio .NET with Visual Basic .NET depends upon the edition you have. To simplify things, I'm using the free trial version of Visual Studio .NET, Professional Edition, which you can order for a small shipping fee.

The trial version will run for 30 days, which should give you plenty of time to decide whether you want to pursue Visual Basic .NET programming further. To get your trial copy of Visual Studio .NET, point your Web browser to http://msdn.microsoft.com/vstudio/nextgen/. Note that this URL is subject to change and may be different by the time you read this book. If this turns out to be the case, a little searching on www.microsoft.com ought to get you to the right place.

If you've already purchased one of the Visual Studio .NET editions, the following installation guidelines should be treated as a general outline of the process. Some details may be different for your edition.

1. Place the Visual Studio .NET CD-ROM in your drive. If you have AutoPlay enabled, the installation program will start automatically. If the installation program doesn't start, manually run the Setup.exe program on the CD-ROM. The Visual Studio .NET Setup window appears, as shown in Figure A.1.

Figure A.1

The Visual Studio .NET Setup window.

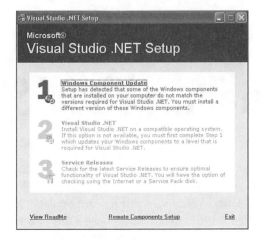

2. Click the Window Component Update selection to update Windows in preparation for Visual Studio .NET. This update includes the installation of the .NET Framework. When you start the update, the end user agreement shown in Figure A.2 appears.

Figure A.2

The Visual Studio .NET end user agreement.

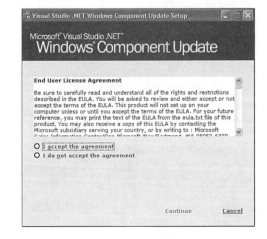

3. To continue the installation, click the I Accept the Agreement option, and then click the Continue option near the bottom of the window. In the next window, click Install Now! When the installation completes, you'll see the window shown in Figure A.3.

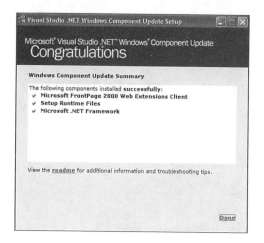

Figure A.3

The Congratulations installation message.

4. Click the Done button. The Visual Studio .NET Setup window reappears, now ready to install Visual Studio .NET, as shown in Figure A.4.

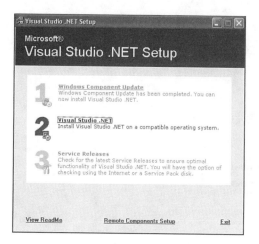

Figure A.4

Ready to install Visual Studio .NET.

5. Click the Visual Studio .NET option. Setup installs some files, and then the Setup window appears. To continue, click the I Accept the Agreement option, and then enter your product code in the space provided, as shown in Figure A.5.

Figure A.5

Accepting the Visual Studio .NET agreement.

6. Click Continue, and the Options windows will appear. On the left side of the window, select the components that you want to install. The components available to you will vary depending upon the version of Visual Studio .NET you're installing. For the programs in this book, you must at least install the Visual Basic .NET component of Visual Studio, as shown in Figure A.6.

Figure A.6

Selecting the Visual Basic .NET component.

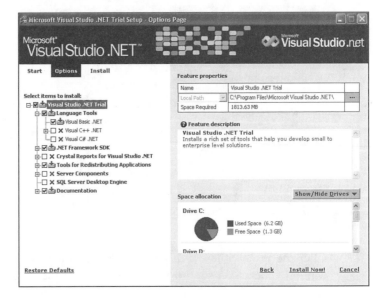

7. On the right side of the window, you can specify where you want to install Visual Studio .NET. However, I strongly suggest that you stick with the defaults, because then your system will be set up exactly as mine was for this book.

8. Click the Install Now option to begin installation. Plan on a long wait—the Visual Studio .NET installation takes freakin' forever!

Speak Like a Geek

argument   A value that's passed to a procedure or function. *See also* parameter.

arithmetic operations   Mathematical operations such as addition, multiplication, subtraction, and division that produce numerical results.

array   A variable that stores a series of values that can be accessed using a subscript.

BASIC (Beginners All-Purpose Symbolic Instruction Code)   The computer language upon which Visual Basic .NET is based.

bit   The smallest piece of information a computer can hold. A bit can be only one of two values, 0 or 1.

Boolean   A data type that represents a value of true or false.

Boolean expression   A combination of terms that evaluate to a value of true or false. For example, (x = 5) And (y = 6).

branching   When program execution jumps from one point in a program to another rather than continuing to execute instructions in sequential order. *See also* conditional branch and unconditional branch.

breakpoint   A point in a program at which program execution should be suspended in order to enable the programmer to examine the results up to that point. By setting breakpoints in a program, you can more easily find errors in your programs. *See also* debugging.

button   A Visual Basic .NET intrinsic control that looks like an on-screen push button. The user clicks the button to initiate the command associated with the button.

byte   A piece of data made up of eight bits. *See also* bit.

CheckBox   A Visual Basic .NET intrinsic control that enables the user to visually toggle an application option on and off. When the user clicks the control with the mouse pointer, a check mark appears or disappears in the control's box.

code window   The Visual Basic .NET window into which you type your program's source code.

ComboBox   A Visual Basic .NET intrinsic control that combines a ListBox with a TextBox, enabling a user to select items from a list or type a selection into the control's text box. *See also* ListBox.

compiler   A programming tool that converts a program's source code into an executable file. Visual Basic .NET automatically employs a compiler when you run a program or select the File menu's Make command to convert the program to an executable file. *See also* interpreter.

concatenate   To join two text strings into one text string. For example, the string "OneTwo" is a concatenation of the two strings "One" and "Two".

conditional branch   When program execution branches to another location in the program based on some sort of condition. An example of a conditional branch is the `If...Then` statement, which causes the program to branch to a program line based on a condition such as `If (x=5)`.

constant   A predefined value that never changes.

container   A control that can hold other controls.

control   An object such as a Button that defines properties and methods and responds to events.

data type   The various kinds of values that a program can store. These values include `Integer`, `Long`, `String`, `Single`, `Double`, and `Boolean`.

debugging   The act of finding and eliminating errors in a program.

decimal   The most precise data type for handling floating-point values. *See also* double and single.

decrement   Decreasing the value of a variable, usually by 1. *See also* increment.

design time   The period when you're creating a program, either by placing controls on the application's form or writing program source code. *See also* runtime.

double   The data type also known as a double-precision floating-point value. *See also* decimal, floating point, and single.

element   One value in an array. *See also* array.

empty string   A string that has a length of 0, denoted in a program by two double quotes. For example, the following example sets a variable called `str1` to an empty string: `str1 = ""`.

encapsulation   An object-oriented-programming term that refers to a class's ability to contain all of an object's properties and methods as well as control which of the properties and methods are visible to other parts of the program.

event   A message that's sent to a program as a result of some interaction between the user and the program.

event procedure   A procedure that enables a program to respond to an event. For example, a Button control named `Button1` might have an event procedure called `Button1_Click` to which Visual Basic .NET jumps when the user clicks the button.

executable file   A file, usually an application, that the computer can load and run. Most executable files end with the file extension .EXE.

file   A named set of data on a disk.

floating point   A numerical value that has a decimal portion. For example, the values 12.75 and 235.7584 are floating-point values. *See also* decimal, double, and single.

form   The .NET Framework object that represents an application's window. The form is the container on which you place the controls that make up your program's user interface.

function   A subprogram that processes data in some way and returns a single value that represents the result of the processing.

global variable   A named value that can be accessed from anywhere within a program module.

GroupBox   A Visual Basic .NET intrinsic control that looks like a rectangle with a label. This control is used to associate related controls into a group.

HScrollBar   A Visual Basic .NET intrinsic control that enables the user to select a value from a range of values. This control looks like the horizontal scroll bars you often see in applications' windows. *See also* VScrollBar.

I/O (Input/Output)   The process of transferring data into or out from the computer. An example of input is when the user types something on the keyboard whereas an example of output is when a program saves data to a disk file.

increment   Increasing the value of a variable, usually by 1. *See also* decrement.

index   The portion of an array reference that indicates which element of the array to access. For example, in the line X = `array1(10)`, 10 is the index, which is also sometimes called an subscript. *See also* array.

infinite loop   A loop that can't end because its conditional expression can never evaluate to true. An infinite loop ends only when the user terminates the program. *See also* loop and loop control variable.

inheritance   An object-oriented-programming term that refers to the ability of a new class to inherit the properties and methods of an existing base class.

initialize   Setting the initial value of a variable.

input devices   Devices, such as the keyboard and mouse, that transmit information into the computer.

integer   A data type that represents whole numbers. The values 240, 128, and 2 are examples of integers. *See also* long.

interpreter   A programming tool that executes source code one line at a time unlike a compiler, which converts an entire program to an executable file before executing any of the program's commands. *See also* compiler.

label   A Visual Basic .NET intrinsic control that represents a line of static text in a window. The user cannot edit static text, but a program can change it through the Text property.

ListBox   A Visual Basic .NET intrinsic control that enables the user to use a mouse to select an item from a list. *See also* ComboBox.

literal   A value in a program that is stated literally. That is, the value is not stored in a variable.

local variable   A variable that can be accessed only from within the subprogram in which it's declared. *See also* global variable and variable scope.

logic error   A programming error that results when a program behaves differently than the programmer intended. For example, the program line `If x = 5 Then Y = 6` is a logical error if the variable x can never equal 5. *See also* runtime error.

logical operator   A symbol that compares two expressions and results in a Boolean value (true or false). For example, in the line `If X = 5 And Y = 10 Then Z = 1`, And is the logical operator. *See also* relational operator.

long   A data type that represents large integer values. *See also* integer.

loop   A block of source code that executes repeatedly until a certain condition is met.

loop control variable   A variable that holds the value that determines whether a loop will continue to execute.

machine language   The only language a computer truly understands. All program source code must be converted to machine language before the computer can run the program.

mathematical expressions   A set of terms that use arithmetic operators to produce in a numerical value. For example, the terms `(x + 10) / (y + 2)` make up a mathematical expression. *See also* arithmetic operations.

message box   A special type of dialog box that can contain a title, a message, and a combination of predefined icons and buttons. A program displays a message box with the `MessageBox.Show` method.

method   A procedure associated with a class, object, or control that represents an ability of the class, object, or control. For example, a Button's `Move` method repositions the button on the form.

modular programming   Breaking a program up into a series of simple tasks.

numerical literal   A literal value that represents a number, such as 125 or 34.87. *See also* literal and string literal.

numerical value   A value that represents a number. This value can be a literal, a variable, or the result of an arithmetic operation.

object   Generally, any piece of data in a program. Specifically in Visual Basic .NET, a set of properties and methods that represent some sort of real-world object or abstract idea. An object is usually created from a class.

object-oriented programming   The programming technique where the programmer thinks in terms of objects, along with their attributes (called properties) and actions (called methods). The programmer creates classes that represent objects and then creates objects from the classes.

order of operations   The order in which Visual Basic .NET resolves arithmetic operations. For example, in the mathematical expression `(x + 5) / (y + 2)`, Visual Basic .NET will perform the two additions before the division. If the parentheses had been left off, such as in the expression `x + 5 / y + 2`, Visual Basic .NET would first divide 5 by Y and then perform the remaining addition operations.

output devices   Devices, such as the screen or a printer, that accept data coming out from the computer. *See also* input devices.

parameter   Often means the same thing as "argument," although some people differentiate argument and parameter, where an argument is the value sent to a procedure or function and a parameter is the variable in the function or procedure that receives the argument. *See also* argument.

PictureBox A Visual Basic .NET intrinsic control that enables a program to display complex images, including high resolution images from a disk file.

polymorphism An object-oriented programming term that refers to the ability of derived classes to perform the same function of a base class in different ways. For example, a Shape base class may have a Draw method that draws a shape. Rectangle and Circle classes derived from the Shape class will also have a Draw method, but the Rectangle class's method will draw a rectangle and the Circle class's method will draw a circle.

procedure A subprogram that performs a task in a program but doesn't return a value. *See also* function.

program A list of instructions for a computer.

program flow The order in which the computer executes the program statements.

programming language A set of English-like keywords and symbols that enable a programmer to write a program without having to use machine language.

Properties window The Visual Basic .NET window that displays a control's properties and their settings.

property A value that represents an attribute of a class, object, or control. For example, a Button control's Text property represents the text that appears inside the button.

RadioButton An intrinsic Visual Basic .NET control that represents a mutually exclusive option in a set of options. For example, several RadioButton controls representing colors might be grouped together, enabling the user to select one and only one color. If the user clicks on a different color, the originally selected color becomes deselected while the new color becomes selected. This type of control is called a radio button because of how a group of these buttons acts like buttons on a car radio, which enable the driver to select only a single radio station at a time.

read-only property A property whose value cannot be changed from within a program. However, the program can retrieve (read) the property's value.

relational operator A symbol that determines the relationship between two expressions. For example, in the expression X > 10, the relational operator is >, which means "greater than." *See also* logical operator.

return value The value that a function sends back to the statement that called the function. *See also* function.

runtime The period when a program is running rather than being designed. *See also* design time.

runtime error   A system error that occurs while a program is running. An example is a divide-by-zero error or a type-mismatch error. Without some sort of error handling, such as that provided by the `Try...Catch` statement, runtime errors can result in a program crash.

scope   *See* variable scope.

single   The data type that represents the least accurate floating-point value, also known as a single-precision floating-point value. *See also* decimal, double, and floating point.

Solution Explorer   The Visual Basic .NET window that displays the current modules in your Visual Basic .NET project.

source code   The lines of commands that make up a program.

string   A data type that represents one or more text characters. For example, in the assignment statement `str1 = "I'm a string."`, the variable `str1` must be of the `String` data type.

string literal   One or more text characters enclosed in double quotes.

subprogram   A block of source code that performs a specific part of a larger task. In Visual Basic .NET, a subprogram can be either a procedure or a function. *See also* procedure and function.

subscript   The portion of an array reference that indicates which element of the array to access. For example, in the line `X = array1(10)`, 10 is the subscript, which is also sometimes called an index. *See also* array.

substring   A small portion of a larger string. For example, the string "One" is a substring of the larger string "OneTwo". *See also* string.

TextBox   An intrinsic Visual Basic .NET control that enables the user to enter and edit text.

third-party controls   Controls that are not part of the original Visual Basic .NET package. These controls can be purchased and added to the Visual Basic .NET toolbox. Some third-party controls can even be freely downloaded from various Web sites.

Timer   An intrinsic Visual Basic .NET control that enables a program to determine when a specific period of time has elapsed.

Toolbox   The area of the Visual Basic .NET main window in which you can select the controls to place on a form.

top-down programming   Organizing procedures in a hierarchy, with general-purpose procedures at the top that call specific-purpose procedures lower in the hierarchy.

unconditional branch   When program execution branches to another location regardless of any conditions. An example of a conditional branch is the `GoTo` statement.

user interface   The visible representation of an application, usually made up of various types of controls, that enables the user to interact with the application.

variable   A named value in a program. This value can be assigned and reassigned a value of the appropriate data type.

variable scope   The area of a program in which a variable can be accessed. For example, the scope of a global variable is anywhere within the program whereas the scope of a local variable is limited to the procedure or function that declares the variable. A variable declared inside a block of code has what's called block scope. *See also* global variable and local variable.

VScrollBar   A Visual Basic .NET intrinsic control that enables the user to select a value from a range of values. This control looks like the vertical scroll bars you often see in applications' windows. *See also* HScrollBar.

Index

C

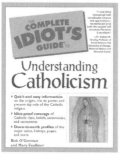

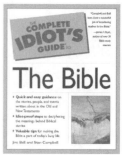

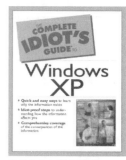